APPROACHES TO *Ulysses*

APPROACHES TO

University of Pittsburgh Press

THOMAS F. STALEY
and
BERNARD BENSTOCK
Editors

ulysses

Ten Essays

To Muffi

and

To Eve

Contents

Introduction

JAMES JOYCE's *Ulysses* was first published by a young American bookseller in Paris nearly fifty years ago—the rest is literary history. No novel written in this century has laid such a large claim on the literature and criticism of our time. *Ulysses* stands as one of the seminal works of our culture, and to say this is not in any sense to make personal claims for it.

The enormous amount of critical material that has been written on *Ulysses* is legend and not the subject for discussion here, except to note the fact that all the previous book-length studies of *Ulysses* have been written by individual authors, each pursuing a special line of inquiry, each developing his own approach through a sustained reading of the book. The quality of these contributions to *Ulysses* criticism, of course, varies, and the time of composition affects the perspective of each author. In the 1930s, for example, Stuart Gilbert's and Frank Budgen's books on *Ulysses* were written with firsthand information from Joyce himself. The nearly dozen book-length studies which have followed represent a wide range in both quality and approach. This volume is the first book-length study to present *Ulysses* from ten different aspects, all by different authors.

It is always dangerous, if not arbitrary, to insist that a collection of essays has a unity of purpose. This is so even with a volume such as this one, whose essays center on a particular literary work. The purpose of this collection is, in fact, based upon multiplicity and diversity rather than upon any idea of unity or singularity of approach.

The inherent value of any collection of essays rests on the quality of the individual contributions, and no editor can ignore this value, but there are others. The editors of this volume were cognizant of these facts: (1) no novel of our century has had more critical attention devoted to it; (2) no novel has been the subject of such a variety of critical approaches; (3) a great number of the individual essays on *Ulysses* have dwelt on one of the eighteen episodes of the novel. With these facts in mind, each author was asked to look at one of the central critical problems in *Ulysses* and deal with it as well as relate it to the novel as a whole, and no essay was to be exclusively devoted to a single episode. This was the extent of editorial intervention with regard to the topic that each author chose. On the basis of their past areas of scholarly interest, however, several authors were asked to pursue their previous areas of inquiry. The most obvious example is Weldon Thornton, who was asked to write about the function of allusion in *Ulysses* after having published his *Allusions in Ulysses*.

Each author was free to work within these broad parameters as he saw fit, and no restrictions or mechanical uniformity was imposed by the editors. The variety, controversy, and scope is a result of the individual approaches and not of premeditated design. The completed essays, if not by design, complement each other in a variety of ways. Thomas F. Staley's and Robert Boyle's essays both deal with the character of Stephen Dedalus and his role in the novel. These two essays reflect in their arguments the wide variety of critical opinion on Stephen's importance in the novel and Joyce's attitude toward him. No two essays could reach more widely divergent conclusions on a character than do those of Darcy O'Brien and David Hayman on Molly Bloom, and yet the ramifications of each argument offer considerable insight into the complexities of the novel itself. The enormous problems of technique and the special way in which Joyce uses literary devices are taken up by Richard M. Kain, William Schutte and Erwin Steinberg, and Weldon Thornton. The essays of Bernard Benstock and H. Frew Waidner each deal with Joyce's specific use of background material—a persistent critical issue in Joyce scholarship. Fritz Senn's essay, which takes up the problem that Joyce poses for translators, reaches far deeper in its implications, for it deals with the basic problems of language.

The variety of these essays attests not so much to the dissimilarity of the contributors but rather to the inherent richness of *Ulysses*. The approaches themselves are, in part at least, a testimony to Joyce's enormous creativity—a creativity which the critic merely approaches.

THOMAS F. STALEY
BERNARD BENSTOCK

APPROACHES TO *Ulysses*

Stephen Dedalus
and the Temper
of the Modern Hero

THOMAS F. STALEY

I am sure, however, that the whole structure of heroism is, and always was, a damned lie and that there cannot be any substitute for the individual passion as the motive power of everything—art and philosophy included.

James Joyce in a letter, 1905

I

STEPHEN DEDALUS'S POSITION as a hero even in the most banal modern sense of that term rests on the weakest kind of claim—gratuitous assertion. After his painful hegira in Paris and before he makes his even more painful and defeating return to Dublin to take up quarters with Buck Mulligan, Stephen hardly seems anything more than an intelligent, self-conscious, urbane, and somewhat irritating misanthrope. A succession of critics have been able to find very little in Stephen to commend him as a potential artist, far less as a hero.[1] Perhaps Joyce's words to his brother,[2] which form the epigraph to this essay, provide an obvious but, at the same time, accurate clue to the purpose behind Joyce's treatment of Stephen Dedalus in *Ulysses*. Critics such as Clive Hart and Stanley Sultan[3] read the character of Stephen in a more favorable light, but both wisely refrain from making terribly generous claims for him. Perhaps the tunneling out of a moral dilemma is strong enough claim to be made for a modern fictional hero. The chief concern of this essay is to raise those issues which have to do with the critic's approach to Stephen Dedalus, for in approaching the character one, in large measure, approaches the novel as a whole.

The Stephen of *Ulysses* who follows Buck Mulligan's bidding and walks up the steps to the top of the Martello Tower on the morning of June 16, 1904, is a far cry from the "priest of eternal imagination, transmuting the daily bread of experience into the radiant body of everlasting life."[4] Mulligan's mock mass stands as a deliberate and careful rebuke to Stephen's earlier aspiration, for it is Mulligan as priest who raises the chalice aloft and performs the priestly ritual. Stephen himself is unable to come to terms with the "daily bread of experience" much less transmute it into "everlasting life." Before transmutation can take place, whatever the materials of life, there must first of all be a synthesis between passion and intellect—art and philosophy. The first three episodes of *Ulysses*, the Telemachia, initiate the battleground for Stephen's unresolved conflict. The battle appears hopeless; like Kafka's "Hunger Artist," Stephen seems to be caught in a static condition where time does not move for him. Past and future are equally horrifying; memory and speculation offer no exodus.

For the present, the morning of June 16, 1904, Stephen

serves Mulligan the mocker, "the Medicineman," as Hugh Kenner has called him.[5] Stephen Dedalus is not a sage, not an artist; he, nevertheless, serves most admirably as a major character in one of the two or three most ambitious novels of our century. Stephen reflects his world and serves Joyce's purpose well, and is not simply deserted for the more light and lively, more human Leopold Bloom, as so many contend. The mind and character of Stephen, insofar as they reflect and contribute to the central themes and purposes of *Ulysses*, are developed so carefully and completely by Joyce that a close scrutiny of them clearly reveals Stephen's larger function within the thematic framework of the entire novel. This point is not to suggest the obviously intricate correspondences which are dependent upon Stephen's function, but rather to insist that insofar as *Ulysses* reflects the impressions of the outside world on the mind and art of James Joyce, so, too, does the character of Stephen reflect the struggle of the sensitive human being with all his weaknesses and strengths as he confronts the modern world—within the microcosm of one day in Dublin. On this day we have ushered in a character who reflects in all his pain and anguish, and even nastiness, the temper of the modern hero. In Stephen Dedalus, Joyce has showed us that the successful creation of a would-be artist's inability to "transmute" living matter into art is itself a most artful creation of a character and a reliable and accurate portrait of the modern hero.

II

William Empson in an essay on *Ulysses* has written: "A critic of *Ulysses* always holds a theory about the intention of Joyce in *Ulysses*, without realizing he is holding it."[6] This is so, Empson contends, because Joyce refuses to tell the reader the end of the story. Empson's point is well taken. For example, in a note to his play *Exiles*, Joyce writes that "the doubt which clouds the end of the play must be conveyed to the audience."[7] The danger for the critic is complicated further when he deals with that intellectual creation, Stephen Dedalus. W. H. Auden reflected the Anglo-Saxon disdain for the intellectual in his discussion of the work of Sainte-Beuve when he wrote that the behavior of intellectuals is "seldom to be taken seriously."[8] Unlike the French, the Anglo-Saxons are at least suspicious or frightened if not openly hostile to intellectuals. This is a fact of life which Stephen clearly grasps within his consciousness and it is a very important element in the world of *Ulysses*.

Although we are not innocent of Empson's caution, it seems proper for us to begin with Joyce's now famous words to his friend Frank Budgen, during the composition of *Ulysses*, concerning Stephen Dedalus: "He has a shape that can't be changed."[9] Stephen, according to Joyce, had reached a fixed position in his mind—he had come to the end in the creative process of bringing a character to life through the medium of words. Joyce had reached that point where he had finally come to terms—in his own mind, at least—with a character who had preoccupied his mind and art for the better part of twenty years.

One may interpret Joyce's words to mean that Stephen had come to life as Joyce wanted him to within *Ulysses*. The questions and problems raised by Stephen were resolved, in Joyce's mind at least. Whatever ambiguity remained lay within the nature of the character. At the same time that Joyce mentioned the fixed shape of Stephen, he also told Budgen that "Stephen no longer interests me to the same extent [that Bloom does]."[10] This statement has been taken by some critics to mean that Joyce abandoned Stephen because of an infatuation with the possibilities of Bloom. Stephen has run aground so to speak and Bloom takes over to allow Joyce the full inventiveness of the comic mode—Bloom becomes the hero for the mature artist and Stephen is left hopelessly entangled in his own narrow world. The violence which this kind of reading does to the novel as a whole is obvious.

The conception of the character of Stephen Dedalus in *Ulysses* was certainly governed by the larger purposes of the novel. *Ulysses* itself provides the world in which Stephen finds definition. The total structure—the purposeful design—of *Ulysses* is what qualifies the attention we give to Stephen.

Joyce did not offer Budgen an explanation for the abandonment of Stephen, but it may be interpreted that he was satisfied with the completion of Stephen. Had he not been he would have started over—Stephen *had* to be fixed in Joyce's mind. His awesome care and persistence with *Ulysses* have been fully documented by Richard Ellmann in his biography and by Joyce himself in his own painful letters. *Ulysses* itself, however, provides the best evidence that Joyce had at last completed his creation of a character who, with all his disenchantment and self-pity, is able to do battle with the world. As the novelist John Fowles has written, "It is only when our characters and events begin to disobey us that they begin to live."[11] Stephen hardly disobeys Joyce, but he is given the necessary autonomy to function as an independent character, and this is evidenced in the tone which is established in the opening pages of the novel. The source of Stephen's problems is particularized, but his reactions to the disparity between his admittedly clouded aspirations and what goals he is able to realize sum up many of the essential traits of the young artist who looks into the twentieth century, and in this summation Joyce offers a picture of what Cleanth Brooks calls "the rift in modern civilization—as reflected in the attitude . . . of an intransigent and sensitive and brilliant young artist."[12] The world which Joyce creates in *Ulysses* is an enormously complex one and Stephen's role in it is essential to every aspect of the novel's creation.

What Georg Lukács wrote of Gorki, Rousseau, Goethe, and Tolstoy applies to Joyce. In the works of many of the great modern narrators, Lukács writes, "the autobiographical element plays a very important part. Those great narrators who summed up the essential traits of their epoch . . . had themselves experienced in their own lives the emergence and maturing of the problems of the age. This process of digesting the historical content of an epoch is itself most characteristic for the epoch."[13] Stephen Dedalus—the literary product of Roman Catholic doctrine, Walter Pater, the late Romantics, Ruskin, Newman, Ibsen, the 1890s—stands on the threshold of a new century weak and impotent, but outraged at his own inability to create. Only his defiance, even in the face of failure, protects life from art and makes him real.

III

There are a number of critical issues surrounding the character of Stephen Dedalus as he lives in *Ulysses*. Earlier stages of Stephen appear in both *Stephen Hero* and *A Portrait*. Any assessment of Stephen in *Ulysses* is complicated if, in fact, not predetermined by his life within these earlier works. It has become commonplace for critics of *Ulysses* who treat Stephen to "bring him up-to-date," so to speak, by tracing what they feel to be the essential elements in his life and aesthetic ideas. The purpose here is not to suggest the contrary to this obvious necessity, for how else can the reader come to terms with a character whose appearance in an earlier work lays the necessary groundwork for his later development? Rather the point is to suggest that in large degree the earlier works have somewhat blunted, in critics' eyes, Stephen Dedalus's overall importance in *Ulysses*. What is being challenged here is the view that Stephen Dedalus of *Ulysses* is finally played out and dropped by Joyce in his excitement over the broad possibilities of Leopold Bloom. Stephen, in this view, becomes merely a thematic and symbolic foil for Joyce's grand design and a clearly lesser creation than Bloom. Joyce's obvious delight in the free reign that the comic mode gave to his talents and later temperament is hardly evidence or argument for such a position.[14] There are other arguments, of course, and one must turn to them.

Following these general assertions, it is necessary to demonstrate with some particularity the development of critical opinion surrounding Stephen Dedalus as he emerges in *Ulysses*. Confronted by the enormous amount of secondary material, it is possible to treat only a select number of important as well as representative critical positions.[15]

Joseph Prescott in his study of the characterization of Stephen Dedalus has looked carefully at the manuscripts, typescripts, and the earlier periodical versions of *Ulysses* in order to determine Joyce's method of creating a character. Prescott writes:

So far as characterization generally is concerned, Joyce's recorded remarks encourage one to believe that he started with large and fluid concepts which he then proceeded to particularize by concrete, detailed illustration. The reader's experience, however, is inductive, and only after building up a character bit by bit can he perceive the pattern of the whole. More importantly, working from the preliminary versions, he begins at a stage that is inductive for both author and reader, the author introducing details, the reader following the author, both building toward the whole, the first from preconceived outlines, the second toward outlines that are yet to be apprehended. Painstakingly, indefatigably, Joyce linked together the innumerable atoms that finally emerge as Stephen Dedalus, Leopold Bloom, the minor characters, and Molly Bloom. With the benefit of hindsight the reader of the published text may fluently formulate these people as products of this, that, and other forces; the process of creation, however, is recaptured only when he retraces the steps which Joyce took in shaping his characters.[16]

Prescott presents a great deal of evidence that the Stephen of *Ulysses* is a continuation of the Stephen of *A Portrait*. The shyness, the aloofness, the self-mockery, and the theological preoccupation are still present and continue to make up much of Stephen's character. Prescott sees this consistency in the continuation of character traits, "in the presentation of patent aspects of personal history, thought, and language, but also with consistency in the very images and metaphors toward which the character inclines in articulating experiences, in the peculiar weave of the individual mind."[17] Prescott has shown clearly and well the genesis of Stephen's character as Joyce developed it from *A Portrait*, but a full analysis of Stephen's function within the context of *Ulysses* lies beyond the range of Prescott's purpose. One can readily admit that Joyce uses his earlier Stephen to develop his later version, but still insist, however, that the Stephen of *Ulysses* is extremely more complex and, more importantly, that he reflects the mature vision of Joyce's expression of the plight of the artist in his time. Even a critical view which deals exclusively with the literary elements or devices which go to make up the interiority of the character, must ultimately look to the fictional world where the character finds his ambience, and Stephen in *Ulysses* is not only in a far more complex world but he is actively engaged in trying to find his place in it rather than build an aesthetic which will allow him to escape from it.

The roots of Stephen's characterization may well lie in Joyce's earlier conceptions of him, but the later Stephen, without the whole stage to himself as he had in *A Portrait*, has been created in large measure by Joyce to illustrate the essential problems of the youthful intellectual whose life has been fragmented by the claims of the past, the dilemmas of the present, and the fears of the future. Birdlike girls and seaborne clouds give way to severed umbilical cords and corpses as the modern artist ponders his place in the world.

The most persistent and influential critical attitude toward Stephen Dedalus of *Ulysses* has been the one expressed by Hugh Kenner.[18] Until S. L. Goldberg in his *The Classical Temper*[19] took strong issue with Kenner's interpretation, it was either accepted or ignored; it remained basically unchallenged. Kenner's thesis holds that the entire work is ironical. This irony grows out of the ten-

sion created by Joyce's disgust with the decayed society—
with Dublin as the microcosm—which imprisons the human spirit. An equally strong argument which Kenner
raises is the importance of language in Joyce's work. The
technique he used, according to Kenner, came out of his
subject matter: Dublin. The scope of Kenner's argument
is obviously far broader than the immediate concerns of
this essay, but insofar as his argument affects an interpretation of Stephen Dedalus it is important for our purposes here. Irony is the guiding principle in *Ulysses* for
Kenner, and Stephen is the victim of this purpose:

> The controlling ideas in *Ulysses* are never stated. They exist,
> like magnetic fields, behind and around the words, apprehen-
> sible through perspectives of triple analogy. Joyce's irony goes
> deep indeed. . . . Stephen . . . is aware that he is Hamlet, but
> his awareness is put to the wrong uses. It provides him with no
> insight. It merely feeds his morbidity. It is a role in which he
> is imprisoned.[20]

Kenner's point throughout his argument is that the moral
values (spiritual values, as Kenner would rightly have it)
lie not in the world of the novel but outside *Ulysses*. Joyce,
the Catholic artist, however unwilling to admit what is
implied by the term *catholic*, has accomplished by the
quality of his irony an abstraction which implies a clear
moral connective. This moral vision grows out of the ironic treatment of his creation. The detached artist reveals
the nature of his antipathy through technique, but a technique which forces interpretation outside of the world of
the novel.[21]

Matthew Hodgart in his excellent study of satire agrees
essentially with Kenner's point that Joyce reveals a broad
humanity in his satire and this accounts for the depth of

vision we see in Stephen and Bloom: "Joyce's attitude to his subject is far more sympathetic and his comprehension of the human condition far wider than those of the traditional satirists."[22]

Regardless of what formed the source of Joyce's implied moral vision, the question which remains to be discussed here is whether or not Stephen is victim of Joyce's ironic vision or foil or both. Stephen is certainly both, but not exclusively either. Obviously that debased Dublin which Joyce holds up for ridicule as the cul-de-sac of the modern world is the subject of his outrage and indignation, but what role does Stephen Dedalus play in this picture? Are Stephen Dedalus's metaphysical self-pity and the world (seen in the Dublin microcosm) which produced and tortures him equal objects of Joyce's irony? Is it not possible by reason and evidence to suggest that Joyce's primary emphasis is upon Stephen as victim? The double turn of Joyce's satiric blade is not flashed at Stephen so much as at the world which produced him. Stephen obviously functions within the absurdity of the mock heroic, but his very absurdity points beyond his own existence to the world of the novel. Regardless of how unattractive Stephen may appear, or however vapid his ideas, he remains a character whose moral being is continually brought into focus by Joyce. S. L. Goldberg's clearly reasoned argument against Kenner's insistence upon Joyce's use of an all-pervasive irony is convincing. He writes: "It is equally possible, and in Joyce's work is in fact the case, that irony is a qualifying criticism, which does not imply a total rejection of its object in the least, . . . nor is there any reason why Stephen's potentialities as an artist should be dismissed because he is very immature and clearly portrayed as such. To think so is surely to miss Joyce's point, to ignore the process of growth upon which he insists."[23] To go back to an earlier point, Kenner's interpretation of the Stephen of *Ulysses* seems to discount any potential growth in the character or any essential change in Joyce's attitude toward him. Joyce's irony certainly plays on Stephen's excessive self-pity but not on the character of Stephen as a whole. Stephen is, of course, not portrayed as the ideal hero to do battle with the forces which confront him in his world, but neither is he helpless.

More to the point, not only is Stephen a character who shows growth within the world of *Ulysses*, but he is also a sentient moral being in spite of his obvious proclivities toward self-pity and arrogance. These latter elements make him all the more human, if, at the same time, more exasperating. Stephen's early argument with Mulligan concerning his refusal to kneel at his mother's deathbed is an indication from the very beginning of Stephen's moral posture. As E. M. W. Tillyard has perceptively commented: "Stephen did not fail in morality when he refused to kneel and pray for his mother's soul as she lay dying. On the contrary, he acted only too strictly in accordance with it and through that very strictness was harassed by remorse."[24] Moreover, it can be argued that Stephen's posture within *Ulysses* provides one of the most crucial foci for Joyce's moral vision. An example of this is cited by Tillyard in conjunction with his earlier point: "And if Joyce pitilessly mauls a bogus kind of Irish patriotism through embodying it in the violent and ridiculous figure of the Citizen in the Cyclops episode he presents in all sincerity, lucidity, and fear the ineluctable dilemma of the genuine Irish patriot through the visions that Stephen has of his own country."[25]

As Tillyard's point makes clear, Stephen Dedalus's role in *Ulysses* was far more broadly conceived by Joyce than most critics are willing to admit. The extreme critical view which has been very much ascribed to in the past and which is certainly not Kenner's view—although it has been erroneously attributed to him—has been the dismissal theory. This theory, in the light of what has been written, needs no comment other than to provide an example: "Through the emergence of Bloom and the rejection of Stephen, Joyce is saying that art is the art of living with oneself and with one's fellow man."[26] Whatever Joyce may be saying in *Ulysses*, it seems a reckless extrapolation, if not a mindless one, to accept this position at all.

IV

It is safe to assert at this stage that Stephen Dedalus, however he is prefigured in Joyce's earlier work, is far more ambitiously conceived by Joyce in *Ulysses*, even if only to the degree demanded by the obviously more ambitious work. It remains necessary, however, to discuss in more specific terms Stephen's function within *Ulysses*.

Stephen's struggle in *Ulysses* in all of its specificity and particularity is Joyce's portrait of the creative individual's struggle in the modern world. Paradox and suffering emerge from the beginning of *Ulysses* as the inevitable conditions of the creative modern temper as it seeks to define itself in its own terms. Traditions which we once venerated, if not false now, at least are no longer adequate. Despair and indifference vie with each other in the grim face of a fallen world; they become the dominant moods in the face of nullity. This nullity which is so pervasively reflected in Stephen dominates *Ulysses*. As Lionel Trilling has remarked, "The power of Joyce's work derives, we must see, not only from the impulse to resist nullity but also, and equally, from the impulse to make nullity prevail."[27] Stephen Dedalus's concerns are both moral and metaphysical, but as he gives way to the latter Stephen ushers into literature the difficult metaphysics of the modern literary hero. After Stephen Dedalus's appearance in *Ulysses* moral concerns which are shaped by an ordered world tend to give way in modern fiction almost completely to metaphysics in the temper of the fictional hero: In a world of nothing, the hero explores the nature of his nothingness. Stephen, however, only dimly perceives this nothingness. He is still frustrated by the assaults of impressions from the past which he must filter and conquer before he can look to the nullity of both past and present.

By looking closely at several important passages in *Ulysses* it is possible to suggest, at least, the depth of Joyce's artful concern and the large human as well as thematic and philosophical role that he has Stephen play in *Ulysses*. One can also examine in this way Joyce's techniques for giving his character depth and meaning.

Much attention has been paid to the plethora of liturgical references throughout *Ulysses*; most, but by no means all, of them rise out of Stephen's stream of consciousness. As was noted earlier, Mulligan's mock elevation from the top of the Martello Tower sets in motion the liturgical motifs. His blasphemous utterance of the opening words of the mass, "*Introibo ad altare Dei*,"[28] is a fitting introduction to the religious references. It should be noted, however, that Mulligan's words do not set up a long series of parodies and blasphemous material. On the contrary, Mulligan is set in careful opposition to Stephen in every way. Stephen

is unable to enter the free amoral world which is Buck
Mulligan's. As we shall see, he is unable to free himself
completely from the spiritual experience behind these
words. In any event, the carelessness and superficiality of
Mulligan's blasphemies could never be accepted by
Stephen. The liturgical references as they come from
Stephen are important for what they reveal of his erratic
psychic condition.

Of extreme importance to Stephen's development is the
way in which Joyce evokes at crucial times in his memory
the phrase from the ritual of prayers for the dying:

*Liliata rutilantium te confessorum turma circumdet: iubilan-
tium te virginum chorus excipiat.* (10)[29]

Stephen's sense of guilt is what triggers his recollection of
this prayer of the priest at the bedside of his dying mother.
Two extremely important elements are joined here and
never separated throughout the novel: guilt and death.
In spite of his efforts to throw off these dominant concerns,
Stephen never succeeds. His immediate reaction solidifies
these preoccupations on a conscious level. He breaks off
the Latin prayer by saying: "Ghoul! Chewer of Corpses!
No mother. Let me be and let me live" (10). In spite of
his struggle to break free from memory, the words of the
prayer come back to him as he walks away from the tower
"along the upwardcurving path" (23).

At the end of the first episode, the *"liliata rutilantium"*
phrase takes on existential meaning for Stephen. It is a
persistent association with his "Agenbite of inwit" and his
feeling of culpability for all his actions. It is also significant
that the phrase should come back to his mind at this point,
for he has just been ousted from the tower by Mulligan

and, at the same time, realizes he cannot go home. He stands at that midpoint of impossibility, unable to return to his past but pitifully vulnerable to the future. It is at this juncture that the words of the prayer repeat themselves in his mind.

The sense of guilt which manifests itself in Stephen's obsession with the deathbed prayer is ingrained in his nature. His refusal to kneel and pray has been the one overt break with his past that has forced him to face directly the human consequences of his intellectual integrity. Sex is not the source of Stephen's obsession with sin; a far wider spectrum of human guilt concerns him. Darcy O'Brien misreads the text when he interprets Stephen's words, "Wombed in sin darkness" (38), as Stephen's "adherence to the puritanical, Irish, Joycean conviction that the sexual act is itself sinful, is perhaps the origin of man's moral weakness."[30] Stephen's phrase refers to the doctrine of Original Sin and not, as Mr. O'Brien suggests, to any implied Joycean conviction on sex. The full sentence reads: "Wombed in sin darkness I was too, made not begotten" (38). The latter part of the phrase is important. The words "made not begotten" echo the Nicene Creed recited in the mass: *Genitum, non factum*, begotten not made. The reference here is to Christ, who was not "wombed in sin darkness" because He was without Original Sin. Theology is a part of the nightmare of history from which Stephen has not escaped.

The *liliata* prayer continues to mark Stephen's obsession with death and his own moral struggle. The most dramatic incident where the words of the *liliata* phrase occurs is, of course, in the Circe episode. Stephen's hallucination of his mother's apparition in this episode culminates in his defiant smashing of the chandelier and his outcry of "Nothung!" Triggered by the imagined words from his father, the vision of his mother comes upon him:

STEPHEN

Ho!
(*Stephen's mother, emaciated, rises stark through the floor in leper grey with a wreath of faded orange blossoms and a torn bridal veil, her face worn and noseless, green with grave mould. Her hair is scant and lank. She fixes her bluecircled hollow eyesockets on Stephen and opens her toothless mouth uttering a silent word. A choir of virgins and confessors sing voicelessly.*)

　　Liliata rutilantium te confessorum . . .
　　Iubilantium te virginum . . .
(*From the top of a tower Buck Mulligan, in particoloured jester's dress of puce and yellow and clown's cap with curling bell, stands gaping at her, a smoking buttered split scone in his hand.*) (579–80)

The prayer itself recalls for Stephen the morning scene with Mulligan and the source of his anger at him:

BUCK MULLIGAN

She's beastly dead. The pity of it! Mulligan meets the afflicted mother. (*He upturns his eyes.*) Mercurial Malachi. (580)

For Mulligan, the materialist, Stephen can only have unmitigated scorn, because Mulligan denies completely the spiritual when he tells Stephen that his mother is "beastly dead." In spite of the entire Hamlet context which provides him with a rationalization of his human failure, Stephen is not, on the other hand, willing to admit to the hyperborean moral freedom in which Mulligan lives. Mulligan's freedom is too superficial for him; it denies too easily the life of the mind as well as what are for Stephen the moral obligations of freedom. Stephen looks upon Mulligan's seemingly happy ambience with the world as based on hypocrisy, and however strong his wish to break away, or however defiant his gestures, the words of the prayer which keep coming back to his mind provide the reader with a clear indication of the depth of his struggle. For all of his defiance Stephen's philosophical nature struggles with an older order. Umberto Eco in his book *Le Poetiche di Joyce* points this out clearly: "il vecchio mondo messo in dubbio non nelle sue manifestazioni accidentali, ma proprio nella sua natura di cosmo ordinato, di universo compiuto e definito in modo univoco secondo le regole in alterabili di una sillogistica che e quella aristotelico-tomesta."[31] Central to the source of Stephen's anguish is the fact that he seems to combine a medieval mind or thought process with a modern sensibility.

The violence of Stephen's action with his ashplant is more than a catharsis, for he appears to have not only broken from the earlier "Non Serviam" gesture with its accompanying recognition and defiance, but has gone beyond it to face the naked reality of a world which simply does not orbit around and is indifferent to his servitude. He accepts his past for something else with this violent gesture, and the single word which he utters, and its association with "nothing," brings word and action to a reflection of Stephen's modern conditioning. Stephen, it can be shown, will accept the responsibility of his rejection as the modern hero accepts his fate. He can enter at last the world which Beckett calls the "absolute absence of the absolute." He enters knowing that he cannot quite accept it, but he cannot go backward either—except in memory. Memory, on the other hand, can no longer trap him; the ethical claims of an empty society will not overcome him. Society and the past, both personal and historical, remain a part of him but will no longer dominate his life. It is left for Stephen to build a new world out of the ruins of the old, for this is the artist's function as Joyce saw it.

The *liliata rutilantium* phrase as it repeats itself in the novel and Stephen's response to it are also reflective of Joyce's careful interest in Giambattista Vico's cyclical theory of history.[32] The course of history flows in a cyclical pattern, running in the rhythm of *corso* and *ricorso*. This pattern is the rhythm of the *liliata rutilantium* allusion as Joyce weaves it through *Ulysses* and associates it with Stephen. The repetition itself is suggestive of the recurrence theme of Vico's and of *Finnegans Wake* which, of course, owes a great deal more to Vico's theory. The final allusion to the prayer occurs with Stephen's last act in the novel. History repeats itself with a difference: there has been a gathering up of all that the stream of time has carried with it. This last reference to the deathbed prayer and Stephen's reaction to it reflect the dominant pattern which was later to evolve in *Finnegans Wake*.

Stephen and Bloom finally bid each other good-bye with a handshake and Stephen leaves 7 Eccles Street. As he leaves, the sound of the peal of the hour from the bells of Saint George's brings the prayer back to his mind:

What echoes of that sound were by both and each heard?
By Stephen:
Liliata rutilantium. Turma circumdet.
Iubilantium te virginum. Chorus excipiat. (704)

The end echoes the beginning and itself becomes a beginning. Throughout *Ulysses* Stephen has been preoccupied with death. Death and guilt have made up his closed world in the sense that both have been deeply internalized; they are at the core of his metaphysical existence in the novel. The repetition of the Latin prayer for the dead frames death and guilt at each occurrence, and it is repeated in the novel at crisis points in Stephen's development. In itself the prayer is neutral, but Stephen's reaction to it is a clear indicator of his psychological condition. The last time the words are repeated in his memory they seem to fall on Stephen quietly. This quiet conclusion is in careful contrast to Stephen's earlier eruption.

The fact that the *liliata* prayer suggests itself to Stephen as his last thought in the novel clearly reveals certain thematic functions. First of all, it appears obvious to Stephen at last that he will never escape the nightmare of history and any attempts to break away from the bond of life, even gestures of the most dramatic kind, are hopeless. On the other hand, the closer he has looked at death, the more willing he appears to be able to accept life. There is no reconciliation between life and death, between guilt and freedom, for the world itself does not offer any. Extremely important to this view of the world is Stephen's life within the novel.

Perhaps the most clearly distinguishing differences the reader notes between Joyce's creation of the earlier Stephen and the Stephen in *Ulysses* are in the mood and style. For example, the entire "art for art's sake" mood which pervades chapters 4 and 5 of *A Portrait* is rejected from the very beginning. The Stephen of *Ulysses* is attempting to reach what Hermann Broch in his essay *James Joyce und die Gegenwart* calls "a cognition that embraces totality."[33] The conscious life of Stephen is progressively forced into isolation, but in his very detachment he reflects the themes of usurpation and betrayal which are such characteristic aspects of the temper of the isolated modern hero.

Arnold Goldman has convincingly argued for the strong influence of Kierkegaard on Joyce's work.[34] Goldman quite accurately suggests that the Stephen of *A Portrait* may be defined in terms of the Kierkegaardian crisis-state. Goldman notes that "Stephen's view of his own experience, as it develops in the *Portrait of the Artist,* projects a Kierkegaardian aesthetical trajectory, a subjectivist interpretation in which outer events serve merely to display basic unchanging characteristics in a permanent and static complex."[35] The Stephen of *Ulysses* moves far beyond this condition however tenuous his ultimate destiny may appear. Stephen's character, in spite of all the symbolic trappings of *Ulysses,* is rooted in the epistemological function of the novel—a novel which attempts to raise life to myth and in so doing presents a comprehensive world view. This latter point is not to suggest that Stephen's epistemological function can in any way be separated from Joyce's conscious art; on the contrary, it is his art which creates Stephen's philosophical and human depth.

Stephen's response to the disorder and disappointment of the world is the typically modern one of suspension—a state which nearly drives him to madness. Stephen is essentially unwilling to engage in battle with the world in the traditional sense; on the other hand, he refuses to make any inauthentic reconciliations. Suspension implies incompleteness and this incompleteness reflects Stephen's particular historical and metaphysical situation. Stephen's reflections throughout *Ulysses* clearly indicate that the religious question is central to his dilemma—central in the sense that it is the focal point of his rejection of the values of the world which produced him.

The Irish Catholicism under which Stephen Dedalus

grew up drew so much of its authority not from a vital spiritual community but rather a Catholicism which wrought a spiritually devastating emphasis on the heresies of Gnosticism, Albigensianism, and Jansenism, all heresies which deny man his goodness and perfection. It was this emphasis which accounted for so much of the paralysis of the Irish spirit of which Joyce wrote so knowingly. The indictment of the Roman Catholic Church of Ireland by Joyce is clearly reflected in Stephen's anguish. There is not one note of joy in Stephen's reflections on the Church. He is the victim not of religion but of a religious cult that had warped the religion of Christ so that it became a vapid organism that systematically denied man his goodness and drained from him recognition of the real essence of Christ's message. This is a large part of the nightmare which Stephen confronts in *Ulysses*. Stephen is a victim, and whatever his own weaknesses, he must do battle with the forces which deny man his independence and freedom of will and at the same time realize that freedom is not gained by mere rejection, or, as in Mulligan's case, by hypocrisy.

Stephen's earlier weapons of "silence, exile and cunning" hardly aid him now: silence turned him inward with his self-lacerating preoccupations; exile turned the world upon him rather than provided an escape; cunning, he realizes, has carried with it its own self-defeat. Stephen had espoused stasis as a condition of life as well as art, but he makes his rejections clear through enactment even if on another level he remains passive. For example, he rejects the contemporary reenactment of the good Samaritan parable. When Bloom finds Stephen, beaten up and drunk, he comes to his aid, brings him home, and offers cocoa. Stephen responds by singing a savagely bitter ballad about the

Christian who is killed by the daughter of the Jew who brought him home. Whatever arrogance one finds in surface actions such as this, the underlying recognition on Stephen's part reveals a much more complex and at the same time more self-defeating attitude: "One of all, the least of all, is the victim predestined" (692). But the posture of self-pity is in no sense final. A few moments later the narrator of the Ithaca episode announces a far different posture on the part of Stephen:

Did Stephen participate in his dejection?
He affirmed his significance as a conscious rational animal procceding syllogistically from the known to the unknown and a conscious rational reagent between a micro- and a macrocosm ineluctably constructed upon the incertitude of the void. (697)

Stephen's "incertitude" is what creates the deep tension between himself and the world. His earlier certitude had been melted by his serious attempts to discover who he was. Throughout *Ulysses* Stephen has held a precarious position in relation to all of those elements in the outside world with which he must somehow come to terms. He faces the uncertain relationship which again and again repeats itself in modern literature: the conflict between the self and the world. The character of Stephen Dedalus as he appears in *Ulysses* does more than particularize this broad thematic concern of so many modern novelists. With Stephen Dedalus, Joyce has given a human vision to one of the oldest themes in literature, and he has also refracted one element of his own substantial vision into the sensibilities of a modern intellectual who, with all his imperfections, carries on a human struggle to find meaning beyond despair.

NOTES

1. See especially Hugh Kenner, *Dublin's Joyce* (London: Chatto & Windus, 1955), and S. L. Goldberg, *The Classical Temper: A Study of James Joyce's "Ulysses"* (London: Chatto & Windus, 1961). Special attention will be given to these two seminal critical studies later in this essay.

2. "To Stanislaus Joyce, 7 February 1905," *Letters of James Joyce*, vol. 2, ed. Richard Ellmann (New York: Viking Press, 1966), p. 81.

3. Clive Hart, *James Joyce's "Ulysses"* (Sydney: Sydney University Press, 1968). Stanley Sultan, *The Argument of "Ulysses"* (Columbus: Ohio State University Press, 1964).

4. James Joyce, *A Portrait of the Artist as a Young Man*, ed. Chester G. Anderson and Richard Ellmann (New York: Viking Press, 1964), p. 221.

5. Kenner, *Dublin's Joyce*, p. 230.

6. William Empson, "The Theme of Ulysses," in *A James Joyce Miscellany*, ed. Marvin Magalaner, 3d series (Carbondale: Southern Illinois University Press, 1962), p. 125.

7. James Joyce, *Exiles* (New York: Compass Books, 1961), p. 125.

8. W. H. Auden, "Talent, Genius and Unhappiness," *The New Yorker*, November 30, 1957, pp. 221–37.

9. Frank Budgen, *James Joyce and the Making of "Ulysses"* (Bloomington: Indiana University Press, 1960), p. 105. Budgen's study was originally published in 1934. The 1960 edition contains some additional material in an appendix entitled "Further Recollections on James Joyce."

10. Ibid.

11. John Fowles, *The French Lieutenant's Woman* (Boston: Little, Brown, 1969), p. 96.

12. Cleanth Brooks, "Joyce's *Ulysses*: Symbolic Poem, Biography or Novel?" in *Imagined Worlds*, ed. Maynard Mack and Ian Gregor (London: Methuen & Co., 1968), p. 438.

13. Georg Lukács, *Studies in European Realism* (New York: Grosset and Dunlap, 1964), p. 221.

14. David Hayman has convincingly demonstrated that the comic element in *Ulysses* is developed from the opening episode and sustained throughout the work. See David Hayman, "Forms of Folly in Joyce: A Study of Clowning in *Ulysses*," *ELH* 34 (1968): 260–83.

15. A more extensive discussion of the various critical positions on *Ulysses* is found in my essay, "*Ulysses* and World Literature," in *James Joyce: His Place in World Literature*, ed. Wolodymyr T. Zyla (Lubbock:

Texas Tech Press, 1969), pp. 39–52. Also see Richard M. Kain, "The Position of *Ulysses* Today," in *James Joyce Today*, ed. Thomas F. Staley (Bloomington: Indiana University Press, 1966), pp. 83–95.

16. Joseph Prescott, *Exploring James Joyce* (Carbondale: Southern Illinois University Press, 1964), p. 60. An earlier version of this chapter appeared in 1959, "The Characterization of Stephen Dedalus in *Ulysses*," *Letterature Moderne* 9 (March–April 1959): 145–63.

17. Ibid., p. 62.

18. Some might take exception to this point, but certainly no one can read Stephen in nearly the same way Wyndham Lewis did after Hugh Kenner's analysis.

19. Goldberg, *The Classical Temper*, see especially pp. 103–12.

20. Kenner, *Dublin's Joyce*, p. 209.

21. L. A. Murillo has treated Kenner's argument succinctly in a recent study: *The Cyclical Night* (Cambridge: Harvard University Press, 1968).

22. Matthew Hodgart, *Satire* (London: Weidenfeld and Nicolson, 1969), p. 232.

23. Goldberg, *The Classical Temper*, p. 110.

24. E. M. W. Tillyard, *The Epic Strain in the English Novel* (London: Chatto & Windus, 1967), p. 188.

25. Ibid., pp. 188–89.

26. Margaret Church, *Time and Reality* (Chapel Hill: University of North Carolina Press, 1963), p. 39. I quote Professor Church not to attack her position individually but rather because of the succinctness of her representative statement.

27. Lionel Trilling, "James Joyce in His Letters," *Commentary* 45:2 (February, 1968), 54.

28. James Joyce, *Ulysses* (New York: Random House, 1961), p. 3. All references to *Ulysses* are to this edition and page numbers are given in parentheses.

29. Weldon Thornton in his *Allusions in "Ulysses"* (Chapel Hill: University of North Carolina Press, 1968) glosses and translates the prayer as follows:

E. R. Steinberg has identified this as coming from the "Ordo Commendationis Animae," a prayer for the dying, which can be found in most Roman Catholic *Rituals* in Tit. V, Cap. 7. The *Ritual* says this prayer is said by the bedside of the dying during the death agony. In the Irish *Ritual* of the time, this passage is translated, "may the lilied throng of radiant Confessors encompass thee: may the choir of rejoicing Virgins welcome thee." (pp. 17-18)

30.   Darcy O'Brien, *The Conscience of James Joyce* (Princeton: Princeton University Press, 1968), pp. 90–91.

31.   Umberto Eco, *Le Poetiche di Joyce* (Milano: Bompiani, 1966), p. 63.

32.   An excellent discussion by A. Walton Litz of Vico's influence on Joyce has appeared recently in *Giambattista Vico: An International Symposium*, ed. Giorgio Tagliacozzo (Baltimore: Johns Hopkins Press, 1969).

33.   Hermann Broch, *James Joyce und die Gegenwart* (Wein-Leipzig-Zurich: Herbert Reichner Verlag, 1936).

34.   Arnold Goldman, *The Joyce Paradox* (Evanston: Northwestern University Press, 1966), pp. 62–73.

35.   Ibid., pp. 72–73.

The Priesthoods
of Stephen
and Buck

ROBERT BOYLE, S. J.

2

THERE ARE MANY PRIESTS, real and metaphorical, operative in *Ulysses*. I intend to concentrate on two of the metaphorical priests, confecters of quite different metaphorical eucharists—Stephen Dedalus and Buck Mulligan. Several aspects of the opposition and attraction of these two figures, so important in the structure of the novel, from their initial union to their eventual sundering, can be clearly perceived in the light of the metaphorical priesthoods to which Joyce has ordained them.

The background for Stephen's priesthood lies in *A Portrait of the Artist as a Young Man.*[1] In "Astroglodyna-monologos," a paper read at the Second International James Joyce Symposium in Dublin, June 1969, I discussed some of the complications of the villanelle imagery. I spoke there too of the value of Robert Scholes's perceptive insight into the treatment of the Temptress as Irish muse, irresistible but destructive.[2] But further work needs to be done on sorting out the priest-Logos-Eucharist-Blessed Virgin complex of imagery in the passage dealing with the composition of the villanelle. It will help to keep in mind that Stephen pictures himself as artist in varied roles—as the God of creation; as the Holy Spirit, source of the sacraments; as the eternal Son; as the consecrator and donor of the true Eucharist; even as like the Blessed Virgin in bringing forth the Word.

In the passage preparing for the villanelle, Stephen pictures himself as seraph, drawn down from heaven by the alluring Temptress. It is necessary to note, however, that the seraph who shows up in the virgin's chamber is Gabriel, the angel Catholics are accustomed to from Luke 1:26 and from the Angelus; he is not at all Stephen. Stephen indeed does elsewhere scoff at the Virgin Birth, but it would not serve his purpose here (which is to elevate in romantic terms the divine role of the artist) to suggest improper activity between the seraph and Mary. Stephen does not do that anywhere, as far as I know. His suggestions elsewhere deal with Mary's relations with God, either God the Holy Ghost or God the Son. The Stephen of *Stephen Hero* does ask if the figure of "the Holy Ghost is intended for a spermatozoon with wings added."[3] He thus prepares the way for a later drunken suggestion of Mary's "knowing" God in some improper way, as I shall later discuss. But I do not find here any suggestion of sexual misbehavior between Mary and the angel.

Stephen has a goal other than lampoon or blasphemy here, anyway. There is here no glance at impropriety on Mary's part, nor is there any identification of Mary with the Temptress. Stephen is here comparing Mary with the artist's imagination, since both bring forth a life-giving word (or, as Stephen might say, Mary in the Catholic myth does something analogous to what the artist does in reality). Mary, having served her function of giving the desirable religious, sacred, sacramental character to the image, drops out of it, leaving only the eternal imagination as the focus of attention. Stephen does not say that Mary allured the seraph. The Temptress allured Stephen from seraphic life, and the seraph comes to Mary's chamber, but those are two distinct images, serving different functions. The second one (Mary and the seraph) is brought into the context of the first one, and profoundly influences it, but does not merge into it.

Further, the image concerning Mary serves to illumine another aspect of Stephen's image different from the alluring, enchanting aspect—namely, the beautiful, life-giving, eternal aspect aspired to in different tone by Yeats in his Fergus poems and in "To a Rose upon the Rood of Time." Mary, under the power of God the Holy Spirit (not of the seraph), conceives and brings forth the Word. The Word, in turn, changes bread into the food of divine life. He embodies his Spirit, the force which vivifies his blood, in wine that (in the Roman Catholic practice that Joyce knew) the priest may offer sacrifice and drink the living Word that brings, in Christ's promise (John 6:54), the possession of eternal life. Thus Stephen pictures the imagination, like another Mary, conceiving its artistic product, its word, under the power of the artist's spirit, which is like another Holy Spirit, and bringing forth an eternal word, the finished literary work, which extends into a true eucharist giving life to those who participate. Joyce employs the beautiful and noble aspirations of Catholic incarnational and eucharistic dogmas to exalt the true achievement of the successful literary artist.

Joyce's use of all these elements, and especially the relating of the Word-made-flesh to the Eucharist, is a natural outgrowth of Catholic thought and attitude. One element in the background lies in the long controversy over the Real Presence, with discussion often centered on whether the flesh of Christ in the Eucharist was the same flesh that Mary brought forth. The same elements that Joyce uses furnish the material for Hopkins's Latin poem, "In Festo Nativitatis, Ad Matrem Virginem, Hymnus Eucharisticus,"[4] written about twenty years before Stephen's villanelle. Here Hopkins links the Incarnation and the Eucharist, comparing the communicant receiving the Eucharist with the Blessed Virgin in her conception and bearing of Jesus. A few passages will show some of the similarities of Hopkins's and Joyce's use of the materials. To express the marvel of the infinite God becoming a human baby, Hopkins writes:

> Non concipiendum,
> Dominum tremendum,
> Sed in te contractum,
> Verbum carnem factum.

> [Not now to be conceived (i.e., understood) by us
> As the terrifying Lord that He is,
> But made small in you (Mary),
> The Infinite Word made flesh.]

To stress the notion of the Word becoming a wordless infant (literally, a nonspeaker), he says:

> Quae tu tum dicebas
> Et quae audiebas?
> Etsi fuit mutus,
> Tamen est locutus,
>
> . . . .
> Qui pro me vult dari,
> Infans mihi fari . . .

[What were you then saying,
And what were you hearing?
For even though he was mute
Nevertheless he spoke (since he is the Word Himself,
  by existing He speaks)
      . . . .
Who wishes to give himself for me,
Non-speaking (an infant) to speak to me (as the Word).]

Thus Hopkins, like Joyce, ties up the Blessed Virgin, the
Incarnation, the Word, the Eucharist, and himself. But of
course there is in the use of these identical elements a vast
difference. Hopkins accepted the Incarnation and the
Eucharist as realities; Stephen struggled to reject them.
Hopkins pictures the Word coming from Mary through the
Eucharist to him. Stephen pictures himself bringing forth
a word-eucharist superior to the one Mary conceived and
brought forth.

But there is another aspect to the villanelle which tem-
pers its beauty, an aspect of horror, of fear, of enchantment
in the sense of black magic, of flowing blood and lustful
flesh—the Black Mass aspect. The human imagination as
Stephen experiences it also fears and dreads reality. For
Stephen, driven insane by visions of hell (as Buck Mulligan
avers), the Manichean downward pull into evil matter is
expressed in the villanelle by many things.

First, the allurement of the Temptress threatens him
with, or has already caused in him, that angelic or Icarian
fall he dreaded (yet desperately desired) in *Portrait*: "He
would fall. He had not yet fallen but he would fall silently,
in an instant" (*P*, 162). The instant turns out to be "that
mysterious instant" which Stephen labels as "the enchantment of the heart" (*P*, 213). And the fall and the enchantment appear in the first tercet of the villanelle. Scholes

deals well with the dark aspects of this enchantment, pointing out the ways in which the Temptress is like the Leanhaun Shee, who lives on the lives of those who submit to her. Stephen fears in his Irish muse the bat-like soul, the cannibalistic sow, that he perceived in the Ireland he passionately but hopelessly loved.

Second, the chalice lifted in the villanelle is excessively full, "flowing to the brim," not with winking beaded bubbles, but with blood—something of a Dracula tonality here. This chalice of the artist is definitely in opposition to the broken chalice of the senile priest in "The Sisters," which "contained nothing." On the symbolism of this latter chalice and of the detailed preparation for later priesthood imagery, see the perceptive article of John William Corrington, "The Sisters."[5]

I should like to digress for a moment to speak of smiles and simony. Corrington is especially good on priestly smiles in Joyce's work. The boy in "The Sisters" returns the old priest's "uncertain, conspiratorial smile, offers the old man absolution of 'simony,' for having tried to 'sell' him [the boy-narrator] a religious vocation which he [Father Flynn] himself found too much to bear."[6] Corrington lists Cranly's priestlike smile, the visiting Jesuit's smile, Father Conmee's smiles. He does not mention, but well could, the unseen smile of the spiritual director: "Stephen smiled again in answer to the smile which he could not see on the priest's shadowed face" (*P*, 155). Here the invitation is to share in the power of the priesthood. Herein lies the simony that Stephen sees in all priests. "Don't you think they are trying to buy me?" Stephen Hero asks Maurice (*SH*, 228). The priests, he thinks, want to barter his freedom for a share of their power.

Stephen is under great pressure from his mother too to enter the priesthood. I agree with William Schutte when he says, "The futility and frustrations of her life were to be redeemed by Stephen's accession to the priesthood."[7] This explains May's animosity even to a Catholic university for Stephen. If her prayers are to be answered, he must be in the seminary, where only orthodox books and ideas would be admitted.

. This pressure and bartering are the background for Stephen's interview with the spiritual director, where, after the almost hysterical sales pitch of the priest couched in terms of power, ending with a semi-blasphemous claim to have power, authority over God Himself, Stephen goes on to think of the sin of Simon Magus (*P*, 158–59). A conspiratorial smile in such circumstances takes on hellish overtones.

To return to the villanelle: the third, and most important, of the ambivalent elements in the villanelle is the smoke of incense rising above the smoke of flame. Incense can indeed have pleasant and romantic aspects for Stephen. Like many Catholic children, the young Stephen was considerably more interested, apparently, in the sight of the rising, swirling clouds of incense, the fragrant smell, and the mysterious symbolism tied up with the mystic East, with Araby and Aladdin and Sinbad and the Thousand and One Nights, than with the Blessed Sacrament that the incense honored. Anyone who has been a young server, or who has dealt with them in their preparations for high mass and for benediction, knows the effort required to keep them from excess in pouring in incense as they prepare the thurible before the ceremony. Their enthusiastic swinging of the censer in the sanctuary sometimes causes them (and the priest as well) to choke on the fumes. Something of this youthful enthusiasm appears in Stephen's pleasure in the incense smoke rising "up in clouds on both sides" as he watches a vigorous acolyte at benediction (*P*, 46).

The older Stephen occasionally saw incense expressing bad or threatening things, as in the "vapour of maddening incense" rising from his vices (*P*, 86), or the corruption of his civilization, "mortal odour, faint incense" (*P*, 184). Sometimes he used it in sickeningly sentimental fashion, as in his reaction to his pseudoconversion and confession, when he timidly approached through "the fragrance of incense" in the church (*P*, 141) and later, in relation to the bitterly ironic cash register image, in maudlin contrast sees "the amount of his purchase start forth immediately in heaven, not as a number but as a frail column of incense or as a slender flower" (*P*, 148).

With such background Stephen approached his image of the earth as "a swinging smoking swaying censer" sending up from the vapory oceans the smoke of her praise, incense ascending from the altar of the world (*P*, 218). George Geckle, in "Stephen Dedalus and W. B. Yeats: The Making of the Villanelle," has well demonstrated how Joyce drew material from Yeats for this imagery.[8] "We can compare Yeats's 'clouds of incense' and 'flame on flame' in 'He remembers Forgotten Beauty' with Stephen's 'above the flame the smoke of praise.'" He stresses Yeats's emphasis on "dream-heavy hour" with Stephen's waking to compose the villanelle.

But there is a darker aspect to this incense, which is here also smoke, and smoke in excess. The poem indeed is packed with excess of romantic baggage, "fallen seraphim," "man's heart ablaze," "the chalice flowing to the brim," and the revoltingly Swinburnian "And still you hold our longing gaze / With languorous look and lavish limb." With all this excess we have smoke rising above oceans of flame "from rim to rim." The Temptress in her dark aspect is the lure who pulls seraphs down to hell (that is, at least, the only place seraphs can go, in Catholic tradition, when they fall; and behind that "lure" I suspect the presence of Shakespeare's Sonnet 129, with its "bait on purpose laid to make the taker mad" and to draw the lustful person to "the heaven that leads men to this hell"). In this dark aspect, she reminds Stephen, I believe, of that "fire of hell" described so vividly in the Jesuit retreat: "It is a neverending storm of darkness, dark flames and dark smoke of burning brimstone" (*P*, 120). In the Black Mass of *Ulysses*, "Brimstone fires spring up. Dense clouds roll past" (*U*, 598).[9] These clouds, like the tower setting of the Black Mass, derive from the "cloud of coalsmoke and fumes of fried grease" of the morning breakfast in Martello Tower, not totally unlike, in smaller scale, the confines of the smoking and fuming prison of hell described in the retreat. In that Black Mass, a mass and a blood-filled chalice operate in relation to flames and smoke, as they also do, with different tonality but with related meaning, in the villanelle.

The lady of the villanelle, praised by incense, foreshadows several ladies of *Ulysses* also related to incense. The decadent sirens of awakening Paris newmaking their tumbled beauties (*U*, 42) do so under the matin incense of wormwood. Gerty MacDowell, under "fragrant incense" and "fragrant names" wafting from the church, thinks, as her heart goes pitapat under Bloom's burning look, of "the perfume of those incense they burned in the church like a kind of waft" (*U*, 357). She coyly fumigates her calculat-

ingly lustful urges with pious incense. The more professionally lustful Nymph emerges through a "pall of incense
smoke" in the Circe chapter (*U*, 544). And in a vein perverse like Gerty's but far more earthy and honest, Molly
ties up lust and incense in imagining herself embraced by
a vested priest with "the smell of incense off him like the
pope" (*U*, 741). Against the background of the languorous
looks and lavish limbs of the Temptress being praised by
the smoke of incense rising ritually from oceans of flame,
Molly's attitude toward incense seems puritanically re-
strained.

For Joyce's priests, incense is approached in a brisk, busi-
nesslike manner. Father Conmee uses it to determine his
bearings on his purposeful wanderings, as he passes St.
Joseph's and mechanically, while considering the conventional virtues and real vices of the inmates, salutes the
Blessed Sacrament (*U*, 221). Canon O'Hanlon, assisted by
Gabriel's brother, Father Conroy, in no-nonsense sentence
structure and diction, goes through the ritual of censing
the Blessed Sacrament, efficiently noting on the second
incensation danger to the flowers (*U*, 359 and 361). Stephen, as priest of the imagination, approaches the matter
of censing, in the villanelle, with far more romantic fervor,
but with him too, as with the actual priests, the incense is
intimately tied up with the Blessed Sacrament. Incense at
high masses is used to honor and praise the host and the
chalice at the elevation. It is not, therefore, surprising that
in the villanelle passage the image of the censer and the
smoke of praise led Stephen, as he meanders through
thoughts of himself as monk (*P*, 219–20) and then of the
conventional priest Father Moran, into the radiant image
of the Eucharist, and thus to the hymns and sacrificing

hands of the mass. Thence he passes into the baptism of her nakedness ("like water with a liquid life"—*P*, 223) and thus has the basis for imagining the new life of one born again—albeit into hell. The villanelle thus, in a way, recounts Stephen's life from his adventures with the ritualistic, perfumed whores, under the gasflames burning as if before an altar, through his pseudoconversion and piety, into his emergence from the grave, his rapturous vision of the girl in midstream, and his soul's Shelleyan "swooning into some new world" (*P*, 172). It is in part the unhealthy poem of a poseur, surely, as Geckle points out in stating that the "weary" of the villanelle stems from the Shelley fragment Stephen quotes earlier, "Art thou pale for weariness." Geckle, in opposing Scholes's view that with this poem Stephen ceases to be an esthete and becomes an artist, says that Stephen "is an esthete who never gets beyond the sentimental stage of erotic lyricism."[10] But, partially true as this statement is, it is not the whole truth, as careful attention to some of Scholes's arguments and, above all, to the symbolism of the mass indicates.

Stephen, then, does set himself up as a priest in the villanelle. He does it in relation to the Eucharist, and forms an image that Joyce later makes use of in varied ways. As priest of eternal imagination, he will transmute the daily bread of experience into the radiant body of overliving life (*P*, 221). I spoke in my paper at the Joyce Symposium of the oddity, from the view of Catholic orthodoxy elsewhere operative in the image, of Stephen's participle, *transmuting*. One would expect *transubstantiating* or *changing*, but not *transmuting*. The denotation of *transmuting* is of course quite right, but the connotation is all wrong, from the point of view of the Catholic doctrine and usage. All the words

can mean a basic shift in substance, but *transmute* carries
with it not only its magical atmosphere from its use in
alchemy (which here goes with *enchanted*), but the notion that once the change is effected, you will be able to
perceive it—you will know it is gold or whatever it has
been changed to, to see it or test it or find it out somehow.
Transubstantiate has since the thirteenth century been in
official use in Roman Catholic teaching, and specifically, in
a religious context, carries with it the notion that no physical means can uncover the change in substance. *Change* is,
clearly, broad enough to encompass the same connotation.
But *transmute*, as it has normally been used, does nothing
of the kind, as a glance at the *O.E.D.* will verify. Hence I
judge that its use in Stephen's image suggests some of the
dark and magical elements that Stephen develops in his
alluring witch (here not a laughing one) who enchants
knights-at-arms. Stephen had tried unsuccessfully to be
the knight, in Jesuit imagery, of the Blessed Virgin (*P*,
105); now he finds himself enthralled by the Temptress,
who turns out to be his own soul, his own imagination, alluring and repulsive all at once.

Stephen compares the work of literary art to the Eucharist on several bases: 1) it is made from something ordinary,
daily experience, as the Eucharist is made from daily
bread; 2) it emerges from the spirit of a man, as the Eucharist (that is, Christ) emerges from the power of the
Holy Spirit; 3) it develops in and proceeds from the imagination, as the Eucharist (that is, Christ) developed in and
proceeded from the Blessed Virgin; 4) it gives life, self-
knowledge, conscience, to those who respond to it, as the
Eucharist brings divine life to the communicants. The
Word-made-flesh, the Logos, is closely tied in with Joyce's

use of the Eucharist image, as we have seen. He heard those words daily, "et Verbum carnem factum est," for all of his early life, in the last gospel of the mass, and he said them three times a day in the Angelus: "And the Word was made flesh, and dwelt among us" (John 1:14). This divine Word became for him the artistic word, and led him to much of the imagery concerning literary art not only in *Portrait* but in *Ulysses* and *Finnegans Wake* too, and not only in relation to Stephen and Shem but in relation to Buck Mulligan and Shaun as well.

Buck appears as usurping priest on the opening pages of *Ulysses*. The stately diction and sentence structure reflect the ritual imagery of the mass: Buck *bears* his bowl as if it were a chalice, as the boy in "Araby" bore his chalice safely, or as Stephen was boatbearer at Clongowes (*P*, 41), an experience Stephen recalls (*U*, 11) as he holds Buck's bowl; Buck intoned; solemnly, he blessed gravely. His dressing-gown is yellow, a liturgical color which can be used any time the proper color is not attainable. His gown is ungirdled, highly appropriate for Buck; the prayer the priest says as he puts on his cincture (or "girds his loins") is a prayer for chastity. The mild morning air does what a server does for the priest in raising the hem of a long chasuble. Buck intones the opening prayer of the mass and then, with a possible allusion, as Edmund Epstein pointed out,[11] to Friar Laurence's "Come forth, thou fearful man,"[12] he indicates both his patronizing attitude toward Stephen in "Kinch" (which I suppose, with Tindall, comes from *Kinchen*, child) and his notion of the kind of priest Stephen is, a Jesuit afraid of hellish reality. Stephen, emerging, gazes at the "untonsured" hair, a companion word to "ungirdled." The *un-* operates here, I take it, as it does, for example, in

Keats's "Thou still unravished bride . . ." where the prefix denies the thing expected, the thing that should be. The urn should, after all these ages, be marred by bustle and time, but against all expectation, is not. In Joyce's text, too, Buck as priest should be girdled and tonsured, but he is not, and his role as usurper is stressed.

Buck now cutely peeps and covers smartly. He is about to make a funny. Sternly he orders, "Back to barracks." I cannot recall seeing any discussion of that puzzling order. I can see two possibilities. Either soldiers in the pubs are being ordered to barracks for emergency assignment or soldiers operating at the front are being ordered to desist and return to barracks. If it is the first, then Buck could be addressing Christ, or "Christine," on the basis of ordering him, or her, to leave the bliss of heaven and get back to Christian soldiering in the Eucharist. This reading is perhaps strengthened by the semiblasphemous statement Joyce puts into the mouth of the spiritual director in *Portrait* (p. 158), ". . . the power, the authority, to make the great God of Heaven come down upon the altar and take the form of bread and wine." Still, interesting as the reading is, it does seem to me less likely than the other possibility, partly because it has never been Catholic teaching that Christ leaves heaven in order to be present in the Eucharist. Buck could be obviously ignoring that fact, which he certainly would know, for his satirical purposes, but, since there is another and, I now tend to believe, better alternative, I think he would realize that the use of something so alien to Catholic attitude would weaken his lampoon, both in his own and in Stephen's eyes.

Buck is more likely speaking to something that once was in barracks, is now here operating, and which must leave for some good reason and get back to barracks. This, I take it, is Buck the scientist lampooning the Catholic doctrine on transubstantiation. Since the Fourth Lateran Council in 1215, when the doctrine was defined and declared to have been traditional in the Church, the term *transubstantiation* has been official for Catholic teaching. There have always been several respectable theological theories about what it means and implies, but in the one Buck evidently is using, some such statement as the following would explain how the Real Presence of Christ in the sacrament is effected: the substance of the bread is replaced by the substance of Christ's living body, while the accidents of the bread (the things apparent to our senses) remain sustained by God in some mysterious way. Buck is probably thinking also of the Aristotelean notion that all material forms emerge from the potency of matter in order to become actual and to operate, and when the being they inform ceases to exist they sink back into the potency of matter. Thus, as he proceeds with his burlesque of the consecration of the mass, Buck suggests that the substance of the lather is not withdrawing fast enough to the barracks (or potency of matter) from which it emerged, thus slowing up the entrance of the substance of Christ's body. He therefore orders it to hurry, in military terms.

The military image derives, I suspect, from his experience with Jesuit spirituality, especially in the *Spiritual Exercises* of the knightly founder of the Jesuits. Jesuit military imagery derives in part from St. Paul, of course, and is familiar to modern readers in the poetry of Gerard Manley Hopkins (who, had he lived ten years longer, might have taught Joyce at University College). We have already seen Stephen limply wishing to be the knight of the Blessed

Virgin (*P*, 105), and in *Stephen Hero*, Stephen speaks of the Pope as Christ's "lieutenant in Rome" (*SH*, 141), which of course implies that Christ, like the General of the Jesuits, is in some way a military commander. In *Finnegans Wake*, in an ecclesiastical context, Shaun, at the end of his sermon, almost immediately following the last blessing of the mass, expresses the "Ite, Missa est" ("Go, the Mass is ended") with the briskly military "Break ranks!"[13]

As he proceeds with his lampoon, Buck, like a Catholic Dowie, preaches the Catholic doctrine of transubstantiation to the faithful. Why "Christine" instead of "Christ"? Harry Blamires ingeniously suggests that Buck says "Christine" because Stephen's grandmother was named Christina and his favorite whore was named Georgina, and since the fox buried his grandmother, and the founder of the Quakers was named George Fox, we perceive why Buck says "Christine."[14] No doubt the point he makes eludes me, because I am left with the question still. I suspect that one good reason for Buck's saying "Christine" instead of "Christ" is that he wants the rhythm and false rhyme which the *-ine* endings provide. He tends to speak in balanced rhythms, jingling rhymes, and alliterative words: "Come up, Kinch"; "Back to barracks"; "Malachi Mulligan"; "snotgreen sea"; "scrotumtightening sea"; "our mighty mother." "Genuine Christ" is abrupt, not at all "tripping and sunny like the buck himself" (*U*, 4). Further, "Christine" is closer to that "Hellenic ring" that Buck desires. When he brings forth his play at the end of the Scylla and Charybdis chapter, he does it in Greek terms, clasping "his paunchbrow with both birthaiding hands," like Zeus bringing forth Pallas Athena (*U*, 208). The artist thus, in the ideal Greek context as God of creation, will bring forth a goddess rather than a god. Moreover, his Greek approach takes off from and opposes Stephen's Trinitarian-Sabellian approach (*U*, 208). Similarly, in these opening pages, Buck opposes his own sunny Hellenic strain to Stephen's dark, sinister, Jesuit strain. Further, if Buck were going to change bread into a person to be consumed, he would prefer (or so he would publicly proclaim) female flesh to male. All the metaphorical priests in the book—Stephen (worshiping his own soul, his muse), Bloom (worshipping Martha and Gerty and Molly), Boylan (sipping his chalice in the Ormond Bar)—adore female flesh. If there is more to the choice of "Christine" than this, I fail to see it.

Now Buck goes on to suggest the activity he was used to at mass, quiet organ music at the time of consecration, the prayerful closing of eyes, the dramatic pauses—and he interjects a scientific jab at the doctrine with the notion that the whole body is there except for the white corpuscles. Then he whistles and pauses. Someone at the Forty Foot or elsewhere nearby hears the whistle and whistles twice in answer. It is possible that this is an echo of the thrice-rung bell at the consecration of the mass. Buck pretends the two whistles are the answer he is waiting for from the Holy Spirit, who is supplying the power for this operation (as He did for the Incarnation, "The Holy Spirit will come upon you, and the power of the Most High will overshadow you"—Luke 1:35), and Buck, understanding this for the signal that the process of transubstantiation is complete, asks that the current be switched off.

Stephen now sees Buck as a prelate, patron of the arts in the Middle Ages. As usurping priest, Buck patronizes Stephen, the true priest of art. Stephen dwells on this notion when he thinks of the old woman serving Haines, her con-

queror, and Buck, her gay betrayer (*U*, 14). And he scorns
her for honoring Buck, the bonesetter, while she slights
the artist. Stephen identifies Buck the doctor with the real
priest giving Extreme Unction (priests are instructed to
omit the anointing of the loins when giving the sacrament
to a woman, and with "unclean" Stephen possibly refers
both to Buck's medical concern for cleanliness and to scriptural ritual uncleanness). Stephen alone, as artist, is a true
priest, and Ireland, in the person of the Old Woman, ig-
nores him.

Buck continues his crushing, patronizing smothering of
Stephen in the Scylla and Charybdis chapter. As Stephen
desperately continues with his proof that in Hamlet and in
Shakespeare, as in the Trinity, the son is consubstantial
with the father (*U*, 197), his "enemy," Buck, answers
"amen" from the doorway, and proceeds to carry out his
role as usurping priest. Against Stephen's exhausting (and
futile) attempt to set up an analysis of Shakespeare's soul
through his plays, Buck, as Zeus, produces his own crudely
realistic mirroring of reality, *Everyman His Own Wife*, in
terms of the male crotch, with the genitals (Toby, Dick,
and Davy), denizens of the pubic bush (Crab), bladder
(Mother Grogan), and, I suppose, kidneys (Nellie and
Rosalie) playing roles. Stephen is for the moment crushed
by the ruthless, materialistic will that fronts him, that of
Buck, and realizes anew the gulf between the two of them.
Bloom passes and looks upon Stephen, as Stephen thinks
of the ritual of augury, background for his dream in which
he flew, ending in the street of harlots where a man offered
him melon, as Bloom will offer him Molly. Buck, in the
manner of Oxenford, always sexually ambiguous in Joyce's
usage and offensive to Stephen, suspects Bloom of having

homosexual designs on Stephen. And two plumes of smoke, like the "crooked smokes" of the newspaper office (*U*, 142) and like the frail column of incense of *Portrait* (*P*, 148), lead Stephen to think again of *Cymbeline* and of the long-past Druid priests, silent (Buck speaks of "a druid silence" on page 416), interpreting mysteries in symbols rather than in speech, sending up, not the thick clouds of the villanelle, but soft crooked smokes from the altar of the wide earth.

Stephen, however, does not follow up his fleeting desire for the peace of Druidic priesthood, but returns to his Christian image in the Oxen of the Sun episode. Here there are elements of the mass scattered throughout the chapter. I fully agree with Ruth M. Walsh that it is vain and erroneous to impose a structure of the mass on Joyce's novels, and I see no definite structure here.[15] But some elements suggest a vague procession distantly like the development of the mass, with the kyrielike invocation, the semiconsecration by Stephen, the echoes of the prayers after mass at the end of the chapter.

Stephen's semiconsecration, set in his discussion of the artist as priest, as (like the Blessed Virgin) producer of the word, as eternal Son (*U*, 391-92), is most closely connected with his previous notions of himself as priest. Stephen sits at the head of the board, surrounded by those who receive drink from his hands and who listen to his wisdom. Stephen has been described in terms that could suggest Christ at the Last Supper ("young Stephen that had the mien of a frere that was at the head of the board"— *U*, 388), and now rises to pray with his chalice in hand. Paraphrasing the words of Christ, he invites them to drink of this cup which is not his body (as, in Catholic doctrine, the wine, as well as the bread, is), but which embodies his soul. I am puzzled by the phrase "my soul's bodiment" (*U*, 391). I suppose Stephen means a play on the word *spirit* as applied to the liquor and to his soul. In his parody of Pope Leo's prayer after mass (*U*, 427), Stephen puns on "spirits" (meaning *bad angels* in the prayer) and "those other licensed spirits" (referring, of course, to the drinks they are having). Perhaps he means also that the drink gives body to his soul by giving him energy and courage to bring forth the word. But I merely guess.

Stephen goes on to a play on words quite as clever and considerably more profound than Buck's "back to barracks." He tells his listeners to drink only and leave the breaking of bread to those who live by bread alone. In terms of Christ's use of the words in Matthew 4:4, such persons would be those who do not trust and follow the word of God. In terms of Catholic communion practice, they would be the laity, who in former practice received only the bread. Bloom observes this on page 81: "Doesn't give them any of it." Hence by these words Joyce sets himself off from the laity, since as priest he can drink from the chalice. As early as his first *Dubliners* story, "The Sisters," Joyce used this symbol of the rejection of the bread in favor of the wine, as Brewster Ghiselin and many later critics have noted. It is in the chalice that Joyce's interest centers—the broken chalice in "The Sisters," the boy's chalice in "Araby," the chalice in the villanelle, Buck's bowl-chalice. And it is drink—Mr. Fogarty's special whiskey in "Grace," a symbol of Greek communion practice; the tea from the East in "Grace," in *Ulysses*, in *Finnegans Wake*; the coffee and cocoa Bloom ritually offers Stephen—that gets most of the symbolic attention. So it is reasonable to understand (as Tindall also does in his *Reader's Guide to*

James Joyce[16]) in Stephen's rejection of the bread in favor
of the wine, the repetition of his villanelle image of himself as the true priest.

Now Stephen shows his companions the glistening coins
of tribute, which prepares for the Peter Piscator passage
to follow,[17] as well as for the house that Jack built (the
Vatican). Then he goes into imagery like that of the villanelle discussion, quoting Blake first, and then explicat-
ing Blake's words in the more romantic manner of the Irish
revival. "Time's ruins" is equated to "Desire's wind blasts
the thorntree." The thorntree which bears a rose is a traditional Catholic image for the Blessed Virgin. For example,
in Hopkins's "Rosa Mystica,"[18] Mary is the rose and she is
also the tree who bears the blossom, Christ. But, though
this Catholic image is certainly in the background, Stephen
is evidently thinking in more general terms, using "thorntree" for the element of danger, cruelty, and pain which
"thorn" can carry, and aiming to symbolize any human being destined to bear the rose, not of Christ as in the Catholic image, but of eternal beauty as in the quote from Yeats
which follows. "Build eternity's mansion" is equated to
"but after it becomes from a bramblebush to be a rose upon
the rood of time." In the Catholic image, as in Hopkins's
poem, the person becomes Christ, shares Christ's eternal
life and the mansions he promised his followers. But Stephen, using the title of Yeats's "To the Rose upon the Rood
of Time," stresses, as Yeats does, the contrast between, in
Yeats's words, the "heavy mortal hopes that toil and pass"
and the poet's finding of "eternal beauty wandering on her
way." No doubt Stephen thinks, as poet-priest, of sharing
Yeats's hope to "learn to chaunt a tongue men do not
know."

Now Stephen proceeds to compare once again the artist to the Blessed Virgin. The artist, in Stephen's view, is greater than she is, because though in her womb the word was made flesh (or, as his present tense suggests, in every mother "word"—meaning, I suppose, creative force—is made flesh), in the artist's spirit flesh becomes everliving word. "The word that shall not pass away" combines reference to Christ as the eternal Word and to Christ's words that will not pass away (Matthew 24:35).

"The postcreation," then, is the artist's creation following upon God's, and better than God's. All flesh comes to God, but then dies. All flesh comes to the artist, and lives.

Now Stephen continues his comparison of the artist with Mary, and his aim will be to show her in a relatively bad light. She is powerful in petition, as Catholic tradition has it, and she is second Eve, undoing the bad work of the first. But there is a problem. And now we have a moral dilemma based on a play on the word *know*, which in scriptural use, as in Mary's words to the angel, "I do not know man," means sexual intercourse.

Stephen states that one of two things must be true: Either Mary had some kind of sexual congress with him—and now the problem rises at once. Who is signified by *him*? Thornton[19] suggests the Holy Spirit, but then how explain "creature of her creature," especially in relation to the quotation from Dante which follows. I think *him* must refer to God the Son, and that Stephen is supposing that the Son as God begot himself upon his mother (as Stephen thinks in his Sabellian Creed (*U*, 197): "He Who Himself begot . . . and Himself sent himself." *Sent* in that final clause refers to the Incarnation, and the first *Himself* is the Divine Son and the second, lower case *himself* is the human

Jesus). Then Mary could be said to be creature (in the sense of toy or puppet or mistress) of her creature (in the sense of being the sole source of human life for Jesus), a statement Stephen chooses to consider analogous to Dante's "daughter of your son."

Or, on the other horn of the dilemma, she did not know him, in the sense of recognizing his divinity, and then she who said "I know not man" is to be blamed as is the denier Peter, who said "I do not know the man" (Matthew 26:72, a passage Stephen and Cranly recall—*P*, 244—as a source of rare liturgical poetry), and as is the ignorant Joseph, who in effect said, "I do not know who the man is who made her pregnant."[20] This last leads Stephen to the thought of Taxil, who answered Joseph's doubt by saying it was the damned pigeon (when *sacré* precedes the noun, I am told, it means *damned*). Taxil speaks of Mary's "fichue position," and this leads Stephen (or I think it does) to his next dichotomy.

With German conjunctions to indicate the weighty *Wissenschaft* involved, he uses two terms common in discussion of the Eucharist, and makes up another by an analogy with the first two. But he clearly does not wish to use them in their proper senses, but applies them to Mary's situation. *Transubstantiality* in the Eucharist does refer to divine substance replacing material substance. Here then it could be applied to a divine person "knowing" a human person, as in the first horn of the dilemma. *Consubstantiality* in the Eucharist refers to both substances being present at once, and the *with* is that of the second horn of the dilemma, where Mary is *with* Peter and Joseph. And the third term, *subsubstantiality*, would refer to one substance *under* another substance, which would be like the conventional po-

sition of a woman in intercourse or "cette fichu position."
Ironically Stephen says "Never that," and all enthusiastically agree. But if there is no sexual activity, there is no joy,
even though it is accompanied, as in Mary's case, with no
pangs, blemish, or bigness. Let the laity, the unlearned,
believe that! We who are true priests, having quaffed the
mazer, will, with the power of our will, withstand such
dogmas as the Virgin Birth. And thus the orgulous and
jealous Stephen the drunken artist (who is also reacting to
his former sentimental and irrational response to the Virgin—compare *P*, 105 and 116) has asserted his priestly
superiority to the Mother of God.

Once again, at the end of the chapter, Buck Mulligan
moves to put down Stephen the artist. Having asserted, in
his discussion of Stephen with Haines in the D.B.C. (*U*,
249), that the Jesuits had driven his wits astray with visions
of hell, so that he could never be the ideal Hellenic poet,
or any poet at all, Buck says of Stephen in the confusion of
Burke's pub, "Jesified orchidised polycimical jesuit!" (*U*,
425). The adjectives raise a number of interesting critical
problems.

The first two of the adjectives clearly refer to the influence the Jesuits have had on Stephen, in Buck's view, and
the third, at least in Stephen's own symbolic context, could
also be seen in this light.

Orchidised is the simplest of the adjectives. Buck is
building on the medical term *orchidectomy* (castration).
The Jesuits, in his judgment, have, by frightening Stephen
into insanity, rendered him artistically sterile.

Polycimical (*many-loused*) brings to mind Stephen's
own musings on his lousiness, his mother's hands bloodied
with her children's lice (*U*, 10), and above all, his symbolic

treatment of his lice in *Portrait*: "A louse crawled over the nape of his neck and, putting his thumb and forefinger deftly beneath his loose collar, he caught it. . . . His mind bred vermin. His thoughts were lice born of the sweat of sloth" (*P*, 233–34). Thus his lice become symbols of false thoughts and images. In such a context, Buck's adjective gains point, though there is no indication that Buck knew such a context. Joyce did, however, and that context may have influenced his choice of the word to give greater depth to Buck's view of Stephen's situation. Joyce's tendency to link lice with Jesuits appears in his letter from Rome to Stanislaus, 12 September 1906, in which he refers to the Jesuits as "black lice."[21] Buck, of course, could well be using the adjective simply because unclean Stephen (*U*, 15) had lice.

But it is *Jesified* that presents problems. I take it that Buck is treating the *-us* of *Jesus* as if it were a Latin ending, and then forming his word on analogy with such words as *magnified* and *ratified*. Thus it literally would mean *Jesus-made* or *made-a-Jesus*. But that is puzzling. *Jesus* was, as Stanislaus tells us,[22] one of Gogarty's favorite words, but Buck uses it only once ("and then you go and slate her drivel to Jaysus"—*U*, 216). Joking Jesus, a bastard, is the butt of Mulligan's song, and this contemptuous attitude probably is the main basis for the present coinage. In the Circe chapter (*U*, 591), Edward the Seventh, appearing in relation to Stephen, wears the garb and halo of Joking Jesus, and sings two lines from the third stanza of Mulligan's song. The whole poem is given in *Letters II*,[23] and Gogarty, who wanted it sent to Joyce, would no doubt have noted how much of the description fits Stephen (as it did Joyce): Joking Jesus doesn't swim, doesn't bathe (hence connection with lice), depends on others for support, breezily soars into the air, and so on. Thus Buck, in making Stephen into a Joking Jesus, could once again express his contempt and dislike (mingled, it is true, with something of friendly concern) for Stephen's accepting and operating by the cursed Jesuit strain injected the wrong way, manifesting itself in fanatical g.p.i. (*U*, 6) and in activities both unnatural and sinister (*U*, 5).

As I worked with this word, I toyed with the notion that Joyce might be hinting at a punning reference to *jess*, the cord keeping the hawk in control. That would fit Stephen's notion of the soaring hawklike man (*P*, 169). It could recall the dramatic scene in the spiritual director's office, where the priest stood "his back to the light . . . slowly dangling and looping the cord of the other blind" with his "deft" priestly fingers (*P*, 153–54). Thus *jesified* would suggest, in relation to castration and lousy dogmas with which the Jesuits had crippled Stephen, that they also used their first syllable on him as a device to keep him inside the maze. Religion, Stephen told Davin (*P*, 203), is one of the nets flung at him to hold him back from flight.

Further, Joyce could have, as could Stephen Hero who read Skeats's *Etymological Dictionary* by the hour (*SH*, 26), run across Skeats's quotation from *Ayenbite of Inwit* under *jesses*: " 'Me ofhalt thane vogel be the ges,' one restrains the bird by the jess." The *Ayenbite* is treating "The Third Step of Sobriety," which would fit particularly well with the close of the Oxen of the Sun episode, and the quotation Skeats gives continues, "that he may not fly according to his will," which, granted that he knew it, could be a background for Stephen's "with will will we withstand, withsay" (*U*, 392). But though I find the supposition particularly tempting, I am able to perceive no probability that Joyce intended such a context, though I do glimpse a bare possibility.

There is of course the possibility also that Buck intends not *Jesus* but *Jesuit* by "Jes-." This seems to me extremely unlikely, because I can find no plausible background for the redundancy "Jesuit-made . . . jesuit" or "Made a-Jesuit . . . jesuit." To say "Made-a-Jesus . . . jesuit" could mean that Stephen was made a Jesus in Buck's notion of the Jesuit pattern, a slavish, fanatical, unscientific, sterile failure. But only vapid repetition results from the other supposition. Further, if Buck meant that, I would expect him to say *Jesuified*, which would make the point clear. Buck's "the jejune jesuit" (*U*, 4) might indeed suggest, in relation, say, to the dried-up Dean of Studies of *Portrait*, the notion of a desiccated Stephen-tailored-into-a-jesuit jesuit, but it does not strike me as likely.

Still, it occurred to me that checking the French and German translations might be helpful. I turned to my friend and knowledgeable colleague, Alan Cohn, Humanities Librarian at Southern Illinois University, asking him to send me the translations from SIU's excellent collection. He did so, with illuminating comments. He found that the spelling of the adjectives is identical in all the editions of *Ulysses*, which indicates that we might have here what Joyce actually wrote. The translations, in which Joyce had some part, follow below according to the years in which they appeared:

First German (1927)—*Jesifizierter testikulierter polycynischer Jesuit.* (Vol. II, p. 458)

French (1929)—*Jesufiant testicouillard polypucique jésuite!* (p. 483)

Second German (1930)—*Jesufizierter testikulierter polycinischer Jesuit.* (Vol. II, p. 76)

The German translator, the brave Goyert, in his first attempt seems to have adopted Buck's own method wholeheartedly, and merely transferred the structure Buck provides without specifying further. *Jesi-* leaves the matter ambiguous, as it is, if the context is not considered, in the original text. In his revision, however, Goyert changes this to *Jesu-*, and thus, it seems to me, tends to specify the meaning toward "Jesus-made" rather than to "Jesuit-made." The *u* of the French committee may have influenced him, but, at any rate, the general effect of the translations seems, insofar as I can diffidently conclude anything from them, to strengthen the ticket of the "Jesus-made" faction. The change from *y* to *i* in *polycinischer* seems to be merely a modernization of the spelling. Why the French has no accent on *Jesufiant* I cannot even guess, unless it is merely the printer's fault.

Ultimately, then, I judge that *jesified* means that Stephen, in Buck's view, has been cut off, by the Jesuits, from hope, from reality, from a reasonable aim in life. Joyce himself apparently thought this about Jesus: "I have written quite enough and before I do any more in this line I must see some reason why—I am not a literary Jesus Christ."[24] It would seem that Joyce, in denying that he is a Jesus, is thinking of a Joking Jesus, who plunges or drifts irrationally ahead with no reasonable aim. Joyce denies that he himself is such a creature, but as I read "jesified," Buck judged Stephen to be precisely that.

Buck leaves the novel at the end of the Oxen of the Sun chapter, but his priesthood, as it exists in Stephen's imagination, reaches its climax and fulfillment in the Circe chapter. The real final sundering of these priests, one of science and one of art, takes place toward the end of the Circe chapter, and with it I conclude my brief inspection of Buck's and Stephen's priesthoods. Stephen's priesthood has a great deal more to do in the book, in relation to the Old and New Testament priesthoods of Leopold Bloom, but that is another chapter.

The elements of the mass in the Circe chapter have received much attention. For the purposes of my own present topic, I will deal only with a detail or two of the Black Mass. In the midst of cosmic brimstone fires and smoke, of darkness and earthquakes, of death and war, in the center of the earth (the omphalos) rises the field altar of St. Barbara (*U*, 598–99). Besides the reasons Adams suggests,[25] Barbara is brought in here because her symbol, which she carries, is a tower. A tower was her prison, and Stephen, now determined never to return to his tower, takes something of that attitude. He pictures Haines and Buck, "the panthersahib and his pointer," without him in the tower, "a shut door of a silent tower entombing their blind bodies" (*U*, 44). Barbara's tower, too, if we may judge by the striking fifteenth-century sculpture which illustrates her article in the *New Catholic Encyclopedia*, looked a good deal like the Martello Tower. And, in the next sentence, we find ourselves back again in the Martello Tower, with the two shafts of light and the smoke described on page 11, where Buck Mulligan's gowned form was carrying on his mass by preparing a breakfast-communion. Now, in the Circe chapter, we have Father Mala-

chi O'Flynn repeating the words with which Buck began
his mass, with the significant change of "Dei" to "diaboli."
Buck's true priesthood, his service of the forces of evil, de-
struction, confusion, and death, now becomes apparent.
Stephen, in his imagination, takes an artist's revenge for
the crushing defeats the successful and admired priest of
science has inflicted on him during the day. Haines Love
faithfully translates all Latin into English, as did Mr.
Fogarty at the communion service in "Grace." As the winds
sustained Buck's gown on the opening page, Haines Love
lifts the celebrant's petticoat, and reveals the influence of
George Moore and of medieval phallic symbolism (as in
the hell paintings of Bosch) on Stephen's (or perhaps, in
this case, on Joyce's) imagination.

   Throughout the book there have been hints that Buck is,
at least in Stephen's mind, a homosexual. The reference to
"Wilde's love that dare not speak its name" (*U*, 49) carries
with it the possibility of some kind of homosexual relationship called up by Stephen's musing on Buck's shoes. The
same reference on page 202 may be influenced not only by
Shakespeare and Willie Hughes but by the presence of the
challenging Buck. In his lineup of bodily shames, Stephen
uses the Wilde reference instead of saying "homosexual
brothers" (*U*, 207). And when Buck praises Dowden's academic justification for Elizabethan pederasty with "Lovely!", Stephen thinks, "Catamite" (*U*, 204). Here in the
Black Mass, Buck wears a petticoat, and when it is lifted
it reveals "grey bare hairy buttocks between which a carrot is stuck" (*U*, 599). The phallic symbolism of the carrot
seems obvious enough. The background for the grey buttocks can be found in Joyce's discussion of George Moore's
The Lake.[26] Moore had named his clerical character after
Gogarty, much to Joyce's cynical amusement, and Joyce

tells Stanislaus: "Father Oliver Gogarty goes out to the lake
to plunge in by moonlight, before which the moon shines
opportunely 'on a firm erect frame and grey buttocks'; and,
on the steamer he reflects that every man has a lake in his
heart and must ungird his loins for the crossing." Father
Malachi in the Black Mass inherits those grey buttocks,
and I suspect that Father Buck Mulligan may have derived the adjective "ungirdled" (U, 3), at least in part, from
that phrase "must ungird his loins."

As in the Nausicaa chapter Joyce counterpointed the
lustful sterile exhibition and masturbation on the beach
with the praise of the purity of the Blessed Virgin, so here
he counterpoints the abuse of the Eucharist with the abuse
of the sexual powers. Buck, with the devil's mark of reversed left feet and under the Freudian umbrella, in the
Black Mass fully exercises his perverse priesthood in a
world of unbearable tension, where hate strains against
love in hideous betrayal, where fire and smoke (sources of
ambiguous praise in the villanelle) destroy the twisted and
perverse world, and where God is balanced (and equalled)
by Dog, the spirit by the beast. And Stephen, deserted by
Judas-Lynch, now literally smashed by Private Carr, lies
in the street with his face to the sky. It is a kind of cruci-
fixion his Judas has left him to undergo, and it is another
Joseph of Arimathea,[27] Bloom, who will take Stephen's
body to his own silent tomb, in this case one where (at least
in Molly's imagination) many men have been laid.

NOTES

1. *A Portrait of the Artist as a Young Man*, ed. Chester G. Anderson
(New York: Viking Press, 1969); all quotations are from this edition.
2. "Stephen Dedalus, Poet or Esthete?" *PMLA* 89 (September 1964):
484–89.

3. *Stephen Hero* (New York: New Directions, 1963), p. 141; all quotations are from this edition.

4. *Poems*, ed. Robert Bridges and W. H. Gardner, 4th ed. (New York: Oxford University Press, 1967), no. 178.

5. John William Corrington, "The Sisters," in *James Joyce's "Dubliners": Critical Essays*, ed. Clive Hart (New York: Viking Press, 1969).

6. "The Sisters," *The Portable James Joyce* (New York: Viking Press, 1967), p. 24.

7. *Joyce and Shakespeare* (New Haven: Yale University Press, 1957), p. 108.

8. George Geckle, "Stephen Dedalus and W. B. Yeats: The Making of the Villanelle," *Modern Fiction Studies* 15 (Spring 1969): 87–96.

9. *Ulysses* (New York: Random House, 1961); all quotations are from this edition.

10. Geckle, op. cit., p. 96.

11. Edmund L. Epstein, "Cruxes in *Ulysses*: Notes Toward an Edition and Annotation," *James Joyce Review* 1 (September 1957): 43.

12. *Romeo and Juliet*, III, iii, 1.

13. *Finnegans Wake* (New York: Viking Press, 1947). p. 469.

14. Harry Blamires, *The Bloomsday Book* (London: Methuen & Co., 1966), p. 197.

15. Ruth M. Walsh, "Joyce's Use of the Mass in *Ulysses*," *James Joyce Quarterly* 6 (Summer 1969): 321–47.

16. *A Reader's Guide to James Joyce* (New York: Farrar, Strauss and Giroux, 1959), p. 201.

17. Compare Matthew 17:27.

18. *Poems*, no. 27.

19. *Allusions in "Ulysses": An Annotated List* (Chapel Hill: University of North Carolina Press, 1961), p. 330.

20. Compare Matthew 1:19.

21. *Letters of James Joyce*, vol. 2, ed. Richard Ellmann (New York: Viking Press, 1966), p. 160.

22. Quoted in Robert M. Adams, *Surface and Symbol: The Consistency of James Joyce's "Ulysses"* (New York: Oxford University Press, 1962), p. 208.

23. *Letters*, vol. 2, p. 127.

24. *Letters*, vol. 2, p. 162. In the same letter Joyce several times refers to Oliver St. John Gogarty as "O. St Jesus."

25. Adams, *Surface and Symbol*, p. 29.

26. Quoted in Richard Ellmann, *James Joyce* (New York: Oxford University Press, 1959), p. 242–43.

27. Compare John 19:41.

Motif as Meaning:
The Case of Leopold Bloom

RICHARD M. KAIN

3

IN THE LATE THIRTIES Joyce was having an afternoon of
Dublin gossip with Niall Sheridan, a recent graduate of
U. C. D. (University College, Dublin). In the midst of a
complicated web of relationships, Joyce suddenly paused,
extended his hand, and traced an arabesque in the air before him. "It all makes a pattern," he mused. The patterns
of which he dreamed throughout his long exile form the
texture of *Ulysses,* and provide readers with some of the
most compelling meanings. Were it not for the vistas that
Ulysses presents, the book would be what many early
readers mistakenly assumed it to be—a haphazard transcription of local minutiae. The trivia that Joyce retained
in his memory became transmuted by his imagination into
poetic metaphors. To cite one instance whereby slight details coalesce to form a major theme: Leopold Bloom is of
Hungarian Jewish descent. In a comprehensive treatment
of this aspect, Robert Tracy elucidates many of the details
which contribute to Bloom's ethnic role as the archetypal
Jew, the Wandering Jew, and as an archetypal Hungarian,

"born in the year of Hungary's rebirth." In this dual role his experiences parallel those of Ireland: "he has been exiled, dispossessed, tyrannized over by foreigners, forced to conform to foreign religions, and his adventures during Bloomsday are a recapitulation of the adventures of his races and of Ireland."[1]

Now for some specific allusions, many of which are to be found in Mr. Tracy's article. To Hungarian patriots of the mid–nineteenth century, Ireland was a brother nation in bondage, and the analogy was made specific by Yeats in 1887, in a poem which the author dropped from his collected work after its appearance in *The Wanderings of Oisin* (1889). The invocation to "How Ferencz Renyi Kept Silent" bears tribute to the *"nation of the bleeding breast"* from Ireland, *"the Hungary of the West."* As early as 1902 Hungary had provided Arthur Griffith an example and a program of independence; in 1904 he published "The Resurrection of Hungary," articles which appeared in pamphlet form by the end of that year. From the Hungarian struggle Griffith evolved the policy of the Sinn Fein party (so named in 1906) which was put into practice by the first Irish Dail in January 1919, when the duly elected members of Parliament refused to go to Westminster and instead sat in Dublin (all but those still in prison and a handful of Unionists). Among minor details noted by Mr. Tracy are the following, testifying to Joyce's penchant for documentation. In the brothel scene of *Ulysses*, Bloom is transformed into various historical characters, five of them Jewish and one Hungarian, the patriot Kossuth. The others, Mr. Tracy shows, "help to reinforce the wanderer theme," or "suggest the art of disguise." The Bloom family (originally Virag) followed the custom of alternating the Hapsburg names Leopold and Rudolph; and, as though for Joyce's own purpose, the English ambassador to Vienna in the year of Hungary's freedom (1866) was Lord Bloomfield!

It was also in 1904 that there circulated through Ireland handbills entitled "The Language of the Outlaw," a newspaper report of John F. Taylor's speech on the Irish language given at University College in October 1901, in Joyce's final academic year.[2] Taylor's comparison between Jewish spirituality and Egyptian materialism became a favorite metaphor for the contrast of Irish and English character traits. On a personal level, Joyce must have been pleased that the college magazine, *St. Stephen's,* compared Taylor's style to that "of our Joyce at his best." Joyce defended Griffith in letters to his brother Stanislaus during 1906, and, after the publication of *Ulysses,* the one passage Joyce chose for a phonograph recording was his own reading of the Taylor speech as recounted in the newsroom chapter. The year of the Griffith articles, his book, and the Taylor pamphlet coincides with that of *Ulysses,* though Joyce violated chronology whenever it suited his purpose.

Hints of the significance of Griffith lie near the surface of the text. Bloom thinks of his gibe about the emblem of the *Freeman's Journal*: "a homerule sun rising up in the northwest from the laneway behind the bank of Ireland." That "Ikey touch" appeals to his sense of humor (57),[3] and he remembers it later in the day (161, 370). At Barney Kiernan's, John Wyse Power recounts the rumor that Bloom "gave the idea for Sinn Fein to Griffith" (329), which is corroborated by Martin Cunningham: "we know that in the castle" (331). Molly looks askance at her hus-

band's consorting "with some of them Sinner Fein," and
finds absurd his notion that Griffith is "the coming man":

talking his usual trash and nonsense he says that little man he
showed me without a neck is very intelligent the coming man
Griffiths [*sic*] is he well he doesnt look it thats all I can say.
(733)

Themes derived from Griffith play a role in Bloom's de-
lusions of grandeur in nighttown (471-75). As he is
being made "emperor-president and king-chairman" of
the Utopian Nova Hibernia, St. Stephen's crown is carried
in the procession, and thirty-two workmen *"from all the
counties of Ireland"* begin to construct the New Bloom-
usalem as *"A sunburst appears in the northwest."* In *The
Resurrection of Hungary* Griffith had described the ceremony of 1867 in which Franz Josef as King of Hungary
pledged himself to defend the Constitution of 1848: "the
monarch was anointed, the royal mantle of St. Stephen
placed upon his shoulders, the iron crown placed upon
his head,"[4] the crown traditionally accepted as that of Stephen the First (975-1038). The procession from the
church was led by representatives of the fifty-two counties of Hungary.

Among minor relevances and associations, we may note
that St. Stephen gave his name to the crown which alone
can command the allegiance of a Hungarian, that Stephen is the name of Joyce's hero, St. Stephen's Green the
square on which the University College was situated, and
St. Stephen's the name of the college paper. Stephen is
Greek for "crown," as we are reminded in *A Portrait*. And
thirty-two is not only the number of the counties in Ireland, but also as "thirty-two feet per second" (71) is
associated in Bloom's mind with the law of gravity.

It all makes a pattern, yes. The art of *Ulysses* is to a great extent that of suggestion and concealment, creating a prismatic illusion of fragmentary and overlapping reflections. The game of investigation can go on and on. We have touched only a few aspects of the Hungarian Jewish theme. There were also Joyce's own Jewish friends, and his admiration for the Jewish character. The publisher of an evening paper in Trieste, *Il Piccolo della Sera*, Teodoro Mayer, of Hungarian Jewish descent, was an Irredentist who sought to sever Trieste from Austrian rule and unite it with Italy. Mayer's political leanings may account for the outlook in the essays Joyce contributed to the newspaper from 1907 to 1912, all of them, even those on Wilde and Shaw, nationalistic in tone. Much of Joyce's knowledge of Jewish culture was learned from his most celebrated language pupil in Trieste, Ettore Schmitz, who, as Italo Svevo, had published two novels—*Una Vita* (1892) and *Senilità* (1898)—which had been neglected by the public. Svevo's mocking but sympathetic irony was not lost on his English tutor, who exclaimed, "Do you know that you are a neglected writer?" As Joyce's plans for *Ulysses* were gestating, the luck of the Irish held; he engaged in rather adolescent infatuations with two young Jewish women—Amalia Popper, the daughter of a businessman surnamed Leopoldo, whom he met in 1913, and, five years later, in Zurich, Marthe Fleischmann. An indirect result of the first acquaintance was the romantic-ironic *Giacomo Joyce* notebook, a sequence of epiphanies which present both hero and heroine in self-conscious poses, easy marks for deflation by writer or reader. The second brief contact left its imprint on the Martha Clifford theme in *Ulysses*. In the words of Richard Ellmann, the

Fleischmann episode "was a final burgeoning of his desire for dark, unknown, passionate, preferably Semitic women who would envelop him in their arms."[5] Heinrich Straumann, however, seems to prove that Marthe was not Jewish, although Joyce may well have thought she was and certainly indicated that he hoped she was.[6]

Himself an exile from country and church, Joyce could identify with the Jew as legendary wanderer, possessing qualities ignored or lost in other civilizations. "Look at them," he said to Frank Budgen, "They are better husbands than we are, better fathers and better sons."[7] Whatever the degree of truth in this observation, there is no doubt that from Joyce the compliment was sincere; few artists have shown such great respect for filial and domestic pieties as did Joyce. Then, when he had finished three-quarters of *Ulysses*, he came across studies of the *Odyssey* by Victor Bérard which confirmed his theory of the Homeric poem's semitic roots. Though Joyce seemed to have little or no contact with Jews in Dublin (Ellmann notices his interest in a divorce case of 1906), much of the local color is authentic, as has been shown by the Dublin emigré to Israel, Louis Hyman of Haifa, who presented a paper at the 1969 Joyce Symposium in Dublin.

Mr. Budgen remarked, apropos Joyce's notetaking technique, "He was always looking and listening for the necessary fact or word; and he was a great believer in his luck."[8] Furthermore, "as, in a sense, the theme of *Ulysses* is the whole of life, there was no end to the variety of material that went to its building." The essential technique was that of the leitmotif, for which Joyce credited the then-forgotten novel of Edouard Dujardin, *Les Lauriers sont coupés*, which appeared in magazine installments in 1887, and in book form the next year. The story of the relationship between Joyce and the man whom he titled "annonciateur de la parole intérieure" need not be recounted here. It is in respect to the leitmotif, its use by Dujardin, and its central role in *Ulysses* that this study is concerned, for it is the leitmotif which forms the tie between naturalism and what Louis Gillet termed "the Pandora's box of Symbolism."

Dujardin's little history of *Le Monologue Intérieur* (1931) provides a summary of antecedents and an account of the author's relation to his "impenitent thief," as Joyce termed himself, though in a letter to Harriet Weaver he wryly regarded his compliment as giving the old man "cake for bread." The comparison, however unkind, is almost completely accurate. Dujardin himself contrasted his "modeste tentative" with Joyce's "géniale réalisation" and called attention to his reprise of the motifs of the prelude at the beginning of the novel's eighth chapter and to the young man's recitation to his mistress of his activities of the day, some accurate, others purposely distorted. These two albeit slight anticipations of Joyce do represent in turn the philosophic-symbolic and the naturalistic aspects of the art. For the first: in the opening pages Dujardin's hero reflects on his position in time and space (a passage similar to the opening of the scenario of *La Derniére Année à Marienbad*):

And, from the chaos of appearance, in this time of all times, this place of places, amid the illusions of things self-begotten and self-conceived, one among others, one like the others yet distinct from them, the same and yet one more, from the infinity of possible lives, I arise. So time and place come to a point; it is the Now and Here, this hour that is striking, and all around me life.

The eighth episode opens:

> The carriage moving along the streets. . . . A single one in the unnumbered host of lives, thus I go my way, one by distinction among the rest; and so the Now, the Here, this hour striking, this world of life, all these come to being within me. . . . And what am I?

Dujardin's naturalistic or psychological use of motif is difficult to present in brief quotation. In recounting the events of the day the young man colors his refusal to see *Ruy Blas* with a boring friend as a sacrifice to his beloved Leah, thus winning the response: "—All for my sake. That was heroic."

Dujardin himself attributed the development of the leitmotif to Wagnerian opera. To paraphrase his statement, the Wagnerian motif carries an emotional signification; it is unrelated to what precedes or to what follows, the order being emotional rather than logical:

> De même que le plus souvent une page de Wagner est une succession de motifs non développés dont chacun exprime un mouvement d'âme, le monologue intérieur est une succession de phrases courtes dont chacune exprime également un mouvement d'âme, avec cette resemblance qu'elles ne sont pas liées les unes aux autres suivant un ordre rationnel mais suivant un ordre purement émotionnel, en dehors de tout arrangement intellectualisé.

Joyce was no perfect Wagnerite, finding the master pretentious, but he knew a good thing for his purposes. Wagner was the rage of the Parisian avant garde in the 1880s, and contributed much to the theory and practice of the Symbolistes. Dujardin was the editor of *La Revue Wagnerienne,* founded in 1885, and in August of that year appeared Mallarmé's ecstatic prose tribute to the composer who had "usurped" the poet's task "with the most open and splendid audacity." Of Mallarmé Arthur Symons wrote in his pioneer study, *The Symbolist Movement in Literature* (1899), that "it is his failure not to be Wagner."

The point of this epigram is elucidated in the scholarly article by William Blissett in *James Joyce Today* (1966), wherein Joyce is depicted as a belated and somewhat dubious Wagnerian.[9] Wagnerism pervaded the cultural climate at the turn of the century, nowhere more than in Ireland. Wagner gave fresh impetus to the romantic identification of nationalism and literature, and Blissett finds that "Yeats and his associates were groping toward the idea of an Irish literary Bayreuth." Joyce stood apart from the provinciality and antiquarianism of folk art but sensed the deeper significance of the Wagnerian principle of racial myth when in his early essay, "Drama and Life" (1900), he argued that a work of art, in any medium, no matter "however subdued the tone of passions" nor however "commonplace the diction," is "drama" only if it "presents the everlasting hopes, desires and hates of us, or deals with a symbolic presentment of our widely related nature." In "Drama and Life" Joyce referred to "the least part of Wagner—his music" and showed his awareness of the possible corruption by the public of the mythic force:

Every race has made its own myths and it is in these that the early drama finds an outlet. The author of Parsifal has recognized this and hence his work is solid as a rock. When the mythus passes over the borderline and invades the temple of worship, the possibilities of its drama have lessened considerably.

Wagner, while never as great an influence on Joyce as Ibsen, was nonetheless always in the wings of Joyce's imagination. Blissett makes the interesting suggestion that a Yeats essay of 1907, "Poetry and Patriotism," may have supplemented the Wagnerian image of forging the conscience: "We were to forge in Ireland a new sword on our old traditional anvil for that great battle that must in the end re-establish the old confident joyous world."

The "smithy of my soul" in which Stephen is to forge "the uncreated conscience of my race" is itself but an intimation of what in *Ulysses* becomes a Wagnerian motif of Wagnerism—the ashplant sword, the exclamation as Stephen smashes the lamp, as well as numerous other references, but, more important than any of these, the final concept of the work of art as a simulacrum of the universe. Mallarmé's failure, to revert to Symons's judgment, was that "Wagner having existed, it was for him to be something more, to complete Wagner," which the French poet was unable to do. In contrast, Joyce's work is comparable to Wagner's in immensity and scope. The two men, in life and in art, became culture heroes and heroes of cults. Blissett observes many interesting resemblances:

Their early struggles in a hinterland of European culture, their marriages (Nora was a happier, more durable Minna), their exile, the demands they made on the time and purse of their friends, their egotism and empire-building, the grandiosity of their artistic ambitions, the time it took them to complete their projects and the completeness of that fulfillment, and, not the least striking of resemblances, the international and polyglot intellectuals that were drawn to them to make a cult of personality as well as of art—all these bring the two into a single, very uncommon category: the culture-hero as total artist, totally fulfilled.

Had Joyce not discarded the Homeric chapter titles of his famed schema, early readers might have been able to proceed from the blue and white cover of the first edition (colors of the Greek flag) and to follow the implications of the title. As it was, divided only into three unequal sections, with chapters indicated by blank spaces and capitalization, the book was readily seen as a transcription of an undifferentiated flux. Thus Gillet, in 1925, commented: "we see in Bloom a reflection of the thousand-and-one aspects of the streets, and at all times, we hear this hum of vulgarities and platitudes, this flow of rubbish."[10] One must remember that it is easy to be wise after the event, but it now seems almost impossible for a perceptive reader not to observe the ambiance of allusion in which the novel exists. At the very opening, the mockery of Stephen as "fearful jesuit," "jejune jesuit," and "you have the cursed jesuit strain in you, only it's injected the wrong way," serve, within four pages, to indicate an emphasis beyond that of mere characterization. Shortly thereafter we find "Agenbite of inwit. Conscience. Yet here's a spot." Together with Stephen's memory of his dying mother, mention of his theory of Hamlet, and three immediately following references to Hamlet ("he himself is the ghost of his own father"; "Japhet in search of a father"; and "The Son striving to be atoned with the Father"), the horizon of interpretation expands as the focus intensifies.

The subtle Homeric analogues are more obscure and seemingly less viable as narrative devices. Without the authorized exegesis by Stuart Gilbert, who worked closely with Joyce and who was granted exclusive rights to the scheme of episodes, what reader would have associated

Mulligan with "Antinous and the other suitors," or remembered "the theotechny of the first Book of the Odyssey," not to speak of the milkwoman as recalling Mentor or Athene?[11] But possibly the reaction against such interpretations has itself gone too far. As Clive Hart points out, in the most recent book devoted to *Ulysses* (1968), "some readers, troubled by the excessive attention which the Homeric parallels have received, are now inclined to underplay their significance."[12]

Examination of the surviving notesheets for *Ulysses* throws light upon Joyce's method of work, though it should not affect our imaginative response to what the final text means to an alert reader. Relatively few of these notes survive, but they are immensely rich in implications. The notebook VIII.A.5 at Buffalo, edited by Phillip F. Herring, contains thirty-six pages of written matter, about five hundred entries altogether.[13] Herring has traced some two hundred of these to Victor Bérard's two-volume *Les Phéniciens et l'Odyssée* (1902), already well known, and has made two happy discoveries of sources: Joyce's use of W. H. Roscher's compendious eight-volume *Ausführliches Lexikon der Griechischen und Römischen Mythologie* (1884–1890), and Joyce's perusal of the plays of Thomas Otway, from which numerous Restoration slang words were taken ("blub," "fubsy," "ringoes," the latter as "ringocandies" in *Ulysses*). Joyce made notations like a scholar, albeit a casual one. His first page of notes mentions the names of the archaeologists Bochart, Helbig, Maspero, Reinach, and Curtius. There is a listing of characters from the *Odyssey*, and a page or so of poetic meters and rhetorical tropes. Surprising is the fact that only about sixty entries can be traced to the pages of *Ulysses*, though possibly

others remain to be discovered, or perhaps enter obliquely.
These specific parallels are not limited to any one episode,
but are scattered throughout, the only marked concentration being in the Lotos-Eaters and the Hades episodes.

Bérard is responsible for many of the equivalents for
oblivion in the Lotos-Eaters chapter, notes having been
made on anesthetic, medicine, purge, lotos, with two interesting items: "nepenthe—anesthetic (Queen Vict.)"
reads one line, and the lotos-shamrock association is made
in another. Scattered among such notes and clues are bits
of Dublin data—"P. Mooney's father bailiff" and "Bought
Hungarian sold me lottery ticket from him (Father Cowley)" are examples. Corresponding passages in *Ulysses* are
Bloom's reflections on "Twilightsleep idea: queen Victoria
was given that" (161) and the remarks of the narrator in
Cyclops: "bitch he married, Mooney, the bumbailiff's
daughter" (303). In contrast to the notesheets in the British Museum, also being edited by Herring, these pages
have few direct references to either of the two main characters. An instance of the omitted or hitherto undiscovered
allusion is the following sequence at the top of page four:

> Eumaios pigherd   good
> Melanthus goatherd—bad
> LB meets pigman

The first two lines were cancelled in blue pencil, presumably having been used or transcribed to another listing, but
no "pigman" appears in *Ulysses*. It is tempting to linger
over many of the other citations, but perhaps enough has
been said to indicate the nature of Joyce's preparation,
both directed and incidental. Frank Budgen recalled the
variety of Joyce's notations:

I have seen him collect in the space of a few hours the oddest assortment of material: a parody on the *House that Jack Built,* the name and action of a poison, the method of caning boys on training ships, the wobbly cessation of a tired unfinished sentence, the nervous trick of a convive turning his glass in inward turning circles, a Swiss music-hall joke turning on a pun in Swiss dialect, a description of the Fitzsimmons shift.[14]

The upshot of all this is that the perfect reader of *Ulysses* can probably never exist, at least after the author's death. Nor can even the best of us imperfect readers ever be sure of our readings, for there is no standard of relevance in a world view wherein everything is relevant. Among the best of imperfect readers is Robert M. Adams, whose investigations have enriched our knowledge of Joyce's world immeasurably. Yet Adams devotes a full page of *Surface and Symbol* to mocking "earnest readers" who have bent their minds "to some determined symbol searching" in regard to the name of the excursion boat "Erin's King," on which Bloom once made a pleasant excursion. As to associating the boat with Parnell, Mr. Adams remarks that "the only people to whom *Erin's King* suggests Parnell are those who do not know that it was a real boat, the only boat one could take on expeditions of this nature."[15] Reality did have a way of playing into Joyce's hands, though, and it need not preclude symbolic or other association. In regard to the "Erin's King," a British Museum notesheet for the Eumaeus chapter has a line: "LB never forget trip in Erin's King (C S P)." There it is, Charles Stewart Parnell.

One may readily sympathize with the impatience and exasperation of readers who begin to realize that they may be missing half the show, and it must be a rare commentator who has not been embarrassed by his own errors and oversights. Years ago the present writer posed the problem

of "the validity of Joyce's analogical method": "Can he be
excused from what seems an inveterate habit of idiosyncratic and irresponsible association?"[16] The question remained open-ended, awaiting further understanding of the
significance of the symbolist tradition and its contemporary relevance. Since that time Richard Ellmann has observed what he happily terms "the blurred margin" in
Joyce: "He introduces much material which he does not
intend to explain, so that his book, like life, gives the impression of having many threads that one cannot follow."[17]
Ellmann was speaking about naturalistic details, but his
remarks apply equally to half-buried symbols. An instance
which comes to mind is suggested by an entry in the British Museum notesheets. Most readers have sensed that
Stephen and Bloom are both keyless, and homeless, but
none, one suspects, would ever recognize the parallel
which Joyce noted: "SD forgets hank. LB—key." The overlooked reference is on the last half page of the Proteus
episode (51).

No one has explored the blurred edges more thoroughly
than Adams, who illumines many obscure corners and dis-
covers almost as many more. He has seen the great book
for what it is, not a mechanically precise contrivance, but
an immense structure containing allusive trifles, loose ends,
errors intentional and accidental—in short, a magnificent
but flawed creation, again, like life itself. Such are the risks
involved, and the rewards to be found, in what Joyce
termed "this chaffering allincluding most farraginous
chronicle" (416). Almost every event has its penumbra of
details, partially recognized or unknown, whether on the
naturalistic or symbolic levels, or, as with the "Erin's King,"
on both levels simultaneously. Thus it matters little that

the book can never be fully comprehended, for the very infinitude of motifs and allusions creates an atmosphere of significances. Even when allusions remain in the notes and do not appear in the text, they may have enriched the imagination of the writer sufficiently before having been discarded. Adams has discovered that Paddy Dignam's death was based on that of one Matthew Kane, who drowned in Dublin bay, but that "Joyce blithely deleted from the novel a death by water, such as an alert archetypalist would have gone far out of his way to introduce."[18] Yes, and no; Dignam did not drown, but, as Adams observed,[19] there are references to "the man that was drowned" (23), and Stephen soon identifies himself with the unknown victim: "With him together down" (46), and, thinking of his mother's recent death, imagines her bringing her son to a like fate: "She will drown me with her" (240). Indeed, Matthew F. Kane himself is listed toward the end of the book, among Bloom's "companions now in various manners in different places defunct" (689), where death by water joins death by war and death by disease in a prose litany. The melancholy roll call (689) has its own muted eloquence:

Of what did bellchime and handtouch and footstep and lonechill remind him?
   Of companions now in various manners in different places defunct: Percy Apjohn (killed in action, Modder River), Philip Gilligan (phthisis, Jervis Street hospital), Matthew F. Kane (accidental drowning, Dublin Bay), Philip Moisel (pyemia, Heytesbury street), Michael Hart (phthisis, Mater Misericordiae hospital), Patrick Dignam (apoplexy, Sandymount).

   As these words are being written, an eloquent description of Joyce's philosophic posture by Father Thomas Merton appears in his posthumously published review, "News of the Joyce Industry." Warning against the temptation toward simplification and reductionism by thesis-ridden commentators, he writes:

The mature critic recognizes that, in a work of such richness and complexity as Joyce's, one must not try to pin everything down, categorize, label, define, explain, classify, and prescribe. The art of Joyce is always rich in suggestion and in open possibilities, in delicate tensions, contrasts, unresolved problems that are meant to be left in the air, questions and polarities that are not meant to be reduced to definitive certainties. The stasis of the Joycean aesthetic is not a full stop in inertia, an end of living contradictions, but a delicate balance between them.[20]

Could Father Merton have had in mind the caustic words of that brilliant and impatient Marxist critic of the thirties, Alick West, who attacked Joyce for what was assumed to be a noncommittal attitude to social change? The formality of Joyce's structure, West argued, implies a stability in society which is contradicted by the flux of the characters and that of their thoughts and emotions. The result is inertia:

Joyce seems to play with the two styles of change and stability, as he plays with his two chief characters. He plays with the contradictions; he does not resolve them. Where in Milton there is advancing movement, Joyce only shifts from one foot to the other, while he sinks deeper into the sandflats.[21]

Surely Father Merton is closer to the truth than the exponents of so many orthodoxies—Catholic, Marxist, symbolist—who would create a Joyce in their image. Were the others right, the appeal of the great works would be limited to those of a single persuasion, or to dilettantes who luxuriate in *l'art pour l'art*.

Ulysses now appears to be neither so haphazard as its early readers found it, nor so meticulously executed as later commentators have claimed. The work embodies two contrasting impulses, in uncertain but vital poise. One is that of strict order: time sequence; chapter unity; Odyssean skeleton; interrelationships of characters, places, events; reflections of the past upon the present. The other principle is one of freedom: associations, allusions, correspondences. The features of order focus inward upon the book itself, insuring *integritas, consonantia,* and *claritas,* those qualities which constitute a work of art, according to Stephen in the *Portrait.* The second thrust is outward, centrifugal, leading to wider areas of significances, and, indeed, as has been suggested, to those shadowy realms where meanings remain obscure or undiscoverable.

The inescapable dilemma of literary criticism is that it is by nature selective and thematic, isolating one or another feature of a book at the expense of others which must be included within the larger view that the book demands. Criticism remains partial, and what it gains in analytic subtlety is too often at the expense of larger views. The present area of investigation is the use of the motif in *Ulysses,* but we should not ignore the fact that larger meanings lie beyond. Robert Tracy's full title is pertinent here: "Leopold Bloom Fourfold: A Hungarian-Hebraic-Hellenic-Hibernian Hero." "Fourfold" is but the beginning. There are countless other echoes and resemblances.

Without stumbling upon Dujardin Joyce might independently have found the value of the motif. Indeed it is surprising that in the 1904 essay, "A Portrait of the Artist," one finds no trace of it, for the subject, the "curve of an emotion," calls for a marshalling of experiences and attitudes. Even so, the essay has considerably more coherent development than the succession of episodes in the near-contemporary *Stephen Hero*. Neither manuscript, however, used repeated key words such as are later found in *A Portrait of the Artist as a Young Man*, where the rose, the color and smell of bogwater, sensations of cold and white, and numerous other experiences constitute the inner world of the growing child. The closest that the young Joyce appears to have come to the technique of the leit-motif is in his sequence of epiphanies, shown as a sequence in the edition of Robert Scholes and Richard M. Kain. Though the brevity of each episode results in discontinuity, the recently discovered numbers on several sheets suggest that Joyce intended them as a suite, an effect barely dis-cernible in the surviving forty (of at least seventy-one, if we may trust the pencil markings). Among the few fairly complete sequences is one series of seven bourgeois banali-ties, four of the last five of which are set at the Sheehy home, and thus have a unity of place. These were indicated as 12–14, 16, 19, 21, 22 (Scholes-Kain numbers 9–15).[22]

In fact it would not have been surprising had Joyce gone farther in this direction at that time, for by 1904 Marcel Proust and Thomas Mann were independently developing similar techniques. Proust, like Joyce, was beginning to revise his autobiographical manuscript, "Jean Santeuil," weaving into it echoed meditations and significant recol-lections. It was in the story of "Tonio Kröger," first pub-lished in 1903, that, as Mann later recalled in his preface to the *Stories of Three Decades*, "I first learned to employ music as a shaping influence in my art."[23] He goes on to observe, however, that the leitmotif is to be found as early as *Buddenbrooks* (1900):

The conception of epic prose-composition as a weaving of themes, as a musical complex of associations, I later on largely employed in *The Magic Mountain.* Only that there the verbal leitmotif is no longer, as in *Buddenbrooks,* employed in the representation of form alone, but has taken on a less mechanical, more musical character, and endeavours to mirror the emotion and the idea.

The most direct anticipation by Joyce of the fragmentary symbol motif in *Ulysses* is to be found in his notes for his play *Exiles.* The tantalizing shadowiness of the play has been attributed to its being an imperfectly objectified autobiography and to its bare Ibsenite style. Two notes, dated November 12 and November 13, 1913, indicate the levels of meaning for which Joyce was striving.[24] The first entry is in itself indecipherable; its later elaboration points to roots in Nora's youth in Galway, her infatuation with a young man now dead (the theme of "The Dead"), and the contrast between Bodkin's humble name, destiny, and tomb, with that of Shelley in Rome:

N. (B.)—12 Nov. 1913
  Garter: precious, Prezioso, Bodkin, music, palegreen, bracelet, cream sweets, lily of the valley, convent garden (Galway), sea.

There are similar entries for "Rat" and "Dagger," but we shall limit comment to the above. The initials, those of Nora Barnacle, can also refer to the play's heroine, Bertha, and, obviously, create a pun on *nota bene.* The following entry identifies or almost identifies the ambiguous motivations which permeate the play:

N. (B.)—13 Nov. 1913
  Moon: Shelley's grave in Rome. He is rising from it: blond she weeps for him. He has fought in vain for an ideal and

died killed by the world. Yet he rises. Graveyard at Rahoon by moonlight where Bodkin's grave is. He lies in the grave. She sees his tomb (family vault) and weeps. The name is homely. Shelley's is strange and wild. He is dark, unrisen, killed by love and life, young. The earth holds him.

The note continues in an embarrassingly personal vein, which reinforces the author's identification with the immortal Shelley:

Bodkin died. Kearns died. In the convent they called her the man-killer: (woman-killer was one of her names for me). I live in soul and body.

A final entry on this day associates her with "the earth, formless, mother," half-desirous of killing, yet unable to kill the Shelley aspect of Richard (the play's hero); and, even more daringly, paralleling Richard (that is, Joyce) not only with Shelley but with the risen Christ:

She is the earth, dark, formless, mother, made beautiful by the moonlit night, darkly conscious of her instincts. Shelley whom she has held in her womb or grave rises: the part of Richard which neither love nor life can do away with; the part for which she loves him: the part she must try to kill, never be able to kill and rejoice at her impotence. Her tears are of worship, Magdalen seeing the rearisen Lord in the garden where he had been laid in the tomb.

The note continues with Bodkin's "attendant images," which are "the trinkets and toys of girlhood (bracelet, cream sweets, palegreen lily of the valley, the convent garden)." Joyce implies a contrast between such "attendant images" and his symbols, "music and the sea, liquid formless earth, in which are drowned soul and body."

Elsewhere in the notes her age is given as the lunar

twenty-eight, and numerous other parallels, images, and associations are cited. It would appear that Joyce's imagination was groping towards meanings, both introspective and universal, which the technique of the well-made play was unfitted to project. *Ulysses* alone was destined to carry the heavy weight of multiple significances.

To read *Ulysses* is to experience a sense of life patterned by verbal dexterity. Joyce achieves an unprecedented degree of intimacy with people and their environments. By the time one comes to the requiem for Bloom's dead friends, he has already known these persons through Bloom's musings about them. As for Dignam's death and funeral, no other event touches so many of the dramatis personae. Bloom is uncertain about the time of the service and is concerned about how warm his dark suit will be. He thinks of speaking of the death to O'Rourke; he does so to M'Coy, who wants his name put down as attending. M'Coy regales the bored Bloom with an account of Doran's maudlin reaction to the death, which we witness in midafternoon at Barney Kiernan's, the intoxicated Doran confusing Dignam's first name:

—The noblest, the truest, says he. And he's gone, poor little Willy, poor little Paddy Dignam.
    And mournful and with a heavy heart he bewept the extinction of that beam of heaven. (297–98)

The funeral chapter is one of the most effective in the book, redolent of local atmosphere and permeated with Bloom's subdued melancholy. There the reporter Hynes lists the names of those present, including the mysterious stranger, the man in the mackintosh (there was to be a similar interloper at Joyce's own funeral). At the news office Hynes turns in his account, which is read in the late evening paper

at the cabman's shelter, with its amusing errors: "*L. Boom,
C. P. M'Coy, — M'Intosh, and several others*" (632).
Bloom's reaction was that of being "Nettled not a little by
L. Boom (as it incorrectly stated) and the line of bitched
type, but tickled to death simultaneously by C. P. M'Coy
and Stephen Dedalus, B. A., who were conspicuous, need-
less to say, by their total absence (to say nothing of
M'Intosh)."

Joyce weaves a network of references to Dignam through
most of the episodes. In the Wandering Rocks chapter we
see Father Conmee setting out to arrange for the orphan
son to be entered at Artane (Thom's *Official Directory*
describes it as the "*O'Brien Institute* for destitute children,
Rev. Br. William A. Swan, director"). Conmee thinks:

Brother Swan was the person to see. Mr. Cunningham's letter.
Yes. Oblige him, if possible. Good practical catholic: useful at
mission time. (216)

Cunningham's missionary activities in behalf of Mr. Kernan
had been recounted by Joyce in the story "Grace." On his
way to the tram Father Conmee passes the funeral establishment where Corny Kelleher is entering costs in the day-
book (218) (Bloom had earlier reflected that Corny probably landed the job of burying Dignam—70). A moment
or so later Corny, in rather less dignified fashion, went to
a coffinlid in the corner, "and, spinning it on its axle, viewed
its shape and brass furnishings" (221). Later in the episode
we hear of Cunningham's efforts to raise a fund for the
widow (242), and he and Power, who had shared the
funeral carriage with Bloom and Simon Dedalus, mention
Dignam to Long John Fanning:

—Decent little soul he was, Mr Power said to the stalwart back

of Long John Fanning ascending towards Long John Fanning
in the mirror.

—Rather lowsized, Dignam of Menton's office that was, Martin Cunningham said.

Long John Fanning could not remember him. (244)

Sic transit! Another reaction to the death occurs later at
Kiernan's, when Alf Bergan cannot believe him dead:
"—Sure I'm after seeing him not five minutes ago, says Alf,
as plain as a pikestaff" (295). Still another view is that of
the son, dawdling along the street, happy to be away from
his "blooming dull" house of mourning, thinking of the
school days he will miss, and anticipating how "they'll all
see it in the paper and read my name printed and pa's
name" (247). Ironically enough, in addition to the mis-
prints, the news article describes *"The deceased gentleman"* as *"a most popular and genial personality,"* at whose
funeral *"many friends of the deceased were present"*
(631), that is, only thirteen in all. And though the newspaper had room for a lengthy effusion of commonplaces,
when it came to the son's name, the abbreviation *"Patk."*
had to suffice (631).

The cycle of life and death occurs in Bloom's thought
during the day, and the mystery of the man in the mackintosh, as well as such superficial items as the name of the
officiating priest and the ridiculous advertisement for
Plumtree's Potted Meat placed under the obituaries. The
list of deceased in the morning paper, "Callan, Coleman,
Dignam" (274), soon becomes distorted into a firm,
"Messrs Callan, Coleman and Co, limited" (275). Bloom
goes to Kiernan's in order to meet Cunningham regarding
the fund (307), and his presence on Sandymount Strand
is occasioned by a visit to Dignam's widow regarding in-

surance. Characteristically, Bloom reflects that the insurance company name, Scottish Widows, "takes it for granted we're going to pop off first" (374). The parents of Gerty MacDowell were neighbors and friends of the Dignams, though her father couldn't attend the funeral, "on account of the gout" (348). Bloom's contribution to the fund is duly listed in his budget for the day (696). Finally, Molly Bloom has the last word on the deceased when she visualizes the shabby group of mourners, "Tom Kernan that drunken little barrelly man" and M'Coy and the rest: "and they call that friendship killing and then burying one another." Yet she professes sympathy for the wife and children of the "comical little tee-totum always stuck up in some pub corner" (759).

The chain of attendant images would include the warm black suit and the scampering rat, Callan and Plumtree, M'Intosh and Mrs. Sinico (subject of "A Painful Case," whose funeral was the last Bloom attended), Father Coffey ("name like a coffin"—102), metempsychosis, Scottish Widows insurance, as well as Bloom's frequent thoughts about death and burial.

Proceeding from these references to the funeral, one could find links to almost every other portion of the book. Each character or place is related to still other persons and occasions. Gerty MacDowell, for instance, is not only in the orbit of the Dignam family, but she admires one of the bicycle riders in the races at Trinity College and knows the dog Garryowen who appears at Kiernan's. As a more obscure example, when the funeral carriages cross the Royal Canal a man on a turf-filled barge "lifted his brown strawhat, saluting Paddy Dignam" (98). Four hours later Father Conmee sees the barge "moored under the trees of

Charleville Mall," on it "a bargeman with a hat of dirty straw seated amidships, smoking and staring at the branch of poplar above him" (218). The good father thinks the scene idyllic, the whole economy of turf providential. A third time the bargeman appears, commenting on the current drought (390).

Akin to music in its development and elaboration of themes, yet often likened to mosaic with contrasting colors on a single plane, *Ulysses* is both dynamic and static. There must be several thousand recurring motifs, and it would require a volume almost the size of the original to expound all of them. It may be, however, that they function best on a subliminal level, just on the threshold of consciousness. There, echoes and associations are subdued, not even fully remembered, but nonetheless carrying tones of things familiar and suggestions of further meanings. On the other hand, when they are discovered they are sources of delight. Take the Bloom-Flower chain of meanings. Virag had anglicized his name to Bloom, and Bloom uses the pseudonym Flower in his clandestine correspondence. Martha Clifford sends him a flower in her letter, and compliments him on his lovely name. As he reclines in the bath his genitals are described as "a languid floating flower" (85). He consummated his love for Molly amid the rhododendron on the Hill of Howth. Molly, "flower of the mountain" (768), loves flowers. Rose of Castille, the Last Rose of Summer, the gardens at Gibraltar—*Ulysses* is a poem of flowers.

An interesting and seldom observed aspect of Joyce's art is his frequent recapitulation of themes and of characters. There are summaries of the persons in the newspaper office (133), of the applauding listeners at the Ormond

Bar (285), of the symposium at the hospital (four times enumerated—382, 389, 391, 410), of the characters who watch the vice-regal cavalcade (248–51). The entire Circe episode is in one sense a review of Bloomsday, and the question and answer technique of the Ithaca chapter places the day *sub specie aeternitatis*. The Sirens overture announces most of the topics of the chapter, which is in itself a model of the musicality of *Ulysses*, as the Wandering Rocks episode is a model of the interrelationships of people and places throughout the book as a whole. Bloom recounts one summary of events (373), the litany of "THE DAUGHTERS OF ERIN" in the Circe chapter provides another (488); for external events there is the *Evening Telegraph* (631–32) and Bloom's list of expenditures (696).

Motifs may serve to integrate the environment—the funeral, the Ascot Gold Cup race, theatrical attractions, the cycle races, and the Mirus Bazaar. The characters on the streets as they appear and reappear fulfill a similar function. Motifs underscore philosophic themes—Agendath Netaim the lure of the East, Agenbite of Inwit the prick of conscience, metempsychosis, parallax, Hamlet. The close intimacy we share with the principal figures arises from our being privy to their meditations.

Leopold Bloom may well be the most exhaustively characterized figure in literature. We are made aware of his possessions, the soap in his pocket, the lotion he has failed to pick up, his newspaper and his good-luck potato. We share his petty concerns over the three bob Hynes owes him, Molly's birthday gift, recollected phrases from the notes from Milly and Martha. We know of his physiological reactions (his reading Beaufoy on the toilet is both a literary and literal catharsis) and his physical and psychological yearnings. In an appendix to my *Fabulous Voyager* (1947) I listed about five hundred items, under the headings of personal habits, intellectual outlook, temperament, and imagination.[25] For many of these items leitmotifs can be cited.

Bloom's stream of consciousness is a comedy of the human mind. His memory is cluttered with his pop culture of science, business, and mass amusements. No writer since Flaubert has been so alert as Joyce to clichés, or so amused at their anticlimactic literary effect, or, more properly, their antiliterary effect. Here we may detect the roots of Joyce's incurable love for parody, a delight in language, and at the same time a mockery of linguistic pretensions.

Like the contents of an abandoned bureau, Bloom's mind is filled with imperfectly understood and half-forgotten knowledge; yet unlike Homais, the commonplace druggist in Flaubert's *Madame Bovary*, Bloom enlists sympathy rather than scorn. He is an early antihero, but in spite of the shallowness of his perceptions, he reveals a canny sense of words and ideas. As M'Coy says:

—He's a cultured allroundman, Bloom is, he said seriously. He's not one of your common or garden . . . you know. . . . There's a touch of the artist about old Bloom. (231–32)

He relishes Molly's phrase "barreltone" (152), and recalls something so casual as the butcher's, "Now, my miss" (68). Tags of popular songs, proverbs, advertising slogans —all the odds and ends of a verbal culture—are at hand, usually with a humorous or ironic effect. His recollections enable us to create a fairly complete biography, with his tender memories of his father, his school days (he must have been a fellow student of W. B. Yeats at Erasmus

Smith High School), his agnostic and political opinions, his jobs, his courtship and marriage, his daughter, and his son's death in babyhood.

An exile in his own home, Bloom is modern, rootless, megalopolitan man. As such he is a comic Chaplinesque antihero. In his charity toward others he is "*Christus* or Bloom" (627), as Stephen mutters in the cab-shelter. He is also an Odysseus, *polytropos*, in Homer's word, "a man of many devices," and as W. B. Stanford has demonstrated in his history of *The Ulysses Theme*,[26] Odysseus himself has been subject to many transformations through the ages, and actually became a man of many disguises. Bloom is a Hamlet, something of a Don Quixote, a Don Giovanni *manqué*, the Wandering Jew, Everyman. Ecce Homo— Behold Bloom!

APPENDIX

A Biography of Leopold Bloom

1815   Rudolph Virag was born in Hungary (a septuagenarian at time of his death—708). He was still in Hungary in 1852, when "an indistinct daguerreotype" of him and his father Leopold was made (708). Molly thinks that Bloom's promotion of Milly's photography was due to Bloom's grandfather (751), but it was actually the second cousin, Stefan, who had the atelier in Szesfchervar, whereas Szombathely was Virag's home (500, 666, 708, 709). Virag's later residences, before settling in Ireland, were Vienna, Budapest, Milan, and London (666), with Florence added in another listing (709). Bloom's greatgrandfather had seen Maria Theresa (709).

Having moved to Dublin, Virag married Ellen Higgins

(475), daughter of Julius Higgins, born Karoly, and Fanny Hegarty (666). In the same year he was converted to Protestantism (178, 701). [Harry Blamires, *The Bloomsday Book* (London: Methuen & Co., 1966) p. 242, notes an inconsistency in Bloom's feeling guilt at his own lack of respect for his father's Jewish observances, since Virag was already a convert to Christianity; Virag may, however, have been as imperfect an Irish Protestant convert as Bloom became as an Irish Catholic convert.] Bloom may have known his grandfather, whose spectre appears in the guise of a sexologist (499–506, 508–11). The ghost of his father also reproaches Bloom (430–31).

Of his mother Bloom recalls her good-luck amulet, a potato (56, 181, 430, 431, 467, 542). He keeps her cameo brooch (705), which she is wearing as her apparition appears (431).

1866   Leopold Bloom was born (eleven years old in 1877– 661). A new star appeared at his birth (685), as novae had coincided with the births of Stephen Dedalus, near, not after, the birth of Rudy Bloom, and a few years after the birth of Shakespeare. [Mark E. Littmann and Charles A. Schweighauser, "Astronomical Allusions, Their Meaning and Purpose in *Ulysses*," *James Joyce Quarterly* 2, no. 4 (Summer 1965): 240, identify these as T Coronae Borealis, 1866, S Andromedae, 1885, T Aurigae, 1891, and "Tycho's Star," Delta of Cassiopeia, 1572.]

In childhood, Bloom heard stories from his father: of Kate Bateman playing in *Leah* (75), and of his European residences (709). He remembers his father's reading European newspapers (406), and the Haggadah (121), which Bloom still has (708), together with the daguerrotype portrait, and his father's copy of Spinoza (280, 693).

Bloom attended Mrs. Ellis's juvenile school, and played

marbles (76, 697). At the age of eleven he submitted poetry to a contest sponsored by the *Shamrock* (662). A glance at this verse would dispel all hopes that he might have won a prize! Like most children, he was scolded for getting his clothes dirty (431).

At Erasmus Smith High School (406) (on Harcourt Street, around the corner from Montague Street—536), Bloom must have been a fellow student of W. B. Yeats.

His high-school friends included Percy Apjohn and Owen Goldberg, with whom he recalls playing (160), and going on an excursion (535). These friendships continued beyond his graduation in 1880 (687), for he carried on discussions with them in 1884 and 1885 (651), as he had in high school days (701). He was photographed by Apjohn (722). Apjohn was killed in action at the Modder River [Boer War, 1899] (689). Another friend was Donald (or Cecil) Turnbull (535, 651). Someone named Wilkins drew a shocking picture of Venus (365).

Vance, the physics teacher, was the only instructor recalled (71, 369, 477). Perhaps he it was who was responsible for Bloom's perennial scientific curiosity.

Athletics (665) and sex (535, 536, 537) were preoccupations. In *Vice Versa* [a play in which Joyce acted at Belvedere College], Bloom took a female part (525).

1880 On finishing high school, Bloom was noted for his agnostic (701) and political opinions (651, 701), so much so, in fact, that the Doyles said he would run for Parliament (756).

Bloom worked as a salesman for his father (330, 406), whose senility he recalls (516, 709). His job at Kellet's may have been at about this time (517).

Bridie Kelly gave him his sexual initiation (406, 434). He was also somewhat interested in Josie Powell, later Breen (156, 437).

In 1882 [the year of Stephen's and Joyce's birth] Bloom had tried squaring the circle (503), and cut his hand in a fall (549). He expressed his theories of colonial expansion and of evolution to his friends (701). He scanned traffic through a pane of glass (665).

1886   Bloom met Molly at Dillon's in Terenure (formerly Roundtown). She wore a yellow dress with black lace. They played musical chairs (271, 530). The meeting was fated (271, 638, 756).

         ❊   ❊   ❊   ❊   ❊   ❊   ❊   ❊

Molly had been born on September 8, 1870 (720). She subtracts a year in thinking she would be 33 in 1904 (736), and in dating her birth from the visit of the Prince of Wales (737). [Weldon Thornton, *Allusions in "Ulysses"* (Chapel Hill: University of North Carolina Press, 1961), p. 490, finds that Edward visited Gibraltar in 1859 and 1876, but not in 1870. Robert M. Adams, *Surface and Symbol* (New York: Oxford University Press, 1962) notes that Molly's recall of Grant's visit in 1877 (742) involves her being on the Rock when her father was fighting at Plevna, Joyce thus "stretching historical circumstance here, in order to bring Molly into contact with a man named Ulysses."]

She was the daughter of Brian Tweedy (449), and Lunita Laredo (746), about whom, unknown to Bloom, there was some scandal, without which Molly would have made a better match (730). Tweedy was promoted for his action at Rorke's Drift, in the Zulu War, January 1879 (449, 581, 741). His rank is usually given as major, reference to him as major-general (449) is Bloom's gratuitous promotion to add prestige in the Circe chapter. He made a corner in stamps (56, 748) but all he left his daughter was an English accent (748) and his trunk (715). Molly has her mother's eyes and figure (748). Bloom remembers Tweedy (370, 694, 714), as, of course, does Molly (726).

Bloom reflects on Molly's girlhood at Gibraltar (373) and she remembers the heat, the storms, the great rock, the lanes and ramps, a bullfight, a band concert on the esplanade, as well as walks over middle hill and windmill hill, with its view across the straits, and coming back from Tarifa on the nightboat (740, 741, 746, 747, 748, 760, 764). Her friend Hester Stanhope moved to Paris (740,767) and left her lonely and bored. Her first romance was with Lieutenant Mulvey, who kissed her under the Moorish Wall (364, 375, 716, 741, 744, 746, 767). He left in May 1886 (745), when the Infante was born [identified by Adams as Alfonso XIII (1886–1941)], hence Molly must have moved to Dublin immediately thereafter, in order to have met Bloom before his father's death in June (Adams, *Surface and Symbol*, p. 189).

She made her singing debut at sixteen, hence just about the time she met Bloom (637). She recalls the meeting (756). The Tweedys lived at Rehoboth Terrace at the time (714, 756), but shortly thereafter they were at Brighton Square (756). [Joyce's birthplace was 41 Brighton Square West.]

Josie Powell aroused Molly's jealousy during Bloom's courtship, particularly at Georgina Simpson's housewarming on Christmas night (362, 437, 727, 728). After the Blooms were married, Josie used to say that Molly looked blooming, but Molly thinks Breen is hardly any better name, and besides, Breen is crazy (746). Molly still suspects her (758).

✿　✿　✿　✿　✿　✿　✿　✿

1886　On June 27, Bloom's father, proprietor of the Queen's Hotel, Ennis (708) committed suicide by poison (89, 95, 330, 669, 680). Because of Bloom's annual vigil, he missed the funeral of Stephen's mother, Mary Goulding Dedalus, on June 26, 1903 (680). Molly recalls Bloom's weeping eyes (726).

In the same year Bloom was occupied with the quadrature of the circle (684) and wrote a sealed prophecy of the consequences of passing the Home Rule bill (705).

1887   The Blooms met Stephen Dedalus at Dillon's (664, 759). It was May, and lilacs were blooming (414). At the same time John Henry Menton danced with Molly (105, 113, 114). Luke Doyle's, in Dolphin's Barn, held other memories. There the young couple played charades, and Bloom saw the sun rise (64, 156, 370, 689, 732).

1888   This was the year of courtship, consummation, and marriage, with an acrostic valentine (662), flirtations (728), a gift of eight poppies (732), and June on Howth amid the rhododendron (173, 370, 373, 768). Bloom enjoyed talking with Tweedy (651).

Their union was consummated on September 10 (173, 267, 370, 537, 721), although they were not married until October 8 (720). Among the wedding gifts were a stuffed owl from Alderman John Hooper (112, 678, 692), a marble clock from the Dillons (678, 692), and a dwarf artificial tree from the Doyles (692).

A political torchlight procession occurred on February 2 [the day Joyce was six years old] (701). Bloom was working for Hely, the stationer (105, 153).

Converted to Roman Catholicism (716), Bloom had been "baptised" three times (as a Protestant, as a Catholic, and in a boyish prank) (666).

1889   Milly Bloom was born, June 15 (66, 677, 720, 727). Molly recalls nursing her (739). Among undated recalls of her infancy and childhood are: Bloom's buying baby food (332); her infant hand (178); cutting teeth (727); her bathing (153); her blond coloring (677); her going to "beddy-house" (154); counting buttons (373, 677) (echoed on 490); shaking her moneybox (677); admiring herself in mirror at age of three (365);

drawing her daddy (705); writing a letter (705); burying a bird (112); illness (755); mumps (752); not being seasick on *Erin's King* excursion (66, 373); having nightmares at six and eight (677); admiring her mother's blouse (362); drying a handkerchief (365); her dreaming (678); her fear when parents hid behind tree at Crumlin (373); her father's teaching her (679). She gave him a moustache cup on his twenty-seventh birthday (62, 661, 679). In adolescence, she put aside hoop and skipping rope, refused to have her picture taken, and turned back on Stamer Street without reason (677). She served her father a cutlet (169), and argued over a bracelet at the X L Cafe (66). She pinched her cheeks to redden them (66). Her first period began on September 15, 1903 (721).

1890   Bloom picked up Parnell's hat (634, 639).

1892   He met Stephen at Breslin's, with Stephen's father and granduncle (664); had discussions with Mastiansky (651); received a Christmas card from Comerfords (705). Mrs. Riordan moved from Stephen's home to live at City Arms Hotel, during 1892, 1893, and 1894 (664).

1893   [Adams, *Surface and Symbol*, pp. 188–89, points out: "A notable circumstance about Bloom's past is that the years 1893 and 1894 (which are the years of confusion) are remarkably rich in specifically dated material. It is possible that Joyce's mind dwelt with special fondness on events separated from 1904 by just a decade."]

Residences during this period are confused, as are jobs. Bloom was on Lombard Street (285, 307, 651, 766), then moved to Raymond Terrace in March, where Rudy was conceived (88, 165, 365); but by error he was still on Lombard Street in 1894 (153, 164). The Blooms were at the City Arms Hotel six weeks before Rudy's birth (332, also 168, 300, 366, 664, 720, 721); it was there that he befriended the aged Mrs. Riordan

(172, 723). He worked for the cattle-dealer Cuffe (59, 392, 664), where his outspokenness was known (402), and brought about his dismissal (309), which Molly tried to alter (737).

Incidental events include a water shortage (655); the canal freeze (738); the Comerford party (738); his closing the carriage door for Mrs. Bellingham (457); the fitting of Dollard's tight trousers (264, 266); the *Sinbad the Sailor* pantomime (662 [for confusion in dating see Adams, pp. 79-80]); Prof. Goodwin's farewell concert (63, 154, 264, 730, 732); sunspots (164).

Molly's pregnancy (88, 149, 159, 332, 390, 725) and the birth of Rudy on December 29 were the most significant events of this year. Rudy died on January 9 (66, 94, 109, 384, 664, 720, 721, 763). The last sexual relations of the Blooms took place on November 27 (720).

1894   Fired by Cuffe, Bloom worked at Thom's, publishers of the Dublin Directory (122, 153, 336, 371), and may have worked for Drimmie's insurance (363, 754, 757), or for the advertising agent M'Glade (152). He seems to have been down and out, for Molly played in the Coffee Palace and dealt in old clothes (264, 266, 366, 619, 738), and thought of posing as an artist's model (738). Bloom sold Molly's hair combings (363), and got involved in a scandal about Hungarian lottery tickets, from which his fellow masons rescued him (154, 308, 338, 476, 706, 732, 757). He suggested starting a musical academy, or renting rooms (750).

The Glencree dinner, where Molly was admired by the Lord Mayor Val Dillon (153, 230–31, 364, 735, 759), took place.

Molly saw Stephen driving with his parents to Kingsbridge Station (759). Bloom conversed with his neighbors Mastiansky (60, 107, 487) initialled O. (532) and named Julius [*sic*] (651, 716) and Citron, of 28 St.

Kevin's Parade, who had a young student staying with him (60, 121, 153, 487, 739). Citron's initial was J. (532). [Thom's *Directory* for 1905 lists a Mr. P. Mastiansky at 16, and Mr. J. Citron at 17, St. Kevin's Parade.]

Bloom's friend Phil Gilligan died of phthisis at Jervis St. Hospital (153, 689).

1895   The Blooms may have moved to Holles Street in 1894 or 1895 (363, 524, 677). Molly recalls various residences (757).

1896   Mrs. Riordan died (96, 665). The clock, wedding gift of Matthew Dillon, stopped (692). Molly's portrait photograph was done by Lafayette (637).

1897   Living on Ontario Terrace (677), with Mary Driscoll as maid (402, 451, 724). Bloom brought home a stray dog (641).

1898   Bloom marked a florin, which he never again saw (681).

1899   Bloom witnessed a riot at Trinity College, when a degree was given to Joseph Chamberlain (160); a pink ribbon from an Easter egg of this year is in Bloom's drawer (706).

1901   A nova appears, presumably heralding the century, just as novae had occurred at or about the births of Shakespeare, Bloom, and Stephen (683) [Thornton, *Allusions*, p. 471, identifies this as Nova Persei]. M'Coy recalls Bloom's buying a bargain copy of Ball's *Story of the Heavens* (230).

1903   Mrs. Dedalus was buried, June 26 (680). The Blooms met Boylan, either at the establishment of the tailor Mesias (717) or at the D. B. C. tearoom (729). Molly's last concert was given at St. Teresa's Hall, Clarendon Street (733). Bloom went to Ennis, as usual (164) and was last at Glasnevin for the funeral of Mrs. Sinico,

October 14 [compare with "A Painful Case"] (113, 680, 695). Cowley lent M'Coy a valise for the Wicklow Regatta concert (75).

1904   May 12:   Bloom weighed himself (11 stone, 4 pounds) (652). Bloom is "5 ft. 9½ inches" tall, with "full build" and "olive complexion" (712). He wears a "size 17" collar and five button waistcoat (695).

May 21:   Bloom borrowed Conan Doyle book from Capel Street Library, now overdue (64, 636, 693).

May 23:   Bloom was stung by bee (68, 96, 160, 380, 418, 695).

May 26:   Bloom lent Hynes three shillings (118, 318, 379, 477).

May 29:   Molly met Boylan by the Tolka, when the band played "The Dance of the Hours" (69, 165, 368, 378, 725).

June: Bloom sent Milly a tam as a birthday present (65, 398).

June 13:   A widow looked at Bloom (374). About this time he saw a girl in Eustace Street arranging her garter (73).

June 15:   Bloom dreamed of Molly wearing Turkish pyjamas (374, 391, 432), scribbled a letter (to Martha?) (724).

Undated Recollections:

I. Accidents:
Bloom sprained his ankle at picnic on Sugarloaf Mt. (153, 723); commode broke (534, 715, 755); lost shoe (428); almost shot (444); ill at City Arms Hotel (723); cut his toe (723); got railway car door open (733); looked for burglars (751).

II. Entertainments:
In box at Gunn's Gaiety Theatre (266, 280, 754); at Gaiety

for Beerbohm Tree's "Trilby" [Thornton, *Allusions*, pp. 494–95, dates this as October 10 and 11, 1895] (752); Bazaar dance (69); on "Erin's King" (66, 150, 373, 537); Hengler's Circus (64, 681); horse show (367); Kingstown train (444); Leopardstown races (441); in Master of Rolls' kitchen (173); at Mutoscope pictures: for men only (362); polo match (72, 458); Theatre Royal (457); Viceregal party (158); trip to Holyhead (610). Molly recalls: Simon Dedalus at cricket match (753); college races (758); open air fête (731); fish supper (763); Killiney Hill picnic (740); Mallow concert (733); Mayer's private opera (759); museum (756); Poole's Myriorama (724); trotting matches (753); with Boylan and Bloom at D. B. C. tearoom (729).

III. Molly's Singing:
Choir in Gardiner Street (79, 81, 284); buying "Blumenlied" (274); her singing (278); with d'Arcy (730).

IV. Recollections of Each Other:
Bloom: her reading while braiding hair (67); her dressing (69, 91); her at window (107); her powers of observation (365); the hurdy-gurdy boy (381). Molly: his smutty photo (458, 723, 738); gave her Byron (728); begged bit of her drawers (731); wrote suggestive letters (731); hobnobs with "Sinner" Fein (733, 757); shopgirl in Grafton Street (737); told boatman at Bray about rowing, and almost sank boat (749); ogled women outside Switzers (752); had row over politics (727); slept on floor (758); bought statue (695, 761).

V. Observations of Other People:
Bloom: a barber (269); Mrs. Dandrade (158); Mrs. Fleming making beds (86); Fleming, an embezzler (85); girls in Meath St. (364), in Coombe (77, 78, 165, 539), in Cecilia Street (274), in lane (285, 616), at Jammet's (365); Dr. Murren (112, 159); Davy Byrne (169); Flynn, to whom he sent postcard (363); Mrs. Bellingham (458); Mrs. Talboys to whom he sent obscene photographs (458); O'Rourke's presents (479). Molly (Dublin only, for Gibraltar see the Penelope chapter—723 ff.): Dr. Collins (755); Menton (724); Father Corrigan (725); Kitty O'Shea (736); voyeurs

(738); medical at Holles Street (742); Mrs. Gillespie (743); Mrs. Dween's letter (743); Nancy Blake (743); Atty Dillon's letters (743); Kathleen Kearney (747); Burke woman at City Arms (750); Milly's leaving, not wanting to kiss her (752); Conny Connolly (752); Mrs. Galbraith (736); countryman at City Arms (742); K. C. in Hardwicke Lane (763).

NOTES

1. Robert Tracy, "Leopold Bloom Fourfold: A Hungarian-Hebraic-Hellenic-Hibernian Hero," *Massachusetts Review* 6 (Spring–Summer 1965): 523–38.

2. "The Language of the Outlaw," in *The Workshop of Daedalus: James Joyce and the Raw Materials for "A Portrait of the Artist as a Young Man,"* Robert Scholes and Richard M. Kain (Evanston: Northwestern University Press, 1965), pp. 153–57.

3. Numbers in parentheses refer to the Random House and Modern Library editions of *Ulysses*, 1934–1960, on which the *Word Index* of Miles L. Hanley and most early criticism are based.

4. Arthur Griffith, *The Resurrection of Hungary* (Dublin: James Duffy & Co., M. H. Gill & Son, Sealy, Bryers & Walker, 1904), p. 75.

5. Richard Ellmann, *James Joyce* (New York: Oxford University Press, 1959), p. 464 and passim.

6. Heinrich Straumann, "Four Letters to Marthe Fleischmann," *Tri-Quarterly* 8 (Winter 1967): 180: "It is remarkable that Joyce first took Martha [*sic*] for a Jewess. Actually her grandfather had been adopted as a homeless boy by the Swiss village community of Ueken (Aargau) in the first part of the 19th century. Whether or not he was of Jewish origin cannot be ascertained, but it is at least unlikely. Her parents and her grandmother were certainly not considered Jewish by the people of that village."

7. Frank Budgen, "James Joyce," *Horizon* 3 (February 1941): 107.

8. Frank Budgen, *James Joyce and the Making of "Ulysses"* (New York: Harrison Smith and Robert Haas, 1934), p. 171.

9. William Blissett, "James Joyce in the Smithy of his Soul," *James Joyce Today*, ed. Thomas F. Staley (Bloomington: Indiana University Press, 1966), pp. 96–134.

10. Louis Gillet, "Joyce's Way," translated from "Du Coté de chez

Joyce," *Revue des Deux Mondes,* August 1, 1925, in *Claybook for James Joyce* (New York: Abelard Schuman, 1958), p. 44. *Claybook* is a translation of the collection of Gillet's articles on Joyce, collected as *Stele pour James Joyce* (Paris: Editions du Sagittaire, 1946).

11.   Stuart Gilbert, *James Joyce's "Ulysses"* (London: Faber & Faber, 1930), pp. 99–100.

12.   Clive Hart, *James Joyce's "Ulysses"* (Sydney: Sydney University Press, 1968), p. 83.

13.   Phillip F. Herring, *"Ulysses* Notebook VIII.A.5 at Buffalo," *Studies in Bibliography* 22 (1969): 287–310.

14.   Frank Budgen, *James Joyce and the Making of "Ulysses,"* p. 172.

15.   Robert M. Adams, *Surface and Symbol: The Consistency of James Joyce's "Ulysses"* (New York: Oxford University Press, 1962), p. 86.

16.   Richard M. Kain, "The Position of Joyce," in Marvin Magalaner and Richard M. Kain, *Joyce: the Man, the Work, the Reputation* (New York: New York University Press, 1956), p. 306.

17.   Richard Ellmann, *James Joyce,* p. 377.

18.   Robert M. Adams, *Surface and Symbol,* p. 64.

19.   Ibid., p. 89.

20.   Thomas Merton, "News of the Joyce Industry," *The Sewanee Review* 77 (Summer 1969): 546.

21.   Alick West, *Crisis and Criticism* (London: Lawrence and Wishart, 1937), p. 179.

22.   Robert Scholes and Richard M. Kain, *The Workshop of Daedalus,* pp. 19–25.

23.   Thomas Mann, *Stories of Three Decades* (New York: Alfred A. Knopf, 1936), p. vi.

24.   James Joyce, *Exiles: A Play in Three Acts, Including Hitherto Unpublished Notes by the Author, Discovered after His Death, and an Introduction by Padraic Colum* (New York: Viking Press, 1951), pp. 117–18.

25.   Richard M. Kain, *Fabulous Voyager: James Joyce's "Ulysses"* (Chicago: University of Chicago Press, 1947), pp. 243–51.

26.   W. B. Stanford, *The Ulysses Theme: A Study in the Adaptability of a Traditional Hero* (Oxford: Basil Blackwell, 1954).

The Empirical Molly

DAVID HAYMAN

4

A WOMAN MUCH DISCUSSED but little understood is Molly. Doubtless, her creator's method is partly at fault. He has underscored her symbolic character and eliminated her voice, presenting her as a public creature or a projection of Bloom's private fears and wishes, before allowing her, like Aeschylus' Cassandra, to spill all or almost all in a chapter that tops even the rough and ready obscenity of Circe. The reader is obliged but apparently unprepared to account for the ironic gap not only between metaphor and flesh but also between her public and private natures. Deprived of ready answers and confused by his choices, he is apt to accept only one or two of the many readings of her character and role and overlook or misread the others. He may see her as a whore, a fertility goddess on strike, a frustrated housewife in provincial Dublin, or a mediated projection of Joyce's anxieties. He may reject her or rejoice in her apparent vitality. Unfortunately, this will not do if we are to understand the book to which Molly provides the final yes. I propose therefore to attempt a

103

balanced assessment not only of Molly as she appears to us in the Penelope chapter but of Joyce's presentation of her, discarding for this purpose both biography and received opinion and focusing on the drama of concealment and revelation.[1]

Who is Molly Bloom? We can begin with some vital statistics from among those doled out so slowly to readers intent on naturalizing and controlling the fictional universe. Born on Gibraltar in 1870 of a Spanish Jewess named Lunita Laredo and an Irish major, Brian Cooper Tweedy, Marion or Molly Bloom is the wife of Leopold, whom she married in October 1888, when she was eighteen. Her daughter, Milly, conceived out of wedlock, is fifteen and a photographer's assistant in the market town of Mullingar, where she has begun her first flirtation. The death of the Blooms' only son, Rudy, at eleven days in 1894 has soured Molly on the whole process of childbearing and turned her marriage awry. Since she has a pleasant and even a strong voice, Molly has made a modest reputation in Dublin as a concert singer, and for a time, when her husband's fortunes were low, she also earned money by renting out evening clothes and playing the piano in a "coffee palace." Though she has lost her girlish figure, she is still, at thirty-two,[2] a ripe southern or Jewish beauty and a potentially merry wife. But here we enter the realm of the subjective since at least one witness, the narrator of the Cyclops episode, sees her as a "fat heap . . . with a back on her like a ballalley" (305),[3] and for Stephen, who knows her only from a photograph taken in 1896, she is only a "large sized lady, with her fleshy charms on evidence . . . her full lips parted, and some perfect teeth" (652). Be that as it may, on June 16, 1904, she is beginning, after ten years of virtual abstinence, her first adulterous affair. It is this fact more than any other that makes the day meaningful for Molly and Leopold.

Our awareness of Molly is woven about, rather than of, such information. Prior to the Penelope chapter, we are engaged by an overblown will-o-the-wisp compounded of sentiment, prejudice, and hearsay: Bloom's Molly, obliquely rendered, interacting with Dublin's Moll and our own fleeting impressions garnered in the Calypso chapter. Virtually wordless, a composite cliché, she engages our imagination because she is of interest to others, because what we know is tantalizingly little, and because Bloom, whom we know so well, needs and desires her. If Joyce initiates us into her mystery, he also deceives us wilfully, projecting a Molly whose public identity makes men lick their lips during barroom conversations and whose behavior *en famille* is at once provocative, slovenly, masterful, and slightly mysterious. He generates an attitude toward her which subtly colors our appreciation of the Penelope chapter and creates a delightful but confusing double vision further complicated by the symbolic implications planted in the text.

Each of the Dubliners seems to have a slightly different view. For an admiring M'Coy, she is the wife's more successful competitor from whose table crumbs may be swept. John Henry Menton, who danced with her "fifteen seventeen golden years ago," recalls the "finelooking woman" and the "good armful" she was at seventeen or eighteen when Bloom courted her at Mat Dillon's (106). For Josie Breen she is the "friend" who captured Bloom's affections and made a good marriage. Simon Dedalus treats her as a figure of fun, turning her clothing business into a doubt-

ful and damaging pun on her morals ("Mrs Marion Bloom
has left off clothes of all descriptions"), quipping about
Tweedy's "Daughter of the regiment" and "My Irish Molly,
O," who is from "the rock of Gibraltar . . . all the way"
(269). Though we may agree with Molly that Simon is
"such a criticiser" (768) and suspect that, like Molière's
Célimène, he is overly jealous of his reputation as a wit in a
Dublin that seems stranded in the eighteenth century, we
are willing to imagine some truth behind these facile jibes.
Isn't Molly beginning an affair with Boylan at this very
moment? Of another order is the left-handed compliment
paid her by a dubious Lidwell: "The wife has a fine voice.
Or had. What?" (288). If Molly has lost her voice along
with her figure and her reputation, what does she have
left?

Lenehan does even more damage when he turns a bit
of fondling into a veritable fabliau. His account of the
stargazing episode that followed the famous Glencree banquet ends equivocally when Molly, eager to distract Bloom,
points to the tiny star Chris Callinan calls a "pinprick"
(235). The picture of a bawdy Moll who accepts and en-
courages the advances of a sponge persists till Molly explains that she tolerated Lenehan because she had been
worked up by "the lord Mayor looking" at her "with his
dirty eyes" (750). Further testimony comes from the narrator of the Cyclops chapter, whose information goes back
to the City Arms hotel period when Molly was apt to weep
over her bad luck and scold Bloom publicly. Given the
speaker's thirst for the scurrilous and his taste for hyper-
bole, the absence of real gossip (for instance, about Molly's
love life before Boylan) is a mark in her favor as is his
negative reaction to her bountiful charms. Most damaging,

though most easily overlooked, is the ambiguous passage planted in the riotous conclusion of the Oxen of the Sun episode:

Know his dona? Yup, sartin, I do. Full of a dure. See her in her dishybilly. Peels off a credit. Lovely lovekin. None of your lean kine, not much. Pull down the blind, love. . . . Got a prime pair of mincepies, no kid. And her take me to rests and her anker of rum. Must be seen to be believed. Your starving eyes and allbeplastered neck you stole my heart, O gluepot. (425)

Whatever our impression, the chief speaker, Dixon, is suggesting only that Molly has undressed in full view of his window. Molly's remarks about Dixon are at once tamer and more compromising since she openly flirted though she did not knowingly exhibit herself to him (as she did when a child to a neighbor on Gibraltar—763).

Molly as others see her complements the woman we have seen in Calypso, the substantial animal lying late abed reading pornographic literature and contemplating her assignation with a lusty Boylan. Our first impression is ambiguous, inconclusive, and unpleasant; for like the demanding cat, goddess of the hearth, Molly is only a footnote to the chapter, and the view we get is a function of Bloom's role as the masochistic servant, a foil for the Stephen of the Telemachus chapter. In passages like the following, with an art reminiscent of the *Portrait*, Joyce invests the air Bloom breathes with positive and negative sexuality (a corollary to Bloom's appetites exposed in the chapter's initial paragraph):

She set the brasses jingling as she raised herself briskly, an elbow on the pillow. He looked calmly down her bulk and between her large soft bubs, sloping within her nightdress like a shegoat's udder. The warmth of her couched body rose on the air, mingling with the fragrance of the tea she poured.

A strip of torn envelope peeped from under the dimpled pillow. In the act of going he stayed to straighten the bedspread. (63)

Molly is presented in terms of the objects, sensations, and actions that make her accessible to her man. Joyce underlines her "bulk," her "large soft bubs," the "warmth" of the body and associates her with the beast of lust. But she is also present in the tea, the strip of envelope that actively peeps from beneath the "dimpled pillow," neither of which is sexual in its own right. Her "brisk" movement and Bloom's hesitating, housewifely action, prelude to a sly question, convey better than dialogue Molly's power and his subservience. Similarly, the rising warmth and aroma amplify his cautious awe while lending the scene a mock-religious quality. It is morning and Molly is at her worst, smelling like "foul flowerwater" and associated with "soiled drawers" and a "twisted grey garter looped around a stocking: rumpled shiny sole" (63). Still, though not yet convinced that there can be no substitute for her in Bloom's life, we are left with the impression that she has retained the appeal of the female animal, ripe and used.

Bloom's version of Molly is naturally colored by his preoccupations and limited by his tastes. Self-possessed and balanced, solvent and healthy, Bloom is still haunted by feelings of guilt and inadequacy. He knows that he is in the process of being cuckolded, but can do nothing about it, since he has courted infidelity for ten years. He is in fact as helpless as the wandering Ulysses, though for different reasons. Consequently, his view is remarkable for what it omits or represses. Much is conveyed through his frequent cries of despair, his muted pride, his shyness in her presence, the trick he has of referring everything to her or to their relationship. Molly has become for him, for this day at least, the measure of most things. For us she becomes increasingly significant and valuable as the objects that surround or adorn her take on a magical and symbolic aura.

Like most husbands, Bloom has accumulated the view he projects of Molly, mingling objective fact with subjective interpretation, experience with desire. His Molly, though heavy enough to break a commode during an amorous experiment, is "not unlike" the *Photo Bits* nymph, and very much the eastern houri. Yet he recognizes and tries to rationalize her feeble wit, while her fading charms and provocative wiles are spiced for him by her "southern" temper and jealousy. Similarly he tends to identify Molly and Milly by ascribing to the mother the appeal of the child and the childish tricks that are no longer her style but which increase her charm in his eyes. Our own confusion is increased by the knowledge that Milly is now going out with Mulligan's friend Bannon. It is natural, therefore, that, when Bloom innocently enough sees Milly following the same road as her mother, we project the girl's "future" in terms of Molly's "past." The truth is less spectacular. Bloom is referring mainly to Molly's precocious sexuality on Gibraltar and anticipating his own loss of an affectionate daughter. Like Mulvey, Bannon, as we find out in the Oxen of the Sun chapter, has not seduced Milly.

As probable adultery becomes an immutable fact and as he makes contact with other women (with Martha by letter, with Josie Breen, with limping-coy Gerty his seaside girl, with the whores and finally with Bella-Bello Cohen), Bloom modifies his anxiety. By Eumaeus and Ithaca, Molly has become more like the woman he meets in his bed. One can imagine a film of *Ulysses* in which Bloom's image of Molly would be developed through a series of extremely brief flashes, distinctive gestures from the distant and immediate past, revealing both her character as reflected in attitudes and reactions and the sort of mannerisms that decorate his memory. There is Molly the enthraller: "Mrs Marion. Reading lying back now, counting the strands of her hair, smiling, braiding" (67). Or the bewitching sloth: "Not up yet. Queen was in her bedroom eating bread and. No book. Blackened court cards laid along her thigh by sevens" (75). Or Molly the scold: "Bad as a row with Molly" (78). As wilful Molly, she "wouldn't let herself be vaccinated again" (76). Bloom recalls with particular pleasure the sensual Molly: "Looking at me, the sheet up to her eyes, Spanish, smelling herself" (84). If he seldom misses a chance to emphasize her exotic background, he never overlooks the animal who "gets swelled after cabbage" (103) or the exhibitionist who wanted "to do it at the window" (108), or Molly pregnant: "Funny sight two of them together, their bellies out. Molly and Mrs. [*sic*] Moisel. Mothers' meeting" (162). Perhaps because of the day's event, he links musical Molly and Molly the flirt:

Walking down by the Tolka . . . . She was humming: The young May moon she's beaming, love. He other side of her. Elbow, arm. He. Glowworm's la-amp is gleaming, love. Touch. Fingers. Asking. Answer. Yes. (167)

Such memories are rendered with delicate precision and painfully expunged, but they convey, even more than Bloom's concern, Molly's appeal. We too are drawn (as well as repelled) by the lush evocation of the proposal on Howth and the seedcake "mumbled sweet and sour with spittle. Joy: I ate it. . . . Screened under ferns she laughed warmfolded" (176). And we delight in Molly at Dillon's, still a girl, flirting with Bloom:

Yellow, black lace she wore. Musical chairs. We two the last . . . Halt. Down she sat. All ousted looked. Lips laughing. Yellow knees. (275)

All of these and other echo-vignettes give us an untidy bundle of impressions but hardly a portrait. Their very inadequacy underlines the complex and shifting role she plays in Bloom's life. References in Nausicaa, the bawdy scene imagined in Circe, bits from Eumaeus reinforce our impression. Every detail helps convince us that, faithful or adulterous, Bloom's Molly is an extension of his ego. But though she fills his need for pleasure and pain, there is a great distance between them that can be defined as their marriage. It is because we are still unaware of that distance and incapable of apprehending the nature of the silent woman that we can accept the list of twenty-five lovers compiled for Bloom by the supposedly objective catechist of the Ithaca chapter.

Like the other major figures in *Ulysses*, Molly is far more than the character Joyce presents. She is the vitality generated by the attitudes we accumulate toward her. Thus, if we agree to accept her in the role of "Gea Tellus," we cannot reject her in the role of Great Whore, and though both of these roles apply on a symbolic level, we must realize that she is also a figure existing in time: a ripe and frustrated woman carrying on a sordid affair in an ordinary house on Eccles Street while her husband wanders keyless and paralysed through Dublin. Further, though we may not admire her behavior, we sense through Joyce's presentation that she is far more of a woman than any of the others we see during this day and perhaps more valuable as a human being. It is in part to this purpose that he has sketched figures like Josie Breen, the pitiful sirens at the Ormond, the self-deceiving virgin Gerty MacDowell, the frustrated Nurse Callan, and the pointlessly fertile Minna Purefoy, to say nothing of the whores in nighttown. Each of these figures ultimately refers to Molly, who subsumes and outshines them all not by virtue of what she does but because of her unrealized potential.

This does not glorify the character on the page who drags us along through her voluminous musings, weaves us into her web, mesmerizes us as she articulates a nature that, despite immense assimilative powers, accepts very little that fails to satisfy her animal needs. Such a creature (Joyce's "perfectly sane full amoral fertilisable untrustworthy engaging shrewd limited prudent indifferent *Weib*")[4] is beyond our judgment in a general sense though we may, and will, judge her in each of her particular modes. We may find her as guilty as Bloom of spoiling their marriage. Though she has till recently not been unfaithful in deed, she is hardly a patient Penelope. If she accepts Bloom at all, it is not because she is tolerant but because she needs him in ways even she cannot comprehend. Yet, having been faithful to Bloom in her fashion, she goes further than he would think of going toward slaying (with words) the suitors on his list. She is only ironically a fertility figure since she rejects the opportunity to produce children. Indeed, we may see her as a neglectful mother, or hardly a mother at all, especially since, unlike Penelope, she is not unhappy when Bloom sends off her daughter to gain experience and learn about the dead past (the family interest in photography). Finally, she is unnecessarily querulous and negative for one who has so much more freedom than most of the Dublin women. Yet, if Mother Earth personifies Nature, all of these are earth-motherly attributes and Molly can be seen to fulfill her functions well enough to keep the globe spinning. We may read in her actions and attitudes a necessity that ultimately justifies her in our eyes. Still, if the impulse which makes us glory in the final yes is the product of the interaction of the attitudes Joyce has generated by his various means, such generalizations, along with the parallels and analogies, reflect only dimly on the "character" that emerges from the texture of Penelope.

To understand Molly's behavior and role we must first reduce her to normal scale by putting aside the metaphors and especially by laying the ghost of her checkered past. In one of the best sections of *Surface and Symbol,*[5] Robert Martin Adams has noted the obvious discrepancies in the list of suitors in the Ithaca chapter, pointing to the fact that only Boylan can be established as a lover. Independently of Adams, whose work he fails to acknowledge, Stanley Sultan has demonstrated Molly's fidelity at length, insisting that this fact underscores the positive *Argument of "Ulysses."*[6] There is no question in my mind that Adams is right and that we need no longer look for ways to validate the list or use it as proof of Molly's turpitude. Still, since for most critics and readers the question is not yet settled, it is best to review and develop the main points in support of Molly's chastity. First, she has only Bloom to measure against Boylan as a sexual partner. Second, she makes too much of her newly acquired status. Third, the wording ("Assuring Mulvey to be the first term of his series"—731) indicates that this is a subjective list or at least a projection arranged by an objective voice in chronological order. If Bloom is the true author, we must ask what the sources of his information are and why they are not more reliable. Perhaps the list is best seen as a product of the narrator's playfulness: a whimsical pandering to Bloom's apprehensions, Molly's aspirations and the reader's expectations. At any rate, though Molly mentions eighteen of the twenty-five names[7] in the course of her monologue, with the vaguely possible exception of Bartell d'Arcy, who kissed her on the choir steps, and Mulvey, with whom she did some cautious petting, she admits having had relations with no one other than Boylan. She also refers to at least seventeen males not on the list,[8] any of whom might have been included and one of whom *should* have been. Lieutenant Gardner was among her most mysterious and best-appreciated suitors. His absence alone should invalidate the rest, since he seems to have gone further than anyone since Mulvey. But apparently, Molly has not mentioned him to Bloom or Bloom has for some reason suppressed his name.[9]

Once the improbable lovers have been swept away, we can begin to examine Molly as a woman engaged in her first affair, basing our projections on an awareness of her predicament. We may also appreciate Bloom's anxiety and uncertainty, both of which become more touching if he has not previously been cuckolded. After ten years of mooning over his failure to produce a son, he is suddenly faced with the fact that he may have lost a wife to a prize bull. (A modern Odysseus has returned home on the day Penelope is to marry Antinous.) Accordingly, he relives his romance and marriage in random memories. In the process, he exposes and faces more or less squarely questions he has been avoiding, as for example, his relationship to a Judaism to which he never subscribed in an Ireland which does not accept him, or again his failures as father, son, husband, lover, and provider. It is not that Molly's infidelity is his only problem but that all of his problems are interrelated: Milly's coming of age removes her as a Molly surrogate in his life and at the same time obliges him to recognize duties he has avoided and risks he has run; the visit to the pork butcher introduces the theme of hopeless exile rendered acute by Molly's behavior and confirmed by his treatment at the hands of his fellow Dubliners; the visit to the cemetery recalls Rudy's death and combines with the coming anniversary of his father's suicide to evoke racial, religious, as well as sexual failures.

Molly's affair with Boylan has many causes, none of which is either simple or conclusive. There is of course Bloom's abstinence over a "period of 10 years, 5 months and 18 days during which carnal intercourse had been incomplete, without ejaculation of semen within the natural female organ" (736). Here, already, the problem is complicated since the statement does not preclude coitus interruptus, cunnilingus (773), or manual stimulation (74), to say nothing of the nightly buttock kiss. When she accuses Bloom of being "so cold never embracing me except sometimes when hes asleep the wrong end of me not knowing I suppose who he has" (777), she seems to suggest that she is losing confidence in her charms: "I suppose he thinks Im finished out and laid on the shelf" (766). Perhaps it is partially to reassure herself that she has accepted Boylan's advances.

If the presence of a son can be seen as a restraint on Ulysses' Penelope, the absence of one has kept Molly relatively chaste if hardly patient. Like Bloom she was "disheartened . . . altogether" (778) by Rudy's death which made her aware that "well Id never have another our 1st death too it was we were never the same since" (778). Her self-control becomes more understandable if we see sex as temporarily spoiled for her by the pathos of Rudy's death and the fear of having another disappointment. Obviously, the fault for their sexual problems is not entirely Bloom's though Molly is hardly ready to accept her role in the failure of their marriage. A more potent and recent obstacle to her philandering was the presence about the house of a normally curious and observant adolescent: "her tongue is a bit too long for my taste your blouse is open too low she says to me" (767). Molly's relationship with Milly may help explain why, after ten years, she has suddenly taken up with the first man who has come her way. Not only is she freer with Milly away, but Milly's recent maturity has reminded her of her own aging and brought back with a rush lost girlish pleasures and frustrated hopes. If Bloom tends to confuse his two women, Molly clearly identifies with her daughter: "they all look at her like me when I was her age" (767). For an attractive and vain woman, who, at thirty-two, sees thirty-five as the end of her sexual life, Milly's maturity can only be an irritant.

We think of Molly as a lazy sloven because we see her lying abed late and still undressed during the Wandering Rocks episode. But there is little reason for her to get out of bed, since, despite the big house, she has all too few friends and duties and only the occasional singing engagement or social event to help pass the time. A passive woman to whom life must come if it is to be greeted, she clearly lacks the resources of her husband. Consequently, boredom is a condition of her existence and a motive for her behavior. But this is nothing new. Even Gibraltar, which she evokes with such romantic gusto at the end of her monologue, "got as dull as the devil after" the Stanhopes left: "I was almost planning to run away mad out of it somewhere were never easy where we are." What then of dear dirty Dublin where once again she is "planning to run away" (757).

Though she guiltily exaggerates the motives for resentment, Molly has a good deal to complain about. Deceived into thinking she was marrying a man of promise, she has followed Bloom through a series of failures and watched him waste his small talent dreaming up impractical schemes. Since Rudy's death she has been increasingly obliged to put up with the sexual quirks that pass for lovemaking. She has had to help with the finances and has sacrificed a career (of sorts) to her marriage while raising a daughter enough in her own image that quarrels were inevitable. Now she feels put upon because, after a succession of shabby dwellings, they have settled in too large a house. Doubtless she is reaching for her complaints, especially when she bemoans Bloom's absence and the inadequacies of Mrs. Fleming: "you have to be walking around after her putting the things in her hands sneezing and farting into the pots well of course shes old she cant help it" (768). After all she shares the responsibility for both and she has just taken advantage of the first. She resembles nothing more than the comical scold when she sighs "every day I get up theres some new thing on sweet God Sweet God well when Im stretched out dead in my grave I suppose Ill have some peace" (769). This last and strongest outburst immediately precedes her discovery "that thing has come on me yes now wouldnt that afflict you" (769). And thus Joyce introduces the most comic and appropriate complaint of the monologue, a good deal of which is spent squatting indecorously, a victim of female nature, on the chamber pot.

Add, as an imponderable cause and partial justification of her infidelity, Bloom's tacit encouragement which we sense everywhere and see clearly in the Circe chapter and which Molly misreads as a dodge to help him justify his own behavior: "hed never have the courage with a married woman thats why he wants me and Boylan" (773). Not only did Bloom encourage Milly to leave for Mullingar (an event he never fully explains), he even brought Molly and Boylan together. Though we may wonder how conscious he was of arranging an affair, there is no doubt that Molly's infidelity serves a psychological need in Bloom. This need (for vicarious association with attractive men), which we also find in Richard Rowan, helps motivate Bloom to try to replace Boylan with Stephen.

Critics in general have tended to exaggerate Molly's sexual vitality, her seductive charms, and her lewdness. We know that she began menstruating even later than Milly (at fifteen), that, before Bloom, she had only two suitors, and that she achieved her first true climax only after four years of marriage: "I never came properly till I was what twenty-two or so" (767). We also know that she was reasonably well satisfied with Bloom's performance until the death of Rudy and we cannot prove that she has had anything other than a mild flirtation since her marriage: a few pats from Lenehan, a kiss on the choir steps from Bartell d'Arcy, and some hot caresses from Lieutenant Gardner. One suspects that much of her pleasure during these barren years has been derived from sexual games like the one described on page 740 during which Bloom would draw "out the thing by the hour question and answer would you do

this that and the other with the coalman yes with a bishop."
(It is from such sessions accompanied by manual stimulation and followed by masturbation that Bloom may have
gotten his list, if we need any more naturalistic grounds for
its presence in the Ithaca chapter.) Despite sixteen years
of marriage and the impressively virile performance of
Boylan, she contemplates with great fervor experiences
that seem little more than adolescent overtures: "theres
nothing like a kiss long and hot down to your soul almost
paralyses you" (740–41). Her recollection of the famous
kiss on Howth is as passionate and as vivid as Bloom's.

We may also question Molly's charm. Though we know
she was a pretty girl and a plump one, that she inspired the
admiration of young girl-starved officers, and that Lenehan
ten years earlier enjoyed her already ample curves, we
also know that Stephen thinks her fat and that Dixon for
whom she is "none of your lean kine" (425) has not been
attracted by her charms on display. Even Bloom's praise
is equivocal, more appropriate to past glory than to the
present. More important perhaps is the reaction of Boylan.
Though he carefully distances us from his fancy man, Joyce
does give us a curious glimpse of his preparations for a
seduction. We may wonder why, before going to Molly,
Boylan has worked himself to an erotic pitch, first with the
girl in the flower shop and then with the flirtatious bargirl,
who gives him the "horn" (267) and sends him jaunting
after love in his chariot, a full half hour late for his ap-
pointment. Molly has reason to be uncertain that she has
pleased him despite the vigor of his performance. First,
he cut short the amorous formalities; second, he interrupted their meeting to rush after the newspaper with its
racing report and then showed his rage (but did not men-

tion that he had plunged on Scepter for her); and finally he gave her a farewell slap on the buttocks. Even his letters are cold and formal. It is not surprising that she is finally eager to exchange him for a young submissive lover, taking on the appropriate role of mother-initiator to an imaginary Stephen, in a foredoomed attempt to recover the joys of her youth.

In characterizing Molly we must bear in mind the contradictions that make her so intriguing: her bold earthiness and curious reticence; her tendency to be by turns masterful and submissive, unsentimentally frank and lyrically sentimental; her pride in her ability to accept what she feels is natural and her harsh judgment of Bloom's "unnatural" behavior. We note that though she is frank about her own animal functions, she is disgusted by a soldier's exhibitionism and by her one experience of the filth in a men's WC. The strong language that expresses her rediscovered sexuality so directly shocks even her: "I wanted to shout out all sorts of things fuck or shit or anything at all only not to look ugly . . . who knows the way [Boylan would] take it . . . they're not all like [Bloom]" (754). Interestingly, the obscene words she uses in the privacy of her monologue express outrage, discomfort, or strain rather than joy or pleasure and for the most part she resorts to simple or elaborate euphemisms. Yet such language is a normal part of the Blooms' sexual relationship, part of a private idiom (781) which also contains expressions of lower case sublimity ("he said I was a flower of the mountain"—782).[10] The point is that Molly is confused by her own nature. The unfettered musings that reveal her to us as readers also permit her to discover in herself, and to rationalize, repressed tendencies. Among these is the need

for the sort of relationship she could have with Bloom, a
duel between de Sade and Sacher-Masoch[11] which would
involve some reversal of traditional sexual roles, but, being
limited to the bedroom, would not oblige her to abandon
her feminine prerogatives or destroy Bloom's masculinity:
a milder version in short of the behavior she contemplates
immediately before she begins the meditation on flowers
that leads us to the final volley of yesses (779-80). What
she needs is perhaps best suggested in the following passage where "penis envy," disgust with woman's functions,
and narcissistic delight are mixed as she sits, a cuckquean,
on her pot:

I bet he never saw a better pair of thighs than that look how
white they are the smoothest place is right there between this
bit here how soft like a peach easy God I wouldn't mind being
a man and get up on a lovely woman O Lord what a row
youre making like the jersey lily easy O how the waters come
down at Lahore. (770)

More than the result of her new condition and the afternoon's adventure, such attitudes are the perfect complement to Bloom's sexual disposition. Given her tastes, Molly
is right to be reticent with the dominant Boylan, who would
not care to sacrifice his prerogatives.[12]

If we are shocked by Molly's openness and impressed
by the vigor of her verbal imagination, we must not exaggerate either quality, and above all, we ought not think
that her monologue is typical of her silent musings. This
is an exceptional effort, the expression of a crisis situation, a cathartic outpouring during which she takes stock
of her past life and in some way prepares for her future.
Certainly, it would take an extraordinary occurrence to
release such a flood of pent-up emotion from so unreflective

a woman. For the first time in ten years she has been satisfied; her mind is warm with pleasure but full of unsettling questions. Her flesh, like the earth it symbolizes, is no longer arid. She has slept deeply between Boylan's departure and the thunderclap that startled Stephen during the Oxen of the Sun chapter. It is spring ("Im always like that in the spring Id like a new fellow every year"—(760) and she is menstruating. Even more crucial, her husband's late return has brought fresh concerns along with the interesting news that a young "professor" is about to enter her life fulfilling the predictions of the cards: "he was on the cards this morning when I laid out the deck union with a young stranger neither dark nor fair" (774). Bloom's request for breakfast in bed, though justified by the lateness of the hour, has altered in her mind his usual role. Suddenly, she feels obliged to cope with the needs of an organism not her own but still not quite distinct from hers. Bloom's nature is after all the nature of the marriage she has violated, but hardly annulled. His request, given the extraordinary circumstance, shocks her into a reappraisal of their life together, a process which begins with condemnation of the negligent spouse and moves gradually toward a recognition of the permanence of their relationship. This is the largest dramatic movement of the monologue and the most startling, for it reverses the apparent direction of Molly's thought and, ideally, alters our attitude toward Bloom.[13]

The process begins with an exhibition of jealousy that seems anomalous, like the pains of an amputee. But then Molly has never really possessed a man as she does Bloom and she has always jealously protected her property. Her suspicions date back at least to the Mary Driscoll incident reviewed in Circe, Bloom's first and last clumsy fling at extramarital sex. They achieve almost epic proportions since she has deprived herself of a servant (for which she naturally blames Bloom) and because she sees him as a Lothario (a veritable Mulligan in fact) who would quickly seduce any available woman. Now, she assumes the worst because Bloom's posterior osculation from which he achieved only a "proximate erection" (735) was not warm enough. She calculates that the last time he "came on my bottom" (740) was the night she met Boylan and doubts that he could go so long without sex. She has also surprised him in the act of writing the letter to Martha and suspects that his account of his day has omitted some details, as it has, though not quite the sort she imagines.

Hers is or could be read as a dog-in-the-manger attitude. Not only would she deny others the pleasure she herself cannot have; she would also deny him the pleasure she does not give. But there is a mitigating circumstance. Molly recalls how much she enjoyed Bloom's courting and doubtless also how much she enjoyed sex with him prior to Rudy's birth:

I like the way he made love then he knew the way to take a woman when he sent me the 8 big poppies because mine was the 8th. (747)

Not only does she have no desire to share the joys of her only real romance with a stranger, but, unconsciously, through her present adventure, she is trying to recapture the lost Bloom along with her lost youth or bloom. Finally, her jealousy of her husband at this moment underlines what she is not quite ready to admit, her basic dissatisfaction with Boylan's tactics.

It is curious that Molly draws more pleasure from the meager gift of fragile but suggestive poppies than she does from the sumptuous basket Boylan sent ahead of him, but then we note that Boylan had her for the asking while Bloom used his ingenuity to win her. The deception is inevitable when the two circumstances are juxtaposed in a mind which makes no real distinction between past and present. True, Boylan's straightforward sex is bound to be compared to Bloom's quirks, as Molly reviews the bedroom secrets of the long-married, those long separated from the initial joys of love. But despite her prudery we suspect she has enjoyed some of them as much as Bloom, and that she craves the strangeness of her husband at the moment she is most fully contented by another man.

Though, like her Homeric model, she is far from being as complete a character as her erring husband, we still know Molly's tastes and see her in a variety of roles. A soldier's child brought up on the rock in virtual isolation, she is by nature a man's woman. Apart from the housekeeper, Mrs. Rubio, who imparted so much Spanish lore to her motherless charge, there is only one reference to a female contact on Gibraltar, Hester, the girlish wife of elderly Mr. Stanhope. This was hardly a conventional relationship, though Hester tried to get Molly interested in books and showed her what it meant to be stylish. Even if her remark: "he was years older than her wogger he was awfully fond of me" (755), probably points more to her naiveté than to any real viciousness, Molly saw herself as Hester's rival. On Hester's side we can discern the brief lesbian infatuation of a dissatisfied married woman for a naive and vibrant young exotic: "we were like cousins what age was I then the night of the storm I slept in her bed she had her arms around me then we were fighting in the morning with the pillow what fun" (756). There is nothing to compare with this girlish romp in the relations Molly had with the Dublin vestals for whom the nubile Molly was probably a bit too spirited and even exotic. Her Irish friendships were utilitarian and short-lived. The closest of them, with Josie Powell Breen, ended shortly after the marriage. In 1904, she has no women friends at all and few kind things to say about her sex, whose members she distrusts individually and en masse.

Molly's gifts are few and of ambiguous value. She is apparently a natural and virtually untrained singer who has mastered concert and choir techniques. But her last appearance was "over a year ago" (748) at a concert very much like the one described in "A Mother" or perhaps even less interesting. Even her role in the projected tour, the fruit of Boylan's passion, will probably bring little fortune and no fame despite Bloom's hopes that they will have "all topnobbers. J. C. Doyle and John MacCormack I hope and. The best, in fact" (93).[14] Though Bloom frequently reflects on Molly's songs, the few remarks she herself makes would indicate that she has little sensitivity and only a low-level interest in that or any other art. Still, her "career" has not gone unnoticed in the fringe musical circles, and she seems to keep up her voice and to interest herself in questions of technique as well as in the best way to show off her charms. Apart from the light classics, Molly has read nothing but bawdy or pornographic works. Her taste in clothing and ornaments is equally undistinguished. The gifts she would have Boylan get her reflect the modest aspirations and deficient imagination of a Dublin house-wife. True, she has, as Bloom remarks, some wit, a shrewd eye for character traits, and a gift for epigrammatic description:

Tom Kernan that drunken little barrelly man that bit his tongue off falling down the mens W C drunk . . . . Ben Dollard base barreltone the night he borrowed the swallowtail . . . . squeezed and squashed into them and grinning all over his big Dolly face like a wellwhipped childs botty. (773-74)

Yet, she is a poor judge of her husband's motives and she seems to have been taken in by Boylan's rather obvious line. She thinks of herself as shrewd, but for all her precautions she has failed to fool Bloom about Boylan. Indeed her most successful deception is a small one: the secret of Cohen's bed from which she draws some of her romantic charm. Paradoxically, the bed relates her most immediately to Bella-Circe, whose husband "old Cohen" may have been. (Bloom's knowledge of Bella's private life surely implies some such explanation.)

At heart a blunt and honest person, Molly opens all three orifices for us in the course of her monologue. But most emphatically she exposes her character as lover and wife, showing herself to be in each case both remarkably innocent and instinctively shrewd, a mixture of bad intentions and healthy responses, of vigor and sloth, of blindness and insight, sentimentality and bawdiness. Certainly, she knows (and always knew) that soldier-loves are passing affairs. Why else would she have given Mulvey's Claddagh ring to Gardner (762). Yet this innocent, half-forgotten, first affair, which brought out and ripened her instincts, gives us a sense of wilful charm that is far fresher than the stale incense exhaled by an untried Gerty MacDowell. She was playing this young man while he was toying with her affections. After enjoying herself, with an openness that must have been rare in girls of that time, she seems to have had no regrets or qualms and little enough prudishness. The sort of barnyard sex she describes remains startlingly fresh and naive. Retelling it, she captures the sensations of the moment with details as brilliant as they are slight. Passages like the following suggest both the level of Joyce's sympathy for the strangeness that is woman and the quality of Molly's memory, which, though it mingles and associates, preserves the texture of an experience:

I wouldn't let him touch me inside my petticoat I had a skirt opening up the side I tortured the life out of him first tickling him I loved rousing that dog in the hotel rrrsssst awokwokawok his eyes shut and a bird flying below us he was shy all the same I liked him that morning I made him blush a little when I got over him that way . . . . Molly darling he called me what was his name Jack Joe Harry Mulvey was it yes I think a lieutenant he was rather fair he had a laughing kind of voice . . . he said hed come back Lord its just like yesterday to me. (760-61)

The interplay of engagement and indifference, of clarity and diffuse perception, the sense that time is one continuous erotic present, that a man aroused is yet another animal, and that the word, the promise, is as good as the deed summarize Molly's sexual nature and epitomize her identity as a lover. No wonder so many critics believe her to be no better than a whore. Like a whore she withholds a part of herself and feels no commitment except to the moment. Still, unlike a whore, she seems to enjoy the moment thoroughly. What she gives is hers to keep. What she holds back is in reserve but somehow fully in play in her memory. She has not gone all the way with Mulvey but in her mind she has committed herself. "Id let him block me now flying," she says of that long-lost love, and in her imagination she really would (761) since Mulvey is now her creature even more than before. The same is probably true of the Stephen she imagines, though her view of this affair is from a maternal rather than a girlish angle.

The passage quoted above smacks neither of woman's periodical literature nor, despite the explicitness, of pornographic writing, because Molly has genuinely experienced and now reexperiences a romantic-erotic moment. By contrast her imagined erotic experiences are grotesque blanks. The encounter with a sailor back from the sea is a literary moment even for her and far beyond her range. Her affair with Boylan also points in this direction and should be seen as part literature and part erotic adventuring, a break in her life pattern which could conceivably change but probably will not. That is, Molly might, as she is ready to believe, become a notorious woman, create a scandal or, more probably, she might prolong indefinitely an affair which has meaning only on the animal level. She might force her lover to give her trivial gifts while continuing to live with Bloom. The point is, however, that this is not Molly's sort of affair and that the passive role she has accepted for the afternoon has already begun to annoy her by the evening. She can still savor the joys of being an adulterous woman and doing "it 4 or 5 times locked in each others arms" (763). (The bookish expression here underlines the degree to which Molly is false to her own instincts.) But she already senses that Boylan is too sure of himself, too masterful, and not sufficiently tender for her. She is proud of having such a "swell" for a lover and admires his clothes and airs and she is intrigued by adultery, which she sees as distinct from harlotry and we may see as a cut above the behavior of Bella Cohen. But she has not yet made the adjustment which the role demands. She does not know how to handle Bloom and is even comically worried that Boylan might find her cheating with her own husband: "its all very well a husband but you cant fool a lover after me telling him we never did anything" (748).

More important is the fact that she feels unsure of her status and uncomfortable in a role which has taken her for the first time beyond fantasy. That is why she refers so frequently to deception, adultery, and whores and why she tries so hard to shift the responsibility for her action to Bloom, exaggerating the degree to which she has been neglected and abused, drawing up her list of comical offenses against common sense and propriety: "if I could only remember the half of the things and write a book out of it the works of Master Poldy" (754). The extent of her discomfort both with Boylan and with the role may be judged by the alacrity with which she mentally jumps from Boylan's bed to Stephen's, by her annoyance at the sudden recollection of her entanglement ("O but then what am I going to do about him though"—776) and by the manner in which she slips back toward Bloom. We may view this development from another angle as the result of Molly's unrecognized son-fixation. Having desired and lost a boy, she has refused to risk motherhood again and even rejected the son-surrogate in Bloom. But, now, an unsatisfactory afternoon of submissiveness combined with the anxieties and appetites stimulated by Bloom's late arrival has restored her through her memory and imagination to an earlier stage. The onus of Rudy's death has been removed paradoxically on the very night of Bloom's release and through the same agency, Stephen's image as boy-man: "I saw him driving down to the Kingsbridge station with his father and mother I was in mourning thats 11 years ago now yes hed be 11" (774). It is this miracle that may finally have been accomplished by the Penelope chapter. Perhaps we can compare Molly's behavior on the sixteenth of June 1904 to that of a man of forty trying desperately to renew a life he sees slipping from him unwilling or unable to drop his old commitments. At any rate the monologue is a rite of passage, a coming of age, rendered grotesque by the circumstance of being mature, but it is not, for all of that, free of pathos.

Whatever her extra or intramural activities, Molly is primarily Bloom's wife, but their relationship is the most complex of all. Whether or not she continues her affair with Boylan, who may not have enjoyed himself in her arms or may be put off by the monthly delay, she will continue in her wifely role and perhaps find ways of satisfying both Bloom and herself. Despite her complaints Molly has to recognize her husband's positive qualities, and we have to recognize her firm attachment, against which the afternoon with Boylan seems a fleeting adventure. Curiously, on the balance sheet, the positive factors outweigh the negative. Her jealousy, her protectiveness, her desire to be in his dreams (741), her appreciation of his kindness and sensitivity—all underline her commitment. From the start Bloom exerted a strange attraction which Molly and perhaps Joyce ascribe to a racial or instinctual appeal: "it was he excited me I dont know how the first night ever we met" (771). The implication, muted at this point in her monologue, is that the appeal persists even now that she knows his promise to be false and his quirks to be absurd. We think of Anna Livia's parting remarks to her man:

I thought you were all glittering with the noblest of carriage. You're only a bumpkin. I thought you the great in all things, in guilt and in glory. You're but a puny.[15]

And we recall her dedication and that of the forsaken Bertha in *Exiles*. Molly accepted the advances of a young man different from the others, a youth with a bit of the artist about him, a look of Byron, and an unusual line, a worshipper whom she felt she could control and who could arouse her sexually by means that were subtly unphysical. Though she denies it, she is still intrigued by his courting methods, his curiosity about her rooms, his fetish hunting, his letters so full of physical reference that they had her "at myself 4 or 5 times a day" (771) and even sent her on an embarrassing trip to the doctor. It is this younger Bloom who now holds her youth in thrall. But the Bloom of her revery is more complete, and in accepting or seeming to accept her young pliant lover, she also accepts the man she has helped to make in the course of sixteen years of marriage.

We might compare Molly's monologue to an Ibsen play where we step into an "obvious" situation but through the action experience a shift in our allegiances and watch the reversal of our preconceptions. The Ithaca chapter has completed the reduction of Bloom to particulars, or seems to have done so, projecting him comically out to the stars. "Penelope" puts the pieces together again in a different, more intricate, and vibrant order while animating Molly and putting her through a moment which is dramatic despite its lack of action and the virtual absence of external complications. The monologue shows her apparently reversing her commitments but actually rediscovering them and in the process discloses the unresolved complexities

of her personality. It reveals beneath a mass of vital contradictions the female complement to Bloom, a woman
whose instincts have remained intact though her circumstances are curiously contorted. Like Anna Livia Plurabelle,
she is *Weib*, a creature, neither good nor bad, who lives
almost entirely within and in terms of herself, disregarding
or dismissing everything that she cannot digest, but paradoxically subsuming all.

Further, as my analysis should indicate, Joyce has in
Ulysses worked out the naturalistic grounds for the sort of
dynamic resolution of opposites which we find in *Finnegans
Wake*. I refer to what L. A. Murillo has brilliantly called
"*dis-tensions* between multiple levels of meaning," and
credited with the power of "permitting the resolution of
those meanings into a monolythic unity."[16] What occurs
in Molly's monologue and constitutes her prime role in the
book is similar to what occurs to Bloom when he experiences himself in the Circe chapter. It is an extension of
the sort of identification he makes between Molly and
Milly. Effectively, Molly finds it in herself or rather in the
liquid medium of her thought to reconcile her old-young
natures and rediscover, for the moment at least, a young-
old Bloom, turning both into archetypes of sorts, figures
for humanity and human relations. On a lower level she
reconciles her dual sexual impulse toward mastery and
feminine submission and accepts, along with Bloom's
limitations, her own. Joyce's method, while adhering to a
principle of psychological plausibility, does not enforce
conclusions about the Blooms' future. But, though neither
the epiphany which occurs at the end of the Circe chapter
nor the final affirmation of the Penelope episode are historical events within the universe of the novel, both Bloom

and Molly have gone a long way down the tunnel toward the light. In the process both have revealed the human psyche in its mythmaking role, discovered in themselves the archetypes of experience.

NOTES

1. There has been an astonishing amount of partial or subjective criticism of Molly, defenses and attacks alike which tend to ignore the text and avoid basic questions. But this is hardly the place to review positions which are frequently marred by a refusal to distinguish between various levels of interpretation and presentation. Instead, I shall refer the reader to a recent article by Phillip Herring ("The Bedsteadfastness of Molly Bloom," *Modern Fiction Studies* 15 [Spring 1969]: 49–61) for a useful summary and partial response to all but the most recent positions. For a detailed treatment of Molly's character traits, see Joseph Prescott's "The Characterization of Molly Bloom" in his *Exploring James Joyce* (Carbondale: Southern Illinois University Press, 1964).

2. To the much-quoted letter to Frank Budgen (16 August 1921), Joyce added a postscript that partly explains the discrepancy between Molly's alleged birthday and her age. By some oversight he apparently forgot that "Molly Bloom was born in 1871." *Letters of James Joyce*, vol. 1, ed. Stuart Gilbert (New York: Viking Press, 1957), p. 170.

3. *Ulysses* (New York: Random House, 1961). All page references in the text refer to this edition.

4. *Letters of James Joyce*, ed. Stuart Gilbert, p. 170.

5. *Surface and Symbol: The Consistency of James Joyce's "Ulysses"* (New York: Oxford University Press, 1962), pp. 35–43. Unfortunately Adams concludes by lamenting Joyce's decision to make the irrepressibly sensual Molly a relatively chaste and faithful wife. Adams's point is that Joyce, the jealous husband, was too involved in Molly's character to make her truly convincing, to give her, that is, the depth he manages to give Stephen and Bloom.

6. *Argument of "Ulysses"* (Columbus: Ohio State University Press, 1964), pp. 431–44. Sultan's view, that Molly's relative fidelity and her return in spirit to a consideration of Bloom bodes well for the couple's relations, is to my mind naive. Nevertheless, Molly's relative inexperience does much to justify both Bloom's anxious behavior and the dramatic develop-

ment of Penelope which brings her to a half-conscious awareness of Bloom's true function in her life. It contributes a degree of pathos hitherto lacking in assessments of the Blooms's situation of June 16 and 17.

7. Mulvey (759-62 and passim), Penrose (754), Bartell d'Arcy (745), Goodwin (747 and passim), Mastiansky (749), Menton (739), Father Corrigan (741), Mat Dillon (758), Valentine Dillon (750), Lenehan (750), unknown gentleman in the Gaiety Theatre (769), Dollard (774), Simon Dedalus (768, 774), Pisser Burke (765), Joseph Cuffe (752–55), Wisdom Hely (753), Dr. Brady (754), and, of course, Boylan.

8. Lieutenant Gardner (746), Henry Doyle (747), Larry O'Rourke (750), a black man whose powers she would like to sample (751), an exhibitionist Highlander (753), a redheaded exhibitionist behind a tree (753), "Wogger" Stanhope who was "awfully fond of" her (755), Dixon to whom she issued a silent invitation (757—and perhaps again on 763 where the context is ambiguous), the "country gougers" at the City Arms hotel (758), Duglacz (763), Nosey Flynn (765), "the fellow in the pit . . . at the Gaicty" (767), the gynecologist Dr. Collins (770), Tom Kernan and Martin Cunningham (773), Freddy Mayers (774), and the KC (King's Council) who gave the fish supper "for me" (777).

9. Gardner, who is not mentioned elsewhere in the book, may have been an afterthought designed not only to discredit the list but to throw further doubts on Molly's fidelity and on the viability of Bloom's marriage. It is probably significant that Joyce asked Budgen for Conan Doyle's *History of South African War* as late as August 1921. The time scheme here seems deliberately confused. Still Gardner's dates are such that one must see him as a surrogate for the lost Mulvey and the strayed Bloom, a suitor who reigned halfway through Molly's ten-year famine. Though he died in South Africa of a fever, it is not clear when he left Ireland. I would suggest, from the scant information given on page 749, that he left sometime between 1899 and 1900 and terminated Molly's brief affair before it got beyond the tentative stage. I can find no reference in Joyce's probable source, A. Conan Doyle's *The Great Boer War* (London: Smith, Elder, & Co., 1900; reprinted in a cheap edition for the Nelson Shilling Library in 1908), to the "8th Bn 2nd East Lancs Rgt," but then even the title is wrong in Joyce's reference (idem).

10. Joyce's letters to Nora are, of course, full of similar effusions.

11. *Exiles* (New York: Viking Press, 1950), p. 124.

12. The Blooms' tendencies should not be overstated, despite the evidence in Circe and Penelope that each covets the other's role. The progress of Bloom's day is toward the mastery and assertiveness that is first expressed when he forces Bella to accept a fair price for the damaged lamp-

shade. What he needs is a role which does not strip him of his pride just as Molly needs one that does not blot her femininity, a delicate balance in fact.

13. Here the *Odyssey* parallel is helpful, for we recall that Penelope, at first cool to her returning husband, accepts him only after he reveals his knowledge of the family secret. In this case it is Bloom's presence that reminds Molly of his secret role in her life and restores him (at least partially) to his place in her life. Here as elsewhere the parallel has a positive as well as a negative thrust.

14. Mr. Adams, who points out that the people connected with the tour are truly the best, places Molly correctly among the lesser Dublin musical lights. *Surface and Symbol,* pp. 67, 75.

15. *Finnegans Wake* (New York: Viking Press, 1947), p. 627.

16. *The Cyclical Night* (Cambridge: Harvard University Press, 1968), p. 98 and passim.

Some
Determinants
of Molly Bloom

DARCY O'BRIEN

SIMPSON, a bank manager in the west of Ireland, is beguiled by Delia the barmaid's slender legs, flat uncorseted stomach, perky breasts, intent serious face, smoky grey eyes, generous mouth, and golden casque of hair. Under her libidinous gaze he consumes Irish amounts of whiskey and stout, rips in twain a pack of cards, and lifts heavy weights. Delia, impressed, calls him Mr. Universe. She leads Simpson down to the shore, he skewers her under "rude thrusting buttocks" by moonlight. The affair prospers. Simpson hammers away at Delia in beds, cars, and under bars amid used glasses, bottles, and butts. But she's treacherous, is Delia. She snips off proud bald Simpson's tiny precious pigtail, she cheats on him, and she gives him a dose of syphilis which causes him to go blind. He beats out her brains against a wall.

I read this recent Irish version of the Samson-Delilah story[1] thinking all the while of Molly Bloom and thinking, all unchanged, unchanged utterly. Irishmen continue to have it in for women, even when they have it out for them.

Fear and contempt for woman as a sexual creature, that is the Irish attitude. And when a different perspective crops up, as in the novels of Edna O'Brien, the censor clamps down. Yeats, you say? His Maude Gonne and his Crazy Jane? But Yeats was no Irishman, as any Irishman will tell you.[2]

Seven men were sitting in a pub in a remote corner of the west. They hadn't seen a woman in weeks and, to paraphrase Molly Bloom, they were dyin' for it. "Marriage is no substitute for drink," one of them was saying, hefting his pint, but suddenly a girl passed by in the street outside and six of the seven men rushed to the window to get a look. Each of the six commented in turn on the shape and walk of the passing girl, each more approving than the other. But the seventh man, who came from Monaghan, still sat sipping his pint, saying nothing. Finally someone turned to him and said, "Whadya think, Paddy?" "Begob," said the man from Monaghan, "I'd use her shite for toothpaste!"

The joke was told to me by a Dubliner as illustrative of the crudeness of Monaghanian sensibilities. But it is generally and typically Irish. It combines praise of the girl's attractiveness with a reminder of the repulsiveness of her (normal) bodily functions, and it manages to circle back to a jibe at the extent to which a man will make a fool of himself for woman's sake. Contempt and fear again.

No one knows how or when this attitude got itself locked into the Irish consciousness. It is one thing to say that every Irishman is nursed by the sour milk of Irish Catholic puritanism, but quite another to answer why Irishmen took to that diet in the first place. Attempts have been made to blame an eighteenth-century Jansenist influence for the sexual meanness of Irish religion, but this argument makes no more sense than the myth that "alien political doctrines" poison and subvert defenseless populations today. Perhaps Ireland was fertile ground for Jansenism, but probably puritanism did not reach its full strength in Ireland until the years of the great famine (1845-49), when birth came to mean death or emigration and sexual abstinence became linked to physical survival. Add to this economic factor the growth of Victorian morality and you have the sexual obsessions of the Irish church as Joyce was born into it in 1882—and as it survives today.

But the origins of this puritanism lie deeper. From stone carvings we know of the presence of the Sheela-na-gig[3]— a whorish creature who seduced and emasculated her victims—in pre-Christian Irish mythology; and Irishmen seemed eager to adopt the celibate monastic life once Christianity was introduced in the fifth century. Mariolatry has provided the Irish with an antidote to the lewdness of merely mortal women: nowhere has the cult of the Virgin been stronger, nowhere is virginity held in higher esteem. Likewise Mother Ireland, for whom there are more than a dozen feminine names, has familiarly been depicted as virginal, loverless, and alone, or loved only by the poet who sings her praises.[4] Devoted to the unattainable, repelled by the available, the Irish mind torments itself. Bryan Merriman's comic-satiric *The Midnight Court* (1790), in which the poet is tied down and soundly beaten by lascivious females as punishment for his celibacy, combines a great deal of ribald talk with the usual Irish portrayal of women as randy birds of prey. The poem, probably the finest example of eighteenth-century verse in the Irish language, reminds us of the continuity of Irish misogyny.

Joyce's portrait of Molly Bloom extends this tradition

and almost, but not quite, transcends it. Tradition can be a trashy word, a way of tossing writers into the same bin, a literary disposal system. For the poet or novelist, tradition can lend coherence but also banality—far easier to surrender oneself to traditional prejudices than to explore one's own. So both the critic and the creative artist must fear the cindery sameness that tradition can induce. But Joyce began by creating Molly Bloom out of his own Irish rib. Began her as a woman the way most Irishmen see woman, an eternally recurring version of Sheela-na-gig. Her untraditional, that is to say her human, aspects emerged much later, probably when he was almost done with her, when she started to become more than just a symbol, more than a simple reversal of chaste Penelope. The artistic process is a familiar one. Cervantes and Flaubert began with clever but shallow satire yet ended up with the unfathomable Knight of the Mournful Countenance and Emma Bovary.

What do we know of Molly before her soliloquy? Little. We feel her as an immense hot presence settled on Bloom's brain. We see her but twice, and a few times more in Bloom's fantasies. Our initial impression, a sound one, is that she is not mistress but master of her household. She lies abed while Bloom busies himself with feeding the cat, with breakfast, with bringing up her tea. Her first spoken word, a "sleepy soft grunt," "—Mn." Then such commands as "Hurry up with that tea" and "Scald the teapot." Her sexuality already overwhelms, as "the warmth of her couched body rose on the air, mingling with the fragrance of the tea she poured."

She contemplates a card from her daughter and a letter from Blazes Boylan, her current lover. She has been reading a smutty novel illustrated with a picture of the heroine naked on the floor, threatened by a fierce Italian with a carriage whip. Bloom answers her impatient question about metempsychosis, goes down to eat his breakfast alone, adjourns to the jakes, and leaves to begin his wanderings. We have already seen enough to join with an anonymous Irish poet of the seventeenth century in addressing "The Careful Husband":

> I am told, sir, you're keeping an eye on your wife,
> But I can't see the reason for that, on my life.
> For if you go out, O most careful of men,
> It is clear that you can't keep an eye on her then.
>
> Even when you're at home and take every care,
> It is only a waste of your trouble, I swear.
> For if you one instant away from her look,
> She'll be off into some inaccessible nook.
>
> If you sit close beside her and don't let her move,
> By the flick of an eyelid she'll signal her love.
> If you keep her in front of you under your eye,
> She will do what she likes and your caution defy.
>
> When she goes out to mass, as she'd have you suppose,
> You must not stay a minute, but go where she goes.
> You must not walk in front nor yet too far behind her.
> But she's got such a start that I doubt if you'll
>   find her.[5]

The situation of the cuckold reminds us as much of Wycherley or Molière as of typically Irish suspicions. But as our impressions of Molly, whom we do not meet again in the flesh until six hundred pages later, build up, the Irishness of it all emerges. These impressions come by way of Bloom's fantasies, which convey to us a woman of insatiable sexual appetite, a woman whose husband has given up all hope of sufficiency himself and so allows her nature to take its course of adultery on a grand and multiple scale. Take, for example, Bloom's recollection of his son's conception: "Must have been that morning in Raymond terrace she was at the window, watching the two dogs at it by the wall of the cease to do evil. And the sergeant grinning up. She had that cream gown on with the rip she never stitched. Give us a touch, Poldy. God, I'm dying for it. How life begins" (89).[6] If a certain mixing of metaphors may be excused, Molly is something of a sexual lightning rod here, a conductor of impersonal sexual energy that comes in through the window by way of two dogs and a leering policeman. What choice had Bloom but to try to assume the role of human dildo?

As we watch Bloom first flee from the sight of Boylan and then sneak into the Ormond to get a look at the man about to cuckold him, we might think of one of Bryan Merriman's frantic husbands, lamenting:

> She never seemed to have enough!
> But I'd still have allowed her a second chance
> And blamed it on youthful extravagance
> Were it not that I saw with my own two eyes
> On the roadway—naked to the skies—
> Herself and a lout from the Durrus bogs
> Going hammer and tongs like a couple of dogs.[7]

Bloom sees as much in his own mind when, in the Circe episode, he imagines Molly and Boylan in bed together and Molly hoarsely, sweetly crying out, "O! Weeshwashtkissimapoisthnapoohuck!" When at last Bloom returns home to the inevitable evidence of Molly's afternoon romp, he can only resign himself—and, shades of the man from

Monaghan, kiss her rump, its twin hemispheres "expressive of mute immutable mature animality" (734).

Most of Molly's soliloquy only adds support to the one-dimensional view we have of her as a symbol of the immutable animality of womankind. She mourns briefly for her lost son, but her attitude toward her daughter seems more than normally callous for a mother. Her leading thoughts are all of sex, and they range through time, space, and several partners. She displays a wonderfully robust vulgar humor, as in her description of Boylan's "great red brute of a thing." But time and again, as when she plans to get money from Bloom by fixing his breakfast and taunting him ("then if he wants to kiss my bottom Ill drag open my drawers and bulge it right out in his face as large as life he can stick his tongue 7 miles up my hole as hes there my brown part then Ill tell him I want £1 or perhaps 30/ . . . then Ill wipe him off me just like a business"—780–81), we remember Sheela-na-gig, we remember all the Irish portraits of the insatiable, conniving female.

Much has been made of the obvious exaggerations in Bloom's list of Molly's twenty-five lovers (731). Father Sebastian of Mount Argus does seem an unlikely paramour, and of another on the list, John Henry Menton, Molly says merely that "he had the impudence to make up to me one time" (739). But not only is the list at least partially accurate; it is likely that there are lovers unknown to Bloom. Of a man called Gardner, for instance, Molly says that she used to touch him with her ring hand outside his trousers "to keep him from doing worse where it was too public" (746) and that Bloom "never knew how to embrace well like Gardner" (747). Gardner is not on Bloom's list. And when Molly says of Boylan, "I never in all my life felt anyone had one the size of that" (742) she obviously implies a good deal of experience. It seems silly to quibble, as critics have done, over lists and numbers with Boylan's visit a fact and with Molly saying "O thanks be to the great God I got somebody to give me what I badly wanted" (758). If Bloom's list is part fantasy it is fantasy based on his knowledge that he alone can never satisfy his wife.

As I have tried to suggest, Joyce's portrait of Molly is consistent with Irish fears and prejudices about women. But aside from nationality, Joyce had other, more personal reasons for making Molly wayward. His own sexual experience affected his writing and placed certain limitations on the kind of sexual situation he was able to portray. This experience was of a singularly unhappy sort.

Joyce suffered from an inability to unite feelings of tenderness and sensuality toward the same woman. (Elsewhere I have written about what I believe to be the principal causes of Joyce's psychosexual malady;[8] it seems sufficient here to describe the problem, to cite evidence of it, and to discuss the way in which it affected his characterization of Molly.) Freud believed that all civilized men experience this difficulty to some degree and that it is the most common psychological cause of impotence. The man who cannot see the woman he loves as a fit sexual object, who believes he is debauching her to go to bed with her, finds himself seeking artificial means to satisfy his desires. He may use prostitutes, take a mistress, or indulge in fantasy in order to stimulate himself. He may imagine his wife as a whore; he may take perverse pleasure in her flirtations with other men; he may even encourage, consciously or unconsciously, her adultery. And always he will feel guilty and hostile to her as a result, because the degradation of the woman he regards as too pure for sex can only bring remorse, perhaps a lust for punishment as well. "Where such men love," Freud wrote, "they have no desire and where they desire they cannot love."[9] He might have been describing Joyce.

The most persuasive, but not the only, evidence we have of Joyce's psychosexual affliction comes from his letters to Nora, particularly from the as yet unpublished portions. The sexual guilt Joyce displays in this correspondence is painful to contemplate. He venerates Nora, tells her she is the blessed virgin of his mature years, and tortures himself because of the physical desire he feels for her. How, he asks in desperate language, can he think of her in such contradictory ways? How can he love her as an innocent flower, a schoolgirl, a virgin, and yet lust after her? He describes his desire for her in deliberately repulsive terms as an assault, a brutalization of her purity. He fears he turns her into a whore and fears still more that he wants her as a whore, delights in her whorishness. He is a hog riding a sow. She and her children do not deserve to be touched by his hands, polluted by his sins. If only the sanctity of his regard for her could redeem him in her eyes—but she too has been corrupted. She has murmured obscene words and phrases to him, she has assented to his demands. He goads his lust and his guilt by asking her to flog him, to soil her letters with her excrement. He recalls with mingled delight and shame her urinating on him.[10]

This complicated pattern of desire, guilt, and masochism shows up again in what we know of Joyce's interest in women other than Nora. According to Richard Ellmann, Joyce never consummated any affair after he began living with Nora, but at least two women, a young pupil in Trieste and Marthe Fleischmann in Zurich, were intensely attractive to him. In the notebook labeled *Giacomo Joyce* he recorded his fantasies about Amalia Popper,[11] and they display the same self-torturing pattern as the letters to Nora. Predictably, her virginity appeals to him; at the same time, her Jewishness excites him because of its exoticism: "rounded by the lathe of intermarriage and ripened in the forcing-house of the seclusion of her race,"[12] he says of her, as though her name were Rappacini. Just as he needs to degrade Nora in order to make her sexually suitable, so he speaks of Signorina Popper's "false smile" and the "rancid yellow humour lurking within the softened pulp of [her] eyes."[13] He craves the deviousness, the corruptness of the wanton. And consider this extraordinary passage:

She coils towards me along the crumpled lounge. I cannot move or speak. Coiling approach of star born flesh. Adultery of wisdom. No. I will go. I will

—Jim, love!—

Soft sucking lips kiss my left armpit: a coiling kiss on myriad veins. I burn! I crumple like a burning leaf! From my right armpit a fang of flame leaps out. A starry snake has kissed me: a cold nightsnake. I am lost!

—Nora![14]

Joyce imagines himself the victim of some preternatural snake of a woman who attacks him, "darting at him for an instant out of her sluggish sidelong eyes a jet of liquorish venom."[15] His extended description of Signorina Popper as a snake suggests a certain confusion of sexual identities, since the snake is the oldest and most common phallic symbol in literature and fantasy. The sense of personal weakness and guilt, the masochistic flavor of the scene—all are of a piece with his fascination for urine and excrement and with his requests for flogging. And the final cry of shame and remorse "—Nora!—" seems especially pathetic when one considers that Joyce is only fantasizing, not recording an actual breach of faith.

Joyce's letters to Marthe Fleischmann (1918–19)[16] give us the same picture of his psychosexual nature. One does not exaggerate to say that he prostrates himself before her—and does so before he so much as knows her name. Her lameness suggests the vulnerability of the virginal to him, and since she is already someone's mistress, the essential whorishness is also there for him. And in order to increase a sense of the exotic and the forbidden, he invents her Jewishness. The letters to Nora reveal deep sexual distress but their candor and intimacy lend some hope of purgation. Alas, nine years later, when Joyce was thirty-seven, his letters to Marthe Fleischmann show him at his most helpless, confessing to a stranger his self-castigations and his guilty need to be sexually dominated.[17] How miserable Eros made him!

I have isolated two strains of influence on Joyce, one national and the other personal, but they are quite compatible. The male Irish mind fears the sexual power of woman, associates it with whorishness, and reserves love for the Virgin and her humbler surrogates on earth. Joyce loved his wife as a Madonna, but sexually needed to degrade her. And when he set out to fashion his image of womankind in Molly Bloom, he began with the ideal of the faithful Penelope and contrasted it with what he regarded as concupiscent realities.[18] His obsession with the idea of cuckoldry—so prominent not only in *Ulysses* but in *Exiles* and *Finnegans Wake* as well—is largely a projection of his own psychological conflicts, of what was both titillating and painful to him.

If we consider, moreover, how much of Joyce's own psychosexual nature went into the characterization of Bloom, we can understand how Molly fascinated Joyce in much the same way as she fascinates Bloom. All of Bloom's perversities—notably his masochism and its expression in desire for punishment by private and public humiliation, by birching, and by sexual betrayal—are drawn from Joyce's own fantasy and experience. That Bloom only imagines much of what happens to him is of no psychological importance whatever: Joyce understood well enough that dreams and fantasies are the keyholes to psychological reality. And in providing Bloom with a wife who is in fact unfaithful, Joyce was imagining the consequence of what to him were erotic speculations.

"A novelist lives in his work," wrote Joseph Conrad. "He stands there, the only reality in an invented world, among imaginary things, happenings and people. Writing about them he is only writing about himself. But the disclosure is not complete. He remains, to a certain extent, a figure behind the veil, a suspected rather than a seen presence— a movement and a voice behind the draperies of fiction."[19]

Conrad's words take us through the present argument and beyond—through what is obvious about Molly and what can be known about Joyce to what we can suspect about both of them. Great lust-lump that she is, what of her dissatisfaction with herself, with her life, with her husband and her lovers? And what, most of all, of her romantic longing for something else? Yes, Molly says of Boylan that he gave her what she badly wanted but she wishes too that "somebody would write me a loveletter his wasnt much and I told him he could write what he liked yours ever Hugh Boylan in Old Madrid silly women believe love is sighing I am dying still if he wrote it I suppose thered be some truth in it true or no it fills up your whole day and life always something to think about every moment and see it all around you like a new world" (758). A new world of love letters and sighing and dying—banal and silly, perhaps, as Molly herself remarks, but expressive of emotions that are neither. Expressive of her yearning for escape from the dismal round, if I may distort one of Beckett's titles, of more pricks and kicks. Such passages garland her soliloquy with the simple wildflowers of love and lust entwined. They are scarce, one has to pick through great masses of rubble to find them, but they are there and at the end of the soliloquy they are everywhere. Take even her fanciful thoughts of becoming Stephen's mistress (776): it's his love poems she wants, and who would blame her thinking it would be grand to have their photographs in the paper, lover and mistress? I find this touching and brave, and all the more so because foolish and impossible.

More than once Molly blames Bloom for her adultery. Allowing for her need to justify herself, allowing for her narcissistic concerns for her own pleasures, still there is much to be said against poor Bloom as a husband. Joyce makes quite clear, though most readers blind themselves to it, Bloom's masochistic delights in Molly's infidelity. We need not take Molly's word to remember Bloom's fantasy of her and Boylan abed, with Bloom at the keyhole taking snapshots and clasping himself gleefully at their orgy. Nor is it from Molly that we learn of his analogous sexual pain-pleasures, including the amusing, teasing, taunting, threat-

ening *billet-rude* from Martha Clifford. Molly merely veri-
fies what we already imagine. She resents having to submit
to Bloom's endless perverse questionings—"would you do
this and that and the other with the coalman yes"—and his
need to think of her with someone else, to make her imagine he is someone else: "who is in your mind now tell me
his name who tell me who the German Emperor is it yes
imagine Im him think of him can you feel him trying to
make a whore of me what he never will he ought to give
it up now at this age of his life simply ruination for any
woman and no satisfaction in it pretending to like it till he
comes and then finish it off myself anyway" (740). Ludicrous but certainly ruination too. Bloom is excited by
Molly's muddy boots and wants her to dirty them more
with horse dung. Kissing her bottom she describes as "the
usual" for him. Of his showing her photo about to other
men she says: "I wonder he didn't make him a present of
it altogether and me too after all why not" (774). She
knows she can excite him by spitting out cruel obscenities—
"smellrump or lick my shit" (781)—just the thing for masochistic Poldy. No wonder she muses, "I wish hed even
smoke a pipe like father to get the smell of a man" (752).

What these and other passages suggest is that Molly puts
up with Bloom in a much greater sense than he puts up
with her. Bloom appears to have ceased to attract her at
all sexually, while Molly remains the center of Bloom's
rather wobbly sexual interests. Sexually she regards him
as a freak and a boring freak at that. With him she knows
herself to be primarily a catalyst for his masturbatory fantasies. The German Emperor indeed! There is a loud, self-
mocking echo here of Joyce's belief that he had corrupted
Nora.

Just as Molly wishes for love letters from Boylan, so she laments the passing of what romantic gestures Bloom once made, flowers for her birthday or promises of journeys to Italy—"he ought to get a leather medal with a putty rim for all the plans he invents" (765). But her sharpest regret is for Lieutenant Mulvey. Unsure now whether his name was Jack, Joe, or Harry, still she recalls numerous details of her brief romance with him. The idea of it, the sea and sky, the flowers and sun, most of all the promise of it—these things move her, and they are lost. She knew they were lost sixteen years before when, lying with Bloom on Howth head, she got him to propose to her, "thinking of so many things he didn't know of," of Mulvey and of her Gibraltar girlhood.[20] She said yes to Bloom but she was saying yes as much to her memories, and she renews those memories to ease the emotional impoverishment which marriage has brought.

Reading the last two pages of her soliloquy, one is moved first by the rhythms and the words, but this is a relatively superficial reaction. That these two pages sum up in a sustained lyrical burst the emptiness of the present and the fullness of the past is the truer, the profounder source of their effectiveness—and affectiveness. "I thought as well him as another," as well say yes to Bloom as to any other, and she has no reason yet to feel differently. Only memory lifts her out of futility now and slips her into sleep.

How significant is it that Molly never actually slept with Mulvey? (More precisely, she says that she wouldn't let him touch her inside her petticoat and that "I pulled him off into my handkerchief"—760.) I think this fact tells us a great deal about Joyce's antisexual bias. His own sexual life was so troubled, sex was for him so destructive a force, that he looked backward to a sexually prelapsarian state for his lyrical images of love and peace.[21] If even the much-sinning Molly was to long for a time when "theres a wonderful feeling there all the time so tender" (760), that time, though involved with sex, had to be less than fully sexual. And Joyce's mind remained sufficiently Catholic that it could make a difference to him whether intercourse had actually taken place. The relative innocence of Molly and Mulvey made it possible for Joyce to use this interlude as the single lyrical focus in all the great bulk of *Ulysses*.

I doubt that Joyce was fully conscious of what he was doing in this regard. I do not doubt that he wanted to transcend his sexual conflicts in his life and in his work, but he was unable to do so in either. Remember Yeats's "first principle" of poetics: "A poet writes always of his personal life, in his finest work out of its tragedy, whatever it be, remorse, lost love, or merely loneliness; he never speaks directly as to someone at the breakfast table, there is always a phantasmagoria."[22] And Joyce's principal characters are the phantasmagoria of his personal life. Nowhere in Joyce's writings do we find an example of sensuality and tenderness combined. The *Chamber Music* poems are wholly asexual; the sexuality of *Dubliners* is either perverse or frustrated; Stephen Dedalus sleeps with only a prostitute; *Exiles* dramatizes sexual confusion; in *Finnegans Wake* only the first encounter of Earwicker and Anna Livia is described lyrically, and at that extremely briefly. In *Ulysses* we have the perversions of Bloom, the frustrations and adulteries of Molly—and Molly's single recollection. In this last Joyce came as close as he ever would to describing sexuality as a positive force. But how limited his attempt was! Mulvey, after all, is totally uncharacterized, a mere shadow. Joyce used Molly and Mulvey's experience because of its adolescent, incomplete quality, because it reached the verge and stopped, still promising, still innocent—at least in Joyce's mind.

Sexually Joyce was and his books are infantile. I use the word in its strict psychological sense, not as a moral judgment and certainly not as a reflection on the genius with which he portrayed this infantilism. In writing *Ulysses* he dissected his own sexual nature piece by piece in the person of Bloom. Molly Bloom emerged out of the complicated interaction of several factors: traditional Irish ideas about woman; Joyce's conception of the sexually powerful woman, necessarily something of a whore; his guilt about the probable effects of his own sexual confusions and inadequacies on a woman; and his faintly understood but strongly felt notion of what tender sexual love might be all about. That Joyce chose to express this notion through the lips of a woman is something worth pondering.

NOTES

1. Patrick Boyle, *Like Any Other Man* (London: MacGibbon and Kee, 1966), a novel. Mr. Boyle's short stories are similar in their sexual themes.

2. Well, not any Irishman, but the disowning of Yeats, as a Protestant aristocrat, an Edwardian Englishman who chanced to be born on Irish soil, is common enough—so much so that Michael Longley saw the need to defend Yeats as an Irishman at the 1969 Yeats Summer School in Sligo. And in Ireland one frequently hears the late poems lamented as the delirium of a dirty old man.

3. Vivian Mercier, *The Irish Comic Tradition* (Oxford: Clarendon Press, 1962).

4. Examples abound, perhaps the most famous being "Roisin Dubh" (sixteenth century) and Mangan's adaptation of it, "Dark Rosaleen," in the 1840s. So dear is this conception of Mother Ireland to the hearts of

Irishmen that when Conor Cruise O'Brien mocked it and gave his countrymen a new portrait of Mother ("Introducing Ireland," in *Conor Cruise O'Brien Introduces Ireland* [London: Andre Deutsch, 1969, pp. 13–20]), he created an uproar the likes of which have not been seen in Ireland since the *Playboy* riots. Dr. O'Brien's Mother Ireland is something of an old slut who has had an affair with her neighbor, is a sloppy and extravagant housekeeper, has a bad name for brawling and untruthfulness, tries to teach her children a language she's forgotten herself, and so forth. For thus slandering Mother, Dr. O'Brien was denounced eight weeks running in the Irish press, and his book became a best seller.

5.   Translated by the Earl of Longford, *1000 Years of Irish Poetry*, ed. Kathleen Hoagland (New York: Devin-Adair Co., 1962), p. 150.

6.   Numbers in parentheses refer to the Random House edition of *Ulysses* published in 1961.

7.   Translated by David Marcus (Dublin: Dolmer Press, 1967), p. 24.

8.   "Some Psychological Determinants of Joyce's View of Love and Sex" in *Papers from the Second International Joyce Symposium, Dublin 1969*, ed. Fritz Senn (Bloomington: Indiana University Press, 1970).

9.   "Degradation in Erotic Life," *Collected Papers*, vol. 4, (London: Basic Books, 1925), p. 207.

10.   The partially expurgated letters to Nora of 1909 can be found in *Letters of James Joyce*, vol. 2, ed. Richard Ellmann (New York: Viking Press, 1966); but the full texts are in the Joyce Collection at the Cornell University Library; see also my discussion of the letters and my paraphrase of the unpublished portions of the letter of 2 December 1909 in my *The Conscience of James Joyce* (Princeton: Princeton University Press, 1968), pp. 35–55, and my discussion of the letters in "Some Psychological Determinants. . . ."

11.   The identification of Amalia Popper remains a delicate matter. For an exchange on the subject see the letters in the *New York Review of Books* (November 20, 1969), pp. 44 f.

12.   *Giacomo Joyce* (New York: Viking Press, 1968), p. 2.

13.   Ibid.

14.   Ibid., p. 15.

15.   Ibid.

16.   See *Letters of James Joyce*, vol. 2, pp. 426–36.

17.   Some readers of Joyce's letters to Nora have been so impressed by their frankness that they have optimistically and mistakenly concluded that Joyce was on the verge of working out his psychosexual difficulties. Confession and psychoanalysis are not the same thing, as Joyce's continuing conflicts attest.

18. Joyce's researches into the post-Homeric tradition of the unfaithful Penelope, as documented by Phillip F. Herring in his "The Bedsteadfastness of Molly Bloom," *Modern Fiction Studies* 15 (Spring 1969): 49–61, is another example of his psychologically-motivated interest in cuckoldry.

19. Quoted in Bernard C. Meyer, M.D., *Joseph Conrad: A Psychoanalytic Biography* (Princeton: Princeton University Press, 1967), p. 3.

20. The most mystifying comment about Molly I have ever read is in the form of a letter to the *Irish Times* of 6 August 1969: "Sir,—What a pity that Molly Bloom hadn't the advantages of a Gibraltarian education! She would surely have acquired the intellectual vision (and the eye for business) to have advocated taking over the whole 'district' long ago. It would have compensated, too, for the restricted course of history in the schools on the Rock, by making Geography a more integrated subject and avoiding all this unpleasantness we read of." Maybe Molly Bloom as Governor-General of the Rock really is the answer to all this unpleasantness?

21. An analogy seems obvious here between Mulvey and Gretta Conroy's lost love, Michael Furey, in "The Dead," who is, according to Richard Ellmann, based partly on a dead sweetheart of Nora's, Michael Bodkin. One thinks also of Shem's riddle in *Finnegans Wake* (New York: Viking Press, 1947), p. 170, which implies, among much else, that innocence vanishes with puberty.

22. "A General Introduction for My Work," *Essays and Introductions* (New York: Macmillan 1968), p. 509.

The Fictional Technique of *Ulysses*

WILLIAM M. SCHUTTE

AND ERWIN R. STEINBERG

6

WHEN JAMES JOYCE's *Ulysses* began to appear serially in the *Little Review* early in 1918 and was issued as a book in 1922, it was bitterly denounced and enthusiastically applauded. But both attackers and defenders agreed that it was revolutionary. So it was! On the other hand, it is clear enough as we look back half a century later that it was also a logical next step in the work of an artist who refrained from exploiting his successful use of certain fictional techniques by repeating them with different subject matter. Instead he was impelled—so his practice clearly indicates—to make each of his productions a unique work of art, constructed in such a way as to be clearly distinguished from his own previous publications and inimitable, except in incidentals, by anyone, presumably including himself.

If one examines carefully the texts of *Stephen Hero*, *Dubliners*, *A Portrait of the Artist as a Young Man*, *Ulysses*, and *Finnegans Wake*, one finds Joyce employing a bewildering variety of techniques. No other modern writer can approach his mastery of his craft. The steady movement toward more and more sophisticated means of storytelling made him the most influential innovator of modern literature. At the same time, however, if we read accurately, we will find an essential consistency in Joyce's aims and a continuity in his narrative method from the beginning to the end of his career.

From *Stephen Hero* to *Finnegans Wake* Joyce was concerned to simulate or to re-create life as he conceived it to be. In a sense, of course, this is what all writers try to do. But for Joyce the methods that had been used from the time of Homer to his own day were inadequate to illuminate his conception of what life in his time truly was. His dissatisfaction with these methods was expressed at the very start of his career in a sketch called, at the suggestion of his brother Stanislaus, "A Portrait of the Artist." It was written in one day during his twenty-second year and is clearly a distillation of the extended meditations on the subject of art, especially literary art, which had been occupying him for several years. One passage is particularly significant as a commentary on contemporaneous methods of fiction, but even more because it provides the basis for everything Joyce wrote thereafter:

The features of infancy are not commonly reproduced in the adolescent portrait for, so capricious are we, that we cannot or will not conceive the past in any other than its iron memorial aspect. Yet the past assuredly implies a fluid succession of presents, the development of an entity of which our actual present is a phase only. Our world, again, recognises its acquaintance chiefly by the characters of beard and inches and is, for the most part, estranged from those of its members who seek through some art, by some process of the mind as yet untabulated, to liberate from the personalized lumps of matter that which is their individuating rhythm, the first or formal relation of their parts. But for such as these a portrait is not an identificative paper but rather the curve of an emotion.[1]

Throughout his career, Joyce absorbed himself completely in the Dublin of his youth and young manhood. In each of his books he attempted to represent a portion of that past, and the persons who were a part of it, in such a way that they could not fall into the "iron memorial" grasp of the traditional novel. He sought through various means to reflect reality by simulating its "fluid succession of presents" and so to liberate the "individuating rhythm" of life. For Joyce, as for all novelists, "life" is seen not statistically but as embodied in the individual: the little boy of "Araby," Eveline, Stephen Dedalus, Leopold Bloom, H. C. Earwicker. "Characters of beard and inches" and similar "identificative" details are not excluded from the novel, but they are subsidiary to the "curve of emotion," the rhythm which, as Joyce said in his Paris notebook and repeated in *A Portrait*, is the formal relation "of part to part in any esthetic whole or of an esthetic whole to its part or parts or of any part to the esthetic whole of which it is a part." Whether in life or in art, these parts "constitute a whole as far as they have a common end."[2]

Perhaps more than any of Joyce's other books, *Ulysses* is an attempt to simulate the rhythms of life by constructing a novel whose parts all work in different ways to achieve the same end, the revelation of what it means to live in the modern world. To this task Joyce brought his immense talent, certain devices developed in his earlier works, especially in *A Portrait*, and a variety of new techniques which must have seemed to him essential to the satisfactory achievement of his ends. To demonstrate how all of these techniques were used is beyond the scope of this article, but a brief survey may help the careful reader explore them himself.

Crucial to an understanding of Joyce's strategy in *Ulysses* is the recognition that like *A Portrait, Dubliners,* and *Finnegans Wake,* this novel is constructed of discrete sections. There are eighteen, the tenth of which (Wandering Rocks) is itself composed of nineteen separate vignettes. Never does one section lead directly into the next. Although the central character may be the same in consecutive chapters, there is always both a gap in time and a change in place. In addition, there is always a shift in the immediate concerns of the central character involved and sometimes, as we shall see, a decisive change in technique.

To illustrate we may look briefly at the first three episodes of the book (usually referred to as the Telemachiad), in all of which Stephen Dedalus is the central figure. (Bloom has yet to be introduced.) It is in many ways the most closely integrated portion of *Ulysses*: each episode concerns itself more narrowly than the preceding one with the mind of Stephen, to the growing exclusion of the interests and thoughts of other characters; each gives us a view of the world more selectively focused through the prism of Stephen's consciousness; each relies more heavily on the stream-of-consciousness technique. Nevertheless, there is neither spatial nor chronological continuity between the episodes, and though many of the same ideas weave their way in and out of the Telemachiad, Stephen's central concern in each episode is quite distinct. In Telemachus it is Stephen's unhappy relations with his friends; in Nestor it is his relations with the older generation and the one to follow him; in Proteus it is his relation to the universe, past and present. In time the sections jump with-

out transition from about 8 A.M. to about 10 A.M. to about
11 A.M.; in space from the Martello Tower to Mr. Deasy's
school at Dalkey to Sandymount Strand. We shift abruptly
from Buck Mulligan waving goodbye from the Forty Foot
to Stephen in the classroom: "You, Cochrane, what city
sent for him?"; from Mr. Deasy's back retreating up the
pathway of his school to "Ineluctable modality of the visible" and Stephen's thoughts as he walks along the beach.
The move to the next section is, of course, even more
abrupt: from Stephen, still on the strand, watching the
Rosevean sailing up Dublin Bay to Leopold Bloom in the
middle of the Blooms's kitchen thinking about cats and
kidneys.

Thus Joyce, eliminating the connective tissue which traditionally holds the scenes of a novel together, provides for
his reader the "fluid succession of presents" which his 1904
manifesto called for. There are thirty-six of these "presents": seventeen developed as major episodes and the nineteen related fragments of the Wandering Rocks chapter.
Each of the episodes, as Joyce tried to suggest in a somewhat confusing chart which he once prepared for Stuart
Gilbert,[3] has its own technique, one which Joyce deemed
appropriate, it would seem, for capturing the essence of
the particular present there recorded. These techniques
vary considerably in the course of the book. But underlying them all is the one which critics promptly labeled
stream of consciousness. This technique was not, of course,
altogether new. One can find stream-of-consciousness passages in such writers as Dickens and Dostoyevsky. Joyce
himself had used it sparingly in *A Portrait of the Artist*. In
Ulysses it emerges as the dominant technique.

With the advantage of hindsight one can see how he arrived at what is probably the fullest and most studied exploitation of this technique in all of literature. First, he had developed his concept of the epiphany:

a sudden spiritual manifestation, whether in the vulgarity of speech or gesture or in a memorable phase of the mind itself. He believed that it was for the man of letters to record these epiphanies with extreme care, seeing that they themselves are the most delicate and evanescent of moments.[4]

The short stories in *Dubliners* and the episodes in *A Portrait of the Artist* and *Ulysses* are either carefully developed epiphanies or scenes designed to culminate in epiphanies. And each effort to catch and fix the meaning of the evanescent epiphany, the "sudden spiritual manifestation," forced Joyce to probe more deeply the mind of the character experiencing it and to rely more fully for its unique expression on the idiosyncratic perspective and language of that character.

There was also Joyce's concept of the artist, who, when writing in the highest, or "dramatic" mode, "like the God of creation, remains within or behind or beyond or above his handiwork, invisible, refined out of existence, indifferent, paring his fingernails."[5] Each successive attempt to withdraw himself from the novelist's traditional position between his characters and his reader, each successive attempt to refine himself (the artist-novelist) out of existence, caused him to seek ways in which he could more "dramatically" present "his image [that is, his work of art] in immediate relation to others."[6]

Thus Joyce's attempt to carry out more fully his aesthetic theories in successive works caused him to move more and more to simulate fully the stream of consciousness of each character he was attempting to present to his reader. This gradually increasing reliance on the stream of consciousness is recapitulated in the development of the Telemachiad, where the reader is gradually accustomed to it.[7] In the first of its three episodes, Telemachus, Joyce depends heavily on the standard devices of the omniscient author. "Solemnly he came forward and mounted the round gunrest. He faced about and blessed gravely thrice the tower, the surrounding country and the awakening mountains" (3).[8] The passage is imbued with the flavor of Stephen's personality and perspective on the world, with its ever-present tinge of mockery, but clearly the author here is presenting the scene. Joyce not only tells *what* Mulligan does. He also tells *how* he does it: solemnly, gravely. He avoids allowing the omniscient author to become too obtrusive, however, by making the first two episodes heavily conversational. By thus avoiding omniscient author sentences and by interspersing in the dialogue a few stream-of-consciousness sentences, he prepares the reader for the longer stream-of-consciousness passages to come. By the time the reader reaches the third episode, Proteus, he is ready to accept and understand an episode employing the stream-of-consciousness technique almost exclusively. Joyce does use omniscient author statements in that episode, but sparingly—only to keep the reader apprised of Stephen's movements and whereabouts and to sketch in certain necessary facts about the physical scene.[9]

Joyce repeats with Leopold Bloom this careful progression from opening presentation by omniscient author to full presentation by stream-of-consciousness technique. Thus Calypso begins with auctorial commentary: "Mr Leopold Bloom ate *with relish* the inner organs of beasts and fowls. He *liked* thick giblet soup, nutty gizzards, a stuffed roast heart" (55). (*Italics ours.*) Not until ninety-four pages later does he present a Bloom chapter (Lestrygonians) employing the full stream-of-consciousness technique.

A comparison of the two full stream-of-consciousness chapters, Proteus and Lestrygonians, shows that each carries—and thus projects for the reader—the stamp of the individual mind it is presenting, the first Stephen's and the second Bloom's. Such a comparison suggests, for example, that in many ways Bloom is a pale, materialistic, and frequently comic echo of Stephen. In Lestrygonians Bloom considers many of the same topics that concern Stephen in Proteus: Irish history, the Roman Catholic church, literature, sense experience (each tries a little experiment with the senses), scientific matters, physical change, and the meaning of change wrought by time. But Bloom's interests, ideas, and comprehensions are always much less sophisticated than Stephen's.[10]

Such a comparison shows, too, that Bloom makes much more frequent use than Stephen of a sentence pattern usually associated with the Irish, in which part of the predicate comes at the beginning rather than at the end of the sentence:

Phosphorous it must be done with. (151)

Live on fleshy fish they have to. (153)

Kill me that would. (161)

Similarly, whereas carefully balanced sentences predominate in Stephen's stream of consciousness, jumbled sentences predominate in Bloom's:

Proteus

Signatures of all things I am here to read, seaspawn and sea-wrack, the nearing tide, that rusty boot. (37)

Houses of decay, mine, his, and all. (39)

Day by day: night by night: lifted, flooded and let fall. (49)

Lestrygonians

Where was that ad some Brimingham firm the luminous crucifix? (151)

The full moon was the night we were Sunday fortnight exactly there is a new moon. (167)

Karma they call that transmigration for sins you did in a past life the reincarnation met him pikehoses. (182)

Thus in presenting Stephen and Bloom as clearly differentiated fictional characters, Joyce not only uses the methods traditionally employed by novelists: having them speak, act, and react in distinctly different ways and at the beginning summarizing as omniscient author the unique thoughts of each. He also employs the stream-of-consciousness technique both to refine himself, the mediating author, out of existence, and to simulate the contents of individual and contrasting minds, each with its own rhythm.

A juxtaposition of the closing lines of Proteus and of Lestrygonians shows clearly how Joyce had succeeded by the end of those chapters and how distinctly different were the two personalities presented by this technique:

Proteus

He took the hilt of his ashplant, lunging with it softly, dallying still. Yes, evening will find itself in me, without me. All days make their end. By the way next when is it? Tuesday will be the longest day. Of all the glad new year, mother, the rum tum tiddledy tum. Lawn Tennyson, gentleman poet. *Già*. For the old hag with the yellow teeth. And Monsieur Drumont, gentleman journalist. *Già*. My teeth are very bad. Why, I wonder? Feel. That one is going too. Shells. Ought I go to a dentist, I wonder, with that money? That one. Toothless Kinch, the superman. Why is that, I wonder, or does it mean something perhaps?

My handkerchief. He threw it. I remember. Did I not take it up?

His hand groped vainly in his pockets. No, I didn't. Better buy one.

He laid the dry snot picked from his nostril on a ledge of rock, carefully. For the rest let look who will.

Behind. Perhaps there is someone.

He turned his face over a shoulder, rere regardant. Moving through the air high spars of a threemaster, her sails brailed up on the crosstrees, homing, upstream, silently moving, a silent ship. (50–51)

Lestrygonians

The flutter of his breath came forth in short sighs. Quick. Cold statues: quiet there. Safe in a minute.

No, didn't see me. After two. Just at the gate.

My heart!

His eyes beating looked steadfastly at cream curves of stone. Sir Thomas Deane was the Greek architecture.

Look for something I.

His hasty hand went quick into a pocket, took out, read unfolded Agendath Netaim. Where did I?

Busy looking for.

He thrust back quickly Agendath.

Afternoon she said.

I am looking for that. Yes, that. Try all pockets. Handker. *Freeman*. Where did I? Ah, yes. Trousers. Purse. Potato. Where did I?

Hurry. Walk quietly. Moment more. My heart.

His hand looking for the where did I put found in his hip pocket soap lotion have to call tepid paper stuck. Ah, soap there! Yes. Gate.

Safe! (183)

When the reader turns to the ninth episode, Scylla and Charybdis, he has been carefully conditioned: twice he has experienced a movement from rather traditional fictional presentations to almost total immersion in a stream of consciousness. He should now be prepared to settle himself comfortably behind the eyes of any character and experience the world as that character experiences it.

But in Scylla and Charybdis there is a subtle shift in technique.[11] Until now the omniscient author sentences have been unobtrusive because they have appeared in the innocuous guise of stage directions or have been camouflaged by the idiom and speech rhythms of the character whom they have located or described. As the reader settles himself once more in Stephen's mind at the beginning of Scylla and Charybdis, however, he finds the omniscient author sentences calling attention to themselves in a way that they did not in Proteus:

He came a step a sinkapace forward on neatsleather creaking and a step backward a sinkapace on the solemn floor. (184)

Twicreakingly analysis he corantoed off. (184)

Stephen's idiom, we might say. Perhaps, but also a display of virtuosity that reminds us that the author, who seemed to have all but refined himself out of existence, is back there behind his characters after all.

The stream of consciousness and dialogue quickly flow in, however, and wash away the traces of the author; once again the occasional omniscient author's sentence becomes a modest stage direction:

He laughed again at the now smiling bearded face. (185)
Mr Best came forward, amiable, towards his colleague. (186)

A dozen pages later, however, the reader's eye encounters for the first time a nonverbal image: a passage from a medieval musical score (197). A little later Joyce suddenly changes the layout on the page to a mock verse-play format which forces the reader to puzzle out not only who is speaking but also where the dialogue stops and the stream of consciousness begins, up to this point not a problem:

> To whom thus Eglinton:
> > You mean the will.
> > That has been explained, I believe, by jurists.
> > She was entitled to her widow's dower
> > At common law. His legal knowledge was great
> > Our judges tell us.
> > > Him Satan fleers,
> > Mocker:
> > > And therefore he left out her name
> > From the first draft but he did not leave out
> > The presents for his granddaughter, for his daughters,
> > For his sister, for his old cronies in Stratford
> > And in London. And therefore when he was urged,
> > As I believe, to name her
> > He left her his
> > Secondbest
> > Bed.
> > > > *Punkt*
> > Leftherhis
> > Secondbest
> > Bestabed
> > Secabest
> > Leftabed. (203)

Half a dozen pages later the dialogue suddenly shifts into the format of an opera libretto, complete with appropriate directions in Italian: *Piano, diminuendo. . . . A tempo. . . . Stringendo* (209).

When Joyce employs his technique in this way, he is no longer using the dramatic form wherein the artist "presents his image in immediate relation to others." Instead the effect—calling the reader's attention as it does to the presence of the author—is more like what he calls the "epic" mode, in which the artist presents his image in *mediate* relation to himself and others. In any event, the spell has been broken, the mystery revealed, the hidden author-God made manifest. Having painstakingly prepared the reader in one hundred and eighty pages to accept the stream-of-consciousness technique, Joyce refuses to continue using it in its pure form. Instead he pushes on to develop new techniques, a different one for every additional episode. We find, then, that although the second half of *Ulysses* contains many stream-of-consciousness passages, what distinguishes episodes ten through eighteen is not the exploitation of the stream-of-consciousness technique but rather the experiments in other techniques.

As if to signify a change, Joyce wrote at the end of one draft of the Scylla and Charybdis chapter: "End of First Part of 'Ulysses,' James Joyce, Universitätstrasse, Zürich, Switzerland, New Year's Eve, 1918."[12] Joyce may have had other thoughts at other times about the parts of *Ulysses*; he did not, for example, divide the text into two parts when he prepared it for publication. But the note is helpful in suggesting that at one time, Joyce was thinking of his book as consisting of two nine-episode halves. Certainly this division is useful for the study of his fictional technique.

In The Wandering Rocks and The Sirens (episodes ten and eleven), the narrative techniques become more and more complex. The former, as we have seen, offers the reader fragments of Dublin life at midafternoon on June 16, 1904. Bloom appears in one vignette, Stephen in two. Otherwise the narrative for the first time—and the only time until the Penelope chapter—moves beyond the consciousness of either Bloom or Stephen. But Joyce does not here abandon the techniques of the first half of the book. Thirteen of the sections, most of which consist largely of conversations involving more than two people, are presented as they might have been by an omniscient author. But in six, each of which presents an individual observing the world around him, there are substantial passages of stream-of-consciousness writing.[13] The inclusion of these passages maintains continuity with the earlier sections without being obtrusive, and the stream of consciousness in each instance seems a natural product of the individual's situation at the moment.

In this episode, on the other hand, Joyce introduces one new technique which, like the headlines of Aeolus, is unnatural in the light of conventional narrative practice. As one reads along in one of the vignettes, he is surprised suddenly to be faced with an omniscient author's statement from another vignette which seems to have no relevance to the vignette being read. As we follow Stephen down Bedford Row in the city, for example, we are suddenly asked to leap two and a half miles to where "Father Conmee, having read his little hours, walked through the hamlet of Donnycarney, murmuring vespers" (242), after which without transition we return to Stephen's thoughts about the books on a cart and continue through the vignette with him. These suddenly inserted statements by the omniscient author, which are much like stage directions, are designed to let us know that certain events of the episode are occurring simultaneously. At the moment when Stephen bends over the book cart, Father Conmee is walking through Donnycarney. At the moment when Simon

Dedalus puts coins in his pocket, the viceregal cavalcade passes out of Parkgate. As Boylan talks to the salesgirl in Thornton's, Bloom scans the books in a hawker's cart several blocks away. There are similar intrusive references also to concurrent activities of characters met in earlier episodes (the two midwives, the reverend Hugh C. Love, Councillor Nannetti, Denis Breen) as well as to Miss Kennedy and Miss Douce, whom the reader has not yet encountered but who will figure prominently in the next episode.

These brief stage directions—at least thirty of them, with twenty-three concentrated in nine of the central vignettes —are far more intrusive than the newspaper headlines of Aeolus. Joyce does attempt to ease the reader into this new technique by making the first insertion involving Professor Maginni so much like a description of something the strolling Father Conmee might see that the unwary reader may not realize that the professor is several blocks away. The second indication that two events are occurring simultaneously—this time separated in space by over a mile—is direct: "Corny Kelleher sped a silent stream of hayjuice arching from his mouth while a generous white arm from a window in Eccles Street flung forth a coin." Thereafter, however, Joyce omits the *while*, and the insertions are completely unprepared for.

The effect of the constant eruption of foreign materials into the vignettes is to throw the reader off balance, to call his attention forcibly to the presence of an author—or, as Joyce would have said, a creator or maker. If the early sections of the novel are designed to suggest that material is being translated directly from life to the printed page, episodes ten through seventeen work in the opposite direction: again and again the reader is reminded that he is reading an intricate, highly artificial construct. It is as if, having brought us into the most intimate contact with the worlds inhabited by Stephen and by Bloom, he wishes now to exile us from those worlds, to force us to see them from a more and more disengaged perspective. Techniques, and even technical acrobatics, are used with a fine disregard for intellectual ease and comfort to subvert any identification the reader may have made with Stephen, with Bloom, or with *Ulysses.*

Thus we face a page and a half of apparently unrelated jabbering at the opening of The Sirens; in Cyclops we struggle through a page which contains only a list of saints and a list of objects they are carrying; The Oxen of the Sun is narrated in a series of paragraphs representing the chronological development of English prose; Circe is a phantasmagoria, an endless array of phantoms of the imagination which defy us to determine their significance; in Ithaca we are required to plow through lengthy, pseudoscientific descriptions, among them one of the Dublin water supply system and another of a desk drawer's accumulation of hoarded objects.

In the eighteenth (and final) episode of *Ulysses*, Penelope, we once again see the world through the mind of a single character, Molly Bloom. But this time instead of simulating Molly's psychological stream of consciousness Joyce gives us an internal monologue or silent soliloquy.[14] As he did with Stephen and Bloom, however, he again projects a unique personality, unique not only in the content of her thoughts but in the way those thoughts are presented. The Penelope chapter and Molly are completely different from anything that has come before.

By putting Molly in bed at night in a dark room where the world impinges relatively little on her consciousness, Joyce relieves himself of the need to trace her movements from place to place (as with the two men) or to describe the world around her. Thus, Penelope needs no omniscient author's statements. Furthermore, his decision not to simulate Molly's stream of consciousness made it unnecessary for Joyce to provide a third such stream so different from those of Stephen and Bloom as to be truly unique. Rather he makes available to himself a distinctly different texture and rhythm with which to present those thoughts and thus to project the character.

Joyce opens the Penelope chapter with a sentence of ninety-eight words to set the rhythm of the episode:

Yes because he never did a thing like that before as ask to get his breakfast in bed with a couple eggs since the *City Arms* hotel when he used to be pretending to be laid up with a sick voice doing his highness to make himself interesting to that old faggot Mrs Riordan that he thought he had a great leg of and she never left us a farthing all for masses for herself and her soul greatest miser ever was actually afraid to lay out 4d for her methylated spirit telling me all her ailments. (738)

The sentence ends, but there is no punctuation, for Joyce wishes to suggest a continuing rhythm. The next thirty-six words read:

she had too much old chat in her about politics and earthquakes and the end of the world let us have a bit of fun first God help the world if all the women were her sort. (738)

Here there is what the linguists would call a "double cross juncture" between "world" and "let" and between "first" and "God." Again Joyce chooses not to put periods there so that he may maintain the illusion of a continuing sentence and thus of an unbroken line.

The content of Molly's brain is also distinctly different from Stephen's and Bloom's. Whereas Bloom's understanding of scientific concepts is much less sophisticated than Stephen's and sometimes completely wrong, Molly is scientifically illiterate. Unlike Stephen and Bloom, she shows no interest in politics. And again unlike the two men, who are not religious but are very much interested in the implications of religion, Molly is merely naively superstitious.

It is clear, therefore, that Joyce uses the internal monologue as a fictional technique to project the character of Molly just as he used the stream-of-consciousness technique earlier to project his two main male characters, Stephen and Bloom. And he is successful enough in using the internal monologue to provide us with a unique female personality. In this instance, however, his attempt to suggest that Molly's monologue is an unbroken stream often confuses the reader and calls attention to technique. In this context Penelope seems to belong where it is, at the end of the second half of *Ulysses* (as the creation of a visible artist-God), rather than at the end of the first half (where the artist-God seems to have been refined out of existence).

The techniques of the other episodes in the second half of *Ulysses* have been carefully examined by critics.[15] We shall not go again over the ground they have covered. Instead it may be more important at this stage in the history of Joyce criticism to agree that Joyce's attempt to write an episode in the form of a fugue is a masterpiece of technical virtuosity; to agree further that his reproduction in miniature of the development of English prose is both interesting and accurate; to admire his ability to sink the level of his prose style to tired, tawdry clichés or to the banalities of popular literature; to be amused (if often bored) by page-long catalogs, excursions into pseudomythology, parodies of scientific prose which go on and on and on; and, of course, to be fascinated by the presentation in dramatic form of the hallucinations of the central characters.

We may well agree, too, with the critical consensus that Joyce's technical control in individual episodes is brilliant. However, ultimately we must ask whether the formidable displays of narrative technique, impressive as each may be in itself, contribute to an artistically integrated whole. If, as Joyce proposed in his early sketch, man's life is "a fluid succession of presents" whose "individuating rhythm" the artist must "liberate," it is easy enough to make a case for Lestrygonians as reflecting the "individuating rhythm" of Leopold Bloom's present during the lunch hour, or of Nestor and Scylla and Charybdis as reflecting the rhythm of Stephen's present at two separate times on June 16, 1904. However, it is more difficult in these terms to justify the use of the fugue form to suggest the particular rhythm of Bloom's present during the hour he spends in the Ormond Bar. The conscientious reader can hardly avoid certain essential questions. Are the shifting tones of mood, sensation, thought, and feeling which suffuse The Sirens best presented through the complex, formal pattern which the fugue imposes? Do the introductory fragments justify themselves? Or, to move to another section, how can one justify the "show" passages in Cyclops? Are the verbal excesses there really necessary to suggest the present of Daniel-Bloom in the lion's den? Or again, granting that the catechistic method of Ithaca does reflect the aridity and hopelessness of the present being shared by Stephen and Bloom, is it not perhaps carried well beyond the point where it serves a legitimate function?

Throughout the second half of *Ulysses* one is forced to ask, unless he is prepared blindly to accept the author as a genius who can do no wrong, whether Joyce has not become so obsessed with technique that he has weakened rather than strengthened his novel. We do not pretend to be able to give an authoritative answer. In the long run the question may not be answerable. But by choosing in the final chapters to underscore rather than to conceal the presence of the maker of the book, Joyce himself forced the issue on his readers.

NOTES

1. Robert Scholes and Richard M. Kain, *The Workshop of Daedalus: James Joyce and the Raw Materials for "A Portrait of the Artist as a Young Man,"* (Evanston: Northwestern University Press, 1965), p. 60.

2. *A Portrait of the Artist as a Young Man* (New York: Viking Press, 1964), p. 206. For a discussion of how Joyce applied these principles to *A Portrait*, see William M. Schutte's introduction to *Twentieth Century Interpretations of "A Portrait of the Artist as a Young Man,"* (Englewood Cliffs, N. J.: Prentice-Hall, 1968).

3. See Stuart Gilbert, *James Joyce's "Ulysses"* (New York: Alfred A. Knopf, 1952), p. 41. Joyce employed such terms as "Narrative: young" (Telemachus), "Narcissism" (Lotus Eaters), "Incubism" (Hades), "Peristaltic" (Lestrygonians), and "Labyrinth" (Wandering Rocks) to describe his techniques. Although of some value in suggesting what he is up to in each section, the labels have not proved to be rigorous enough for critics to use with any success. Even Gilbert does little with them.

4. *Stephen Hero* (Norfolk, Connecticut: New Directions, 1955), p. 211. See also *The Workshop of Daedalus*, pp. 3–51.

5. *A Portrait*, p. 215.

6. See Stephen's statement that

art necessarily divides itself into three forms progressing from one to the next. These forms are: the lyrical form, the form wherein the artist presents his image in immediate relation to himself; the epical form, the form wherein he presents his image in mediate relation to himself and others; the dramatic form, the form wherein he presents his image in immediate relation to others. *A Portrait*, p. 214.

(Joyce made an almost identical statement in his Paris notebook. See Herbert Gorman, *James Joyce* [New York: Rinehart, 1948], pp. 97-98.) Shortly after this statement, Stephen says, "The esthetic image in the dramatic form is life purified in and reprojected from the human imagination" (*A Portrait*, p. 215), and two sentences later makes the statement about the artist, "like the God of creation," remaining "invisible, refined out of existence," quoted above.

7. Joyce might, like Edouard Dujardin in *Les Lauriers sont coupés*, have thrown the reader into a full-blown stream-of-consciousness episode without any preparation, but he seems to have felt that the gradual approach to it would be more effective.

8. Numbers in parentheses refer to the Random House edition of *Ulysses* published in 1961.

9. For a fuller discussion of this development, see Erwin R. Steinberg, "Introducing the Stream-of-Consciousness Technique in *Ulysses*," *Style* 2 (Winter 1968): 49-58.

10. See Erwin R. Steinberg, " 'Lestrygonians,' a Pale 'Proteus'?", *Modern Fiction Studies* 15 (Spring 1969): 73-86.

11. One might think on hasty inspection of the text that Aeolus contains a major technical innovation. There Joyce did insert newspaper captions. He did so, however, after he had completed the text. Without them this episode conforms to the regular pattern for the "First Part."

12. In the Rosenbach Manuscript, now owned by the Philip and A. S. W. Rosenbach Foundation.

13. These vignettes are: 1) Father Conmee; 7) Miss Dunne; 10) Bloom; 12) Kernan; 13) Stephen; and 18) Master Dignam.

14. For a fuller discussion of the difference between internal monologue and stream of consciousness, see Erwin R. Steinberg, "The steady monologue of the interiors; the pardonable confusion," *James Joyce Quarterly* 6 (Spring 1969): 185-98. Briefly, we would use the term "internal monologue" when a character speaks silently to himself, in his own mind. We would reserve "stream of consciousness" to characterize the less well organized level of thought which Joyce simulates in Proteus and Lestrygonians, some of which is preverbal.

15. See, for example, Lawrence L. Levin, "The Sirens Episode as

Music: Joyce's Experiment in Prose Polyphony," *James Joyce Quarterly* 3 (Fall 1965): 12-24; Ruth Bauerle, "A Sober Drunken Speech: Stephen's Parodies in 'The Oxen of the Sun,' " *James Joyce Quarterly* 5 (Fall 1967): 40–46; Richard E. Madtes, "Joyce and the Building of 'Ithaca,' " *ELH: A Journal of English Literary History* 21 (March 1964): 443-59.

Ulysses
by Way of
Culture and Anarchy

H. FREW WAIDNER, III

7

IT IS A COMMON and, I believe, apt criticism that one of the principal themes of *Ulysses* is the desirability of wholeness in man—his very fullest self-realization. Such development may be viewed as embracing what are perhaps the two most dominant tendencies in the history of western thought: the moral and the (disinterestedly) intellectual. The relationship between these tendencies has engaged thinkers for centuries, and where so vast a subject as the intellectual background of *Ulysses* is concerned (a topic that it was felt should at least be touched upon in this book of essays on Joyce's masterpiece) the two probably provide as incisive an index as can be found.

Talk, as this is, of conscience vis-à-vis consciousness readily brings to mind Matthew Arnold and his 1869 *Culture and Anarchy* wherein are elaborated the particular energies of Hebraism and Hellenism. In assessing the temper of his race and time Arnold wrote:

We may regard this energy driving at practice, this paramount sense of the obligation of duty, self-control, and work, this earnestness in going manfully with the best light we have, as one force. And we may regard the intelligence driving at those ideas which are, after all, the basis of right practice, the ardent sense for all the new and changing combinations of them which man's development brings with it, the indomitable impulse to know and adjust them perfectly, as another force. And these two forces we may regard as in some sense rivals,—rivals not by the necessity of their own nature, but as exhibited in man and his history,—and rivals dividing the empire of the world between them. And to give these forces names from the two races of men who have supplied the most signal and splendid manifestations of them, we may call them respectively the forces of Hebraism and Hellenism.[1]

Later in this fourth chapter Arnold is seen at his rhetorical best, the balanced phrasing being suggestive: "The governing idea of Hellenism is *spontaneity of consciousness*; that of Hebraism, *strictness of conscience*."[2]

I have said that one is readily put in mind of this Arnoldian dichotomy when considering the intellectual background of *Ulysses*, but my statement more precisely bears witness to the provocative-associative powers of Professor Harry Levin who wrote, before very much had appeared on Joyce:

One by critical precept, the other by awful example, mark the distance between culture and philistinism. Matthew Arnold, though painfully conscious of this distance, might not have recognized them as unhonored prophets of Hellenism and Hebraism. The strains and stresses of middle-class life have alienated Stephen and vulgarized Bloom, have introverted the Hellene and extraverted the Hebrew. Still, somewhere between Stephen's esthetic feeling and Bloom's civic sense, between individual expression and social morality, lies our only hope for the good life. "Hebraism and Hellenism," Arnold has written, "—between these two points of influence moves our world. At one time it feels more powerfully the attraction of one of them, at another time of the other; and it ought to be, though it never is, evenly and happily balanced between them."[3]

The most basic distinction of Arnold's 1869 treatise is that between the man of culture and the Philistine. Briefly the former is he who strives to assimilate—with a mind toward its universal promulgation—the best that has been thought and known in the world, whereas the latter is he whose inclinations—invariably acted upon—proceed not from what Arnold calls his "best self" but rather his ordinary self, and eventuate in materialism, mechanism, individualism, and inflexibility (all being productive of the titular *Anarchy*). The other major distinction is that previously introduced between the person in whom Hebraism holds sway and him in whom Hellenism prevails. It should be observed, by way of relating these concepts, that an excessive regard for *strictness of conscience* can lead to Philistinism (morality become mechanical) just as an achieving of equilibrium between the moral and intellectual energies, provided these be energies sufficient, can result in a state of culture.

In his dialectic of history (spanning Pagan, early and medieval Christian, Renascence,[4] Reformation, and modern times) Arnold treats the two forces as alternately predominating movements. It is my opinion that Professor Levin's estimate of Bloom and Stephen, in its partial eschewing of Arnold's "either-or" susceptibility where individuals rather than peoples are concerned, is a just one, but that beheld yet more hypostatically the two characters may in fact be seen to share not a few, and indeed most, attributes. This is to say, that they may be regarded not only in contrast to each other (one level) but also (Ahab's "little lower layer") as *individually* ranging the compass of human potentiality, as being representative—each one—of a totality of tendency, Hellenic *and* Hebraic, the divergence between them being accounted for naturalistically along the lines of either Flaubertian or Zolaesque heredity and environment. They thus may be read not as radically differing but rather analogous "demonstrations" of the theme of the desirability of wholeness in man, and—by virtue of their similitude—what is more at issue, of the possibility of such wholeness.

If the above construction seems errant or tenuous, let me direct the reader's attention (before endeavoring to make the point myself) to what Richard Ellmann has written on the matter:

Now that Joyce was free to devote himself to *Ulysses*, he often discussed topics related to the book. One such subject was the similarity of the Jews and the Irish, on which Joyce insisted. They were alike, he declared, in being impulsive, given to fantasy, addicted to associative thinking, wanting in rational discipline. [*Ellmann's footnote*: These are made qualities of Bloom's mind.] He held, perhaps with Arnold's "Hebraism and Hellenism" in mind, that there were two basically different ways of thinking, the Greek and the Jewish, and that the Greek was logical and rational. One day he and Weiss were walking and met a Greek, with whom they talked for a long time. Afterwards Joyce remarked, "It's strange—you spoke like a Greek and he spoke like a Jew." He had perhaps already conceived the brothel scene in *Ulysses*, when Bloom and Stephen come together and Joyce writes, "Extremes meet. Jewgreek meets greekjew," following which Bloom becomes utterly rational and self-contained, and Stephen is impulsive. Joyce recognized his own affinities to both groups.[5]

It may at this juncture be asked if such an approach as that proposed (one more with an eye toward homogeneity than heterogeneity) conduces to descanting upon the subject of the intellectual background of *Ulysses*. My answer is simply that this approach, being somewhat static, better befits the nature of the book, a nature deemed by Levin, Joseph Frank,[6] and others (if for a different reason) to be more spatial than temporal.

Probably the readiest way of pointing up what I think to be a certain similarity between Bloom and Stephen is to indicate wherein the Jew is more Hellenic in spirit, and the young man more Hebraic, than is generally conceded. If Bloom is Hellenic, we must be able to observe in him the foremost Hellenic characteristic, "spontaneity of consciousness," what Arnold was to amplify as "the free spontaneous play of consciousness with which culture tries to float our stock habits of thinking and acting."[7] In a word, "flexibility"[8] must attach to the central figure of *Ulysses*. Now Bloom's thought has somewhat indiscriminately been labeled Philistine, bourgeois, by more than one Joyce critic, indiscriminately—I say—for two reasons: first, that Bloom is capable of transcending such mentation; and second, that his general broadmindedness is at variance with what is frequently the circumscribed character of demotic thinking. Among passages that may be adduced in support of Bloom's transcendence of Philistine thought one is particularly notable, as running counter to an ism which even in 1904 retained much of its influence. I refer to Utilitarianism[9] which Bloom weighs and succinctly dismisses, as the following shows:

Forgotten. I too. And one day she with. Leave her: get tired. Suffer then. Snivel. Big Spanishy eyes goggling at nothing. Her wavyavyeavyheavyeavyevyevy hair un comb: 'd.
    Yet too much happy bores.[10] (Italics added)

Respecting liberality of mind in Bloom—and we do well to recollect that Joyce's name for the hero of his originally contemplated short story version of *Ulysses* was Hunter[11]— we find him depicted as "a conscious reactor against the void incertitude" (734). Now the wish to dispel doubt can be as much a bourgeois trait as an, intellectually speaking, patrician one. Ortega y Gasset is instructive here in a manner so redolent of Arnold as to invite quotation:

That man is intellectually of the mass who, in face of any problem, is satisfied with thinking the first thing he finds in his head. On the contrary, the excellent man is he who contemns what he finds in his mind without previous effort, and only accepts as worthy of him what is still far above him and what requires a further effort in order to be reached.[12]

Bloom we perceive too infrequently and inconclusively to exert himself so to qualify as an excellent man but, every bit as conspicuously, too latitudinarian very thoroughly to reflect mass mind. It would be a gross critical error, naturally, to overlook in Bloom the *existence* of "stock habits of thinking and acting"; but the man, if a repository and executor of these, is seldom their slave. Consider the unprovincial spirit which thwarts their bondage:

Night Michael Gunn gave us the box. Tuning up. Shah of Persia liked that best. Remind him of home sweet home. Wiped his nose in curtain too. Custom his country perhaps. That's music too. (284)

Bloom with his *but don't you see?* and *but on the other hand.* (306)

Circumstances alter cases. (550)

Colours depend on the light you see. Stare the sun for example like the eagle then look at a shoe see a blotch blob yellowish. (378)

Related to the above is a word, concept, which engages Bloom throughout his day:

Fascinating little book that is of sir Robert Ball's. Parallax. I never exactly understood. There's a priest. Could ask him. Par it's Greek: parallel, parallax. (154)

Greek, Hellenic, indeed is *parallax*, the apparent displacement of an object resulting from the change in the direction or position from which it is viewed. Bloom may never quite grasp the term, but he is a practitioner of what it signifies—the seeing of something differently, from another perspective. And lest we miss the point, Joyce has larded his text with illustrations of parallax, one of the more salient being Bloom's pursuit by the mongrel in the Cyclops episode, and how Gerty MacDowell seven pages later is made to reflect upon this selfsame canis: "the photograph of grandpapa Giltrap's lovely dog Garryowen that almost talked, it was so human" (352). S. L. Goldberg, in his excellent *The Classical Temper*, perhaps most effectively puts to rest the notion that Bloom carries the Philistine values of turn-of-the-century Dublin, calling Tom Kernan— for example—Bloom's "parody."[13]

Let us now address ourselves to Stephen Dedalus, Bloom coming in for further individual scrutiny later, by noting two features of similarity between him and the canvasser: their both preferring "a continental to an insular manner of life" (with all about psychic flexibility therein implicit) and their "disbelief in many orthodox religions, national, social and ethical doctrines" (666). The latter of these Hellenic points of correspondence is open, I think, to some question where Stephen is concerned (Joyce's ostensibly declarative tone notwithstanding), for this young man may prove more Hebraic in tendency than is usually recognized. There can be no doubt that Stephen time and again evinces a spontaneity of consciousness, a flexibility, quintessentially Hellenic. (It is worth remarking in support of Bloom's Hellenism how Leopold is seen to parallel Stephen in the profession of open-mindedness, objectivity—Stephen: "Signatures of all things I am here to read"—[37]; Bloom: "Everything speaks in its own way"—[121].) And he sounds an inward note of rejection of the mechano-materialist phase of Philistinism from the outset, though not so much in reacting to Mulligan's thrusts as in parrying the well-meant admonitions of the master of the school in which he teaches:

—Three, Mr Deasy said, turning his little savingsbox about in his hand. These are handy things to have. See. This is for sovereigns. This is for shillings, sixpences, halfcrowns. And here crowns. See.

. . . .

Stephen's hand, free again, went back to the hollow shells. Symbols too of beauty and of power. A lump in my pocket. Symbols soiled by greed and misery.
—Don't carry it like that, Mr Deasy said. You'll pull it out somewhere and lose it. You just buy one of these machines. You'll find them very handy.
Answer something.

. . . .

—Because you don't save, Mr Deasy said, pointing his finger. You don't know yet what money is. Money is power, when you have lived as long as I have. I know, I know. If youth but knew. But what does Shakespeare say? *Put but money in thy purse.*
—Iago, Stephen murmured.

. . . .

—He knew what money was, Mr Deasy said. He made money. A poet but an Englishman too. (30)

Compare the above juxtaposing of the Elizabethan-Jacobean and the present-day mechanical with this portion of *Culture and Anarchy*:

Faith in machinery is, I said, our besetting danger. . . . what is coal but machinery? . . . Our coal, thousands of people were saying, is the real basis of our national greatness; if our coal runs short, there is an end of the greatness of England. But what *is* greatness?—culture makes us ask. Greatness is a spiritual condition worthy to excite love, interest, and admiration; and the outward proof of possessing greatness is that we excite love, interest, and admiration. If England were swallowed up by the sea tomorrow, which of the two, a hundred years hence, would most excite the love, interest, and admiration of mankind,—would most, therefore, show the evidences of having possessed greatness,—the England of the last twenty years, or the England of Elizabeth, of a time of splendid spiritual effort, but when our coal, and our industrial operations depending on coal, were very little developed?[14]

Such a mind as Stephen possesses might well be expected to yield him certain truths about life, or at least what he might construc to be truths. And yet it has been said by Richard Kain[15] and others that he believes in nothing. Now conviction in matters at all metempiric we realize to be contestable, but we have nevertheless to conclude that Stephen has made scant use of his endowments to come up so empty-handed. Unless, unless there is at work within him something decidedly inimical to the unfettered play of mind. And just such a thing does propose itself to us in Arnold's psychic schema—Hebraism, "strictness of conscience," "Agenbite of inwit" (16). Remorse of conscience in Stephen is largely to be associated with his refusal to pray for his mother on her deathbed. But he is also pricked at not relieving the pecuniary distress of his younger brothers and sisters, and there is even cause to think that his personal experience has brought him to recognize in literature a greater ethical incumbency than he is normally considered to uphold:

—He can find no trace of hell in ancient Irish myth, Haines said, amid the cheerful cups. The moral idea seems lacking, the sense of destiny, of retribution. Rather strange he should have just that fixed idea. (249)

His mood is decidedly remorseful at the beginning of the book, and remains so pretty much throughout, the very last glimpse we are afforded into his mind reflecting compunction (the prayer he would not repeat):

What sound accompanied the union of their tangent, the disunion of their (respectively) centrifugal and centripetal hands?
    The sound of the peal of the hour of the night by the chime of the bells in the church of Saint George.
    What echoes of that sound were by both and each heard?
    By Stephen:
    Liliata rutilantium. Turma circumdet.
    Iubilantium te virginum. Chorus excipiat. (704)

To say that it is absolute guilt which Stephen feels is too categorically to judge the matter, for he opposes even self-imputations in a way consistent with his native intransigence of mind. But it does seem fair to conclude that the presence of this uneasiness is sufficiently corrosive to preclude all chance of achieving a stable and productive world view. Arnold might have diagnosed Stephen's plight as follows:

Under the name of sin, the difficulties of knowing oneself and conquering oneself which impede man's passage to perfection, become, for Hebraism, a positive, active entity hostile to man. . . . As Hellenism speaks of thinking clearly, seeing things in their essence and beauty, as a grand and precious feat for man to achieve, so Hebraism speaks of becoming conscious of sin, of awakening to a sense of sin, as a feat of this kind. It is obvious to what wide divergence these differing tendencies, actively followed, must lead. As one passes and repasses from Hellenism to Hebraism, from Plato to St. Paul, one feels inclined to rub one's eyes and ask oneself whether man is indeed a gentle and simple being, showing the traces of a noble and divine nature; or an unhappy chained captive, labouring with groanings that cannot be uttered to free himself from the body of this death.[16]

Now the way in which Arnold depicts Hellenism is strikingly similar to that in which Joyce delineates Stephen's aesthetic in *A Portrait of the Artist as a Young Man*:[17]

To get rid of one's ignorance, to see things as they are, and by seeing them as they are to see them in their beauty, is the simple and attractive ideal which Hellenism holds out before human nature; and from the simplicity and charm of this ideal, Hellenism, and human life in the hands of Hellenism, is invested with a kind of aërial ease, clearness, and radiancy; they are full of what we call sweetness and light.[18]

Stephen of course cites a far older authority, but the echo is a significant one:

Aquinas says: *ad pulcritudinem tria requiruntur, integritas, consonantia, claritas.* I translate it so: *Three things are needed for beauty, wholeness, harmony and radiance.* . . . I thought he might mean that *claritas* is the artistic discovery and representation of the divine purpose in anything or a force of generalisation which would make the esthetic image a universal one, make it outshine its proper conditions. But that is literary talk. I understand it so. When you have apprehended that basket as one thing and have then analysed it according to its form and apprehended it as a thing you make the only synthesis which is logically and esthetically permissible. You see that it is that thing which it is and no other thing. The radiance of which he speaks is the scholastic *quidditas*, the *whatness* of a thing. This supreme quality is felt by the artist when the esthetic image is first conceived in his imagination. The mind in that mysterious instant Shelley likened beautifully to a fading coal. The instant wherein that supreme quality of beauty, the clear radiance of the esthetic image, is apprehended luminously by the mind which has been arrested by its wholeness and fascinated by its harmony is the luminous silent stasis of esthetic pleasure, a spiritual state very like to that cardiac condition which the Italian physiologist Luigi Galvani, using a phrase almost as beautiful as Shelley's, called the enchantment of the heart.[19]

But Arnold continues:

Difficulties are kept out of view, and the beauty and rationalness of the ideal have all our thoughts.[20]

Where Stephen is concerned (the post-Paris Stephen), difficulties patently are not kept out of view, and one important reason for this is his carking suspicion that the moral (messily mundane) has insufficiently been accorded its due.[21]

In a much-cited passage Joyce is reported to have remarked to Frank Budgen: "Stephen no longer interests me to the same extent [that Bloom does]. He has a shape that can't be changed."[22] This inflexibility of form is usually explained by Stephen's being, and being no more than, an aesthete. Yet in the light of his Hebraic tendencies, might not that rigidity be accounted for by his being held in a state of suspension, guy-wired as it were, between the claims both of the moral and the intellectual? An obvious difficulty with this explanation is its corollary that Bloom, who retains his author's interest, is similarly suspended. But Bloom's is a suspension—if I may so loosely express myself—at a lower level of consciousness whereon the two forces are less widely divergent and there is some "slack." Of this more presently.

Regarding certain other of those qualities which Arnold deems ingredient to a state of culture, we see Stephen as less than exemplary. Consider the following:

And because men are all members of one great whole, and the sympathy which is in human nature will not allow one member to be indifferent to the rest or to have a perfect welfare independent of the rest, the expansion of our humanity, to suit the idea of perfection which culture forms, must be a *general* expansion. Perfection, as culture conceives it, is not possible while the individual remains isolated. The individual is required, under pain of being stunted and enfeebled in his own development if he disobeys, to carry others along with him in his march towards perfection, to be continually doing all he can to enlarge and increase the volume of the human stream sweeping thitherward.[23]

And ponder (still allowing for Stephen's youth) this:

The great men of culture are those who have had a passion for diffusing, for making prevail, for carrying from one end of society to the other, the best knowledge, the best ideas of their time; who have laboured to divest knowledge of all that was harsh, uncouth, difficult, abstract, professional, exclusive; to humanise it, to make it efficient outside the clique of the cultivated and learned, yet still remaining the *best* knowledge and thought of the time, and a true source, therefore, of sweetness and light.[24]

And finally this:

that spirit of indulgence which is a necessary part of sweetness, and which, indeed, when our culture is complete, is, as I have said, inexhaustible.[25]

As does beseem the Hellene, though, Stephen is general-

ly opposed to preclusion within the intellectual-explana-
tory province; to an arid "Ineluctable modality of the visible" he poses a "Shut your eyes and see" (37). Yet an
equally significant and perhaps more telling indication of
this animus to preserve the possible lies within the moral
sphere:

> Stephen had these words following. . . . what of those God-
> possibled souls that we nightly impossibilise, which is the sin
> against the Holy Ghost, Very God, Lord and Giver of Life?
> For, sirs, he said, our lust is brief. We are means to those small
> creatures within us and nature has other ends than we. (389)

"Copulation without population" (423) is anathema to
him, just as it is to the church he thinks to repudiate.
Whereas Bloom—to whom let us now revert—is a known
possessor of contraceptives (721), his antipathy to "im-
possibilising" falling (or seeming to fall) within the world
of speculation. But speculation of a distinct kind. Bloom's
anti-impossibilizing is bodied forth as often as otherwise in
his deficient grasp of such unrecondite matters as the effect
a dark surface has upon light, or the inimicality of salt and
submergence:

> Where was the chap I saw in that picture somewhere? Ah, in
> the dead sea, floating on his back, reading a book with a parasol
> open. Couldn't sink if you tried: so thick with salt. Because the
> weight of the water, no, the weight of the body in the water is
> equal to the weight of the. Or is it the volume is equal of the
> weight? It's a law something like that. (72)

Simple ignorance, it may be protested, antipreclusion we
would be better without. But there are facets at play here
and a dimension to be found which not only improve Joyce
but impair Arnold. What I allude to is the former's recognition and the latter's suspicion of the unconscious. Let us

examine (our first example) Bloom's puzzlement over the effect darkness exerts upon light and see what it suggests.

He crossed to the bright side, avoiding the loose cellarflap of number seventyfive. The sun was nearing the steeple of George's church. Be a warm day I fancy. Specially in these black clothes feel it more. Black conducts, reflects (refracts is it?), the heat. But I couldn't go in that light suit. Make a picnic of it. (57)

In extenuation of Bloom's having too many explanations for a natural phenomenon might be mentioned the sheer fecundity he displays, Bloom whose ability to hold forth at length on any subject excites comment from the narrator of the Cyclops episode (316). Ignorance, clearly it is, not to know, but an ignorance the far side of vacuity and one thus reflective of a certain *quantity* of experience. Experience with what, it will be queried, with light, heat, blackness? Yes, both physical and psychic. For what Bloom has done in frequent contradistinction to Stephen is to have censored little or nothing out of his apprehension of reality[26] . . . such that the resultant purview is an agglomerate of mind and heart and sense, a veritable potpourri of possibility which, if replete with error, does partake of something like the breadth of life . . . and life's complexity.

In a world where words like *unenlightened, blindness,* and *benightment* are unambiguously expressive of ignorance, is it not singular that Joyce shows on occasion in *Ulysses* intimations (and then some) of the belief in a *positive* relationship between light and darkness?

Gone too from the world, Averroes and Moses Maimonides, dark men in mien and movement, flashing in their mocking mirrors the obscure soul of the world, a darkness shining in brightness which brightness could not comprehend. (28)

And, inasmuch as the above are Stephen's ruminations, ponder something we are told of Bloom (our being practiced enough to know that Joyce is often at his most serious when endeavoring facetiae):

With what meditations did Bloom accompany his demonstration to his companion of various constellations?
Meditations of evolution increasingly vaster: of the moon invisible in incipient lunation, approaching perigee: of *the infinite lattiginous scintillating uncondensed milky way, discernible by daylight by an observer placed at the lower end of a cylindrical vertical shaft 5000 ft deep sunk from the surface towards the centre of the earth.* (698) (Italics added)

Darkness not only as tolerant of light but as out-and-out productive!

A bit earlier I described Bloom's consciousness as being at a lower level than Stephen's, a level whereon the energies of moral cognizance (Hebraism) and dispassionately intellectual awareness (Hellenism) were less divergent, with the result that Bloom is spared Stephen's particular rigidity. In point of fact, there is in Bloom a decided overlapping of the two impulses, which might account for his frequently precarious purchase on things intellectual. For alienation, rejection, of several sorts has caused his moral vision to double, treble, even quadruple, that he might somehow be able to "account" for things, explanatorily "accommodate" them; and this accommodation, multiplicity of accountableness, accordingly (given the specific psyche in question) finds its way into areas of explanation other than moral. The upshot of all of which is that what underlies Bloom's especial ignorance is the very thing for which we esteem him—his indulgence, tolerance, broad recognition of human variability. Darkness in him, then, at least one kind of darkness, may be seen to originate in his fundamental decency—"brightest" surely of human differentiae.

As noted, Arnold throughout *Culture and Anarchy* evidences a distrust of what Ibsen calls in *The Wild Duck* the "night side of existence." And perhaps Joyce indicates an awareness of this deficiency in his predecessor when he gives us in Circe (both masked with Arnold's face) Philip Drunk and Philip Sober (518), twins who—in addition to Weldon Thornton's Philip of Macedon association[27]—hark back, it seems to me, to Tacitus's remarks on the Teutonic reverence for irrationality:

Drinking bouts, lasting a day and night, are not considered in any way disgraceful. Such quarrels as inevitably arise over the cups are seldom settled by mere hard words, more often by blows and wounds. None the less, they often make banquets an occasion for discussing such serious affairs as the reconciliation of enemies, the forming of marriage alliances, the adoption of new chiefs, and even the choice of peace or war. At no other time, they feel, is the heart so open to frank suggestions or so quick to warm to a great appeal. The Germans are neither canny nor cunning, and take advantage of the occasion to unbosom themselves of their most secret thoughts; every soul is naked and exposed. The next day, comes reconsideration, and so due account is taken of both occasions. They debate at a time which cuts out pretence, they decide at a time that precludes mistake.[28]

Notwithstanding, Arnold does provide us with a way of viewing *Ulysses* that, while obscure at times, opens upon certain areas wherein commonplaces in Joyce criticism (such as that commonplace of the incommensurability of Bloom and Stephen) are revealed as somewhat equivocal. In a work so vast in intellectual background, may it be that

Joyce was trying to warn us against too fixed, small an interpretation when of the sandwich men, sign bearers, advertising (Bloom's métier) H. E. L. Y. S.—*Wisdom* Hely's—it was the *Y* which lagged behind? (154)

NOTES

1. Matthew Arnold, *Culture and Anarchy*, ed. R. H. Super (Ann Arbor: University of Michigan Press, 1965), p. 163. All subsequent citations are from this edition.

2. Arnold, op. cit., p. 165.

3. Harry Levin, *James Joyce; A Critical Introduction* (Norfolk, Connecticut: New Directions, 1960), pp. 85–86.

4. In a footnote Arnold explains that he gives the foreign word *Renaissance* an English form in anticipation of the movement it denotes coming increasingly to interest his compatriots.

5. Richard Ellmann, *James Joyce* (New York: Oxford University Press, 1959), pp. 407–08.

6. Joseph Frank, "Spatial Form in Modern Literature," *Sewanee Review* 53 (Spring, Summer, and Autumn 1945).

7. Arnold, op. cit., p. 220.

8. Ibid., p. 104.

9. "I am delivered from the bondage of Bentham! the fanaticism of his adherents can touch me no longer. I feel the inadequacy of his mind and ideas for supplying the rule of human society, for perfection. Culture tends always thus to deal with the men of a system, of disciples, of a school; with men like Comte, or the late Mr. Buckle, or Mr. Mill." Ibid., p. 111.

10. James Joyce, *Ulysses* (New York: Random House, 1961), p. 277. All subsequent citations are from this edition.

11. The fact that there actually was a Dublin Jew called Hunter reported to be a cuckold and twice met by Joyce fails, of course, to diminish the import of the name. Consider Farrington's watchful employer in "Counterparts," Mr. Alleyne (all-eyes), and the circumstance that John Stanislaus Joyce had an astringent business associate named Henry Alleyn.

12. José Ortega y Gasset, *The Revolt of the Masses* (New York: Norton, 1957), p. 63.

13. S. L. Goldberg, *The Classical Temper, A Study of James Joyce's "Ulysses"* (London: Chatto & Windus, 1961), p. 258.

14. Arnold, op. cit., pp. 96–97.

15. Richard Kain, *Fabulous Voyager: A Study of James Joyce's "Ulysses"* (New York: Viking Press, 1959), p. 97.

16. Arnold, op. cit., pp. 168–69.

17. That it is legitimate to employ the earlier work to augment our understanding of Stephen is made apparent any number of times in *Ulysses;* for example, Stephen's being exposed in the Aeolus episode to the words "I see it in your face" and being reminded of the unfair pandying at Clongowes Wood.

18. Arnold, op. cit., p. 167.

19. James Joyce, *A Portrait of the Artist as a Young Man* (New York: Viking Press, 1968), pp. 212–13.

20. Arnold, op. cit., p. 167.

21. Warren D. Anderson has pointed out, in his *Matthew Arnold and the Classical Tradition* (Ann Arbor: University of Michigan Press, 1965), that Hellenism was very much concerned with right conduct and not exclusively intellectual clarity, Stephen thus amending through example a prescription—Arnold's—not so carefully written as it might have been . . . or, as prescriptions ought never to be, hyperbolically set down.

22. Frank Budgen, *James Joyce and the Making of "Ulysses"* (Bloomington: Indiana University Press, 1960), p. 105.

23. Arnold, op. cit., p. 94.

24. Ibid., p. 113.

25. Ibid., p. 143.

26. Weigh Bloom's inability to censor that which to him is most repugnant during his June-day wanderings—the Boylan-Molly rendezvous—an inability not altogether to be diagnosed as masochistic.

27. Weldon Thornton, *Allusions in "Ulysses": An Annotated List* (Chapel Hill: University of North Carolina Press, 1968), p. 398.

28. Cornelius Tacitus, *Germania* in *On Britain and Germany*, trans. H. Mattingly (Baltimore: Penguin Books, n.d.), pp. 119–20.

Ulysses: The Making of an Irish Myth

BERNARD BENSTOCK

8

TRIESTE- ZÜRICH-PARIS, 1914–1921: the subscript on the last page of *Ulysses*[1] capsulizes the Joycean odyssey across the European continent in search of a stasis suitable for literary work. In the process the novel was conceived, completed, and published, a self-exile's account of his turbulent affair of the heart with the most impossible of mistresses, that virgin-whore called Ireland. Of *Dubliners* Joyce had commented to a prospective publisher that he intended it as a "chapter in the moral history" of Ireland; *Ulysses* proved to be no less so, but a gigantic augmentation of the running quarrel, containing the indignations of a lacerated heart and the painstaking fidelity with which the Irish writer recollected in exile the specific details of the face he could never forget. What he recaptured is primarily a fictionalized depiction of the lives of typical Dubliners (and several rare ones) against the backdrop of the city as it existed in 1904: persistent memory, a Thom's *Official Directory*, Dublin newspapers, and responses culled from correspondents at home contributed the pieces for the mosaic.

In addition he embellished his epic novel with the debris of Ireland's history, mythology, folklore, and contemporary politics, boasting to Frank Budgen: "I want . . . to give a picture of Dublin so complete that if the city one day suddenly disappeared from the earth it could be constructed out of my book."[2] Like the face of Jamey Tyrone, *Ulysses* has the map of Ireland all over it.

What Joyce facetiously passed off as the "cultic twalette" in *Finnegans Wake* was in its ascendancy when the artist as a young man was attempting to gain a foothold in the dominant literary circles of Dublin. An awareness of the long existence of a Celtic Ireland inspired the generation of writers that immediately preceded Joyce, and held its own with Joyce's generation as well; nor did it leave Joyce himself untouched: although his attitude may have remained sardonic, he nonetheless kept himself thoroughly versed. It is with malicious mirth that Joyce introduces Hibernicism in *Ulysses* as the preoccupation of the unappetizing Englishman, Haines: he is in Dublin investigating Irish folklore, and neither of his two Irish hosts seems to share his enthusiasms. Haines attempts to speak Gaelic to the ignorant milkwoman (she thinks it might be French) and soon finds himself being mocked by Buck Mulligan, who whimsically passes off his bit of modern Irish wit as mock folklore:

—That's folk, he said very earnestly, for your book, Haines. Five lines of text and ten pages of notes about the folk and the fish-gods of Dundrum. Printed by the weird sisters in the year of the big wind.

He turned to Stephen and asked in a fine puzzled voice, lifting his brows:

—Can you recall, brother, is mother Grogan's tea and water

pot spoken of in the Mabinogion or is it in the Upanishads?
(12–13)

A professed admirer of Stephen's contemporary mode of
wit, Haines nonetheless owes his primary allegiance to
Celtic lore, so that when Stephen is delivering his promised
exegesis of *Hamlet,* Haines is off at the bookshops in quest
of Douglas Hyde's *Lovesongs of Connacht.* Joyce reserves
the prerogative for a final jab, the momentary appearance
of the English student in the Lying-in Hospital to arrange
an assignation with Mulligan; the Gothic novel style serves
Joyce well to pinpoint Haines: "He had a portfolio full of
Celtic literature in one hand, in the other a phial marked
Poison" (412).

Haines's Irish interests are magnified by the citizen's
Irish obsessions. That larger-than-lifesized cycloptic an-
tagonist lives exclusively in an imaginary world of Celtic
mythology, interrupted only by bitter recollection that his
native land is under constant seige by an inferior race. His
Ireland harks back to the dawn of history; its flag precedes
any harp-encrusted emblem, "the oldest flag afloat, the flag
of the province of Desmond and Thomond, three crowns
on a blue field, the three sons of Milesius" (328). By contrast Leopold Bloom is indeed a Johnny-come-lately Irishman who still swears by the Irish harp, "Only the harp.
Lovely gold glowering light. . . . Poop of a lovely. . . .
Golden ship. Erin. The harp that once or twice" (271),
whereas the citizen denounces that presumably Irish symbol—"none of your Henry Tudor's harps, no" (328). The
legendary Celtic founding of Ireland by the sons of Milesius, a keystone of the citizen's patriotism, receives only
mocking lip-service from Stephen Dedalus during the

drinking bout in the hospital: "Return, return, Clan Milly:
forget me not, O Milesian" (393).

During the course of the Cyclops chapter the booming
voice of the citizen is countered often by several others, the
least of which is the voice of sweet reason that is Bloom's.
The anonymous narrator sneers constantly at the citizen
(within the safe confines of his private thoughts), while
vignettes of mock-heroic giganticism are added by Joyce
to hound the citizen's exaggerated pronouncements. The
sotto voce of the narrator is contemptuous, but the epic
digressions resound loudly with mockery for such subjects
as "the ranns of ancient Celtic bards" (312), the revival of
the Gaelic language ("the winged speech of the sea-divided
Gael"—324), the artwork of the ancient Irish ("tastefully
executed in the style of ancient Celtic ornament, a work
which reflects credit on the makers, Messrs Jacob *agus*
Jacob"—243), and their tribal customs: "then lifted he
in his rude great brawny strengthy hands the medher of
dark strong foamy ale and, uttering his tribal slogan *Lamh
Dearg Abu*, he drank to the undoing of his foes" (325).
Every gesture of the superpatriot, from the handling of the
Jacobs biscuit tin to the downing of his pint, is augmented
in grandiose style. His pocket handkerchief balloons into
a "muchtreasured and intricately embroidered ancient
Irish facecloth attributed to Solomon of Droma and Manus
Tomaltach og MacDonogh" (331), while his advocacy of
the Irish language and the Gaelic League is deflated by the
narrator: "one night I went in with a fellow into one of
their musical evenings, song and dance about she could get
up on a truss of hay she could my Maureen Lay, and there
was a fellow with a Ballyhooly blue ribbon badge spiffing
out of him in Irish and a lot of colleen bawns going about

with temperance beverages" (311). And long after the five o'clock session at Bernard Kiernan's, the mocking of the citizen continues in *Ulysses:* his insistence upon ancient Irish athletic events in lieu of effete English games like tennis brings forth Irish funeral sports in which "Tom Rochford, winner in athlete's singlet and breeches, arrives at the head of the national hurdle handicap and leaps into the void. He is followed by a race of runners and leapers" (598). Whereas Homer needed only one Odysseyan No-man to take the measure of the giant Polyphemus, Joyce avails himself of a host of mockers to drown out the chauvinism of the blustering citizen.

From Joyce's viewpoint a mystique of absurd proportions had grown up around matters Celtic, abetted by the hothouse gardening of his enthusiastic countrymen, and he set out in *Ulysses* to satirize the monstrous myth. The Cyclops chapter has the fullest complement of Joycean satire, so that even a prosaic matter like a will being probated in a Dublin courtroom requires the services of so august a body of jurors as "the high sinhedrim of the twelve tribes of Iar, for every tribe one man, of the tribe of Patrick and of the tribe of Hugh and of the tribe of Owen and of the tribe of Conn and of the tribe of Oscar and of the tribe of Fergus and of the tribe of Finn and of the tribe of Dermot and of the tribe of Cormac and of the tribe of Kevin and of the tribe of Caolte and of the tribe of Ossian, there being in all twelve good men and true" (323)—if the Irish fancy themselves as an Israel unto themselves, Joyce contributes his commemoration in true Old Testament style. A ceremonial hanging is attended by a group called the F. O. T. E. I. (a "picturesque foreign delegation known as the Friends of the Emerald Isle"—307) who engage in a battle royal over the dating of Saint Patrick's birth; after the mammoth donnybrook the question is settled by ingenious compromise whereby the two contending dates, March 8 and March 9, are added together to form March 17. In the hospital Irish medicine is exalted ("hostels, leperyards, sweating chambers, plaguegraves"—384), while in the Circe chapter the Tuatha de Danann sea-god, Mananaan MacLir, celebrated by the conquering Milesians, is ushered in by an epic stage direction: "In the cone of the searchlight behind the coalscuttle, ollave, holyeyed, the bearded figure of Mananaan MacLir broods, chin on knees. He rises slowly. A cold seawind blows from his druid mantle. About his head writhe eels and elvers. He is encrusted with weeds and shells. His right hand hold a bicycle pump. His left hand grasps a huge crayfish by its two talons" (510). In Bloom's kitchen Stephen insists that the dating of St. Patrick's conversion of the Irish requires rectification, since he could not have been sent by a fifth-century pope to an Ireland ruled by a third-century monarch. The Stephen-Bloom exchange of fragmental knowledge of the Gaelic and Hebrew languages produces still another travesty in which "both having been taught on the plain of Shinar 242 years after the deluge in the seminary instituted by Fenius Farsaigh, descendant of Noah, progenitor of Israel, and ascendant of Heber and Heremon, progenitors of Ireland: their archeological, genealogical, hagiographical, exegetical, homilectic, toponomastic, historical and religious literatures comprising the works of rabbis and culdees, Torah, Talmud (Mischna and Ghemara) Massor, Pentateuch, Book of the Dun Cow, Book of Ballymote, Garland of Howth, Book of Kells" (688). It is left to the literal view of Leopold Bloom, however, to isolate the mundane item of reality into which overblown myth is eventually reduced: the Eblana name that Ptolemy gave to the Dublin area, celebrated in the epic narrations of the Cyclops chapter, appears to Bloom in prosaic form as he passes the Dublin docks and gazes "abstractedly for the space of half a second or so in the direction of a bucket dredger, rejoicing in the farfamed name of Eblana, moored alongside Customhouse Quay and quite possibly out of repair" (619).

From legend to history there exists an Erin magnified into absolute glory by the reverence of the supercitizen, while an ironic Joyce follows along, charting a much lower road along the same course. Christian history begins in Ireland with Patrick, about whom Stephen expresses some doubts in dating and whose name he mockingly attaches to the nation itself. "Saint Patrick would want to land again at Ballykinlar and convert us, says the citizen [in reaction to the presence of Bloom in Ireland], after allowing things like that to contaminate our shores" (338). Thereafter appears a gigantic ecclesiastical procession of church dignitaries and luminaries, including such Irish (and pseudo-Irish) saints as "S. Laurence O'Toole and S. James of Dingle . . . and S. Columcille and S. Columba and S. Celestine and S. Colman and S. Kevin and S. Brendan and S. Frigidian and S. Senan and S. Fachtna and S. Columbanus and S. Gall and S. Fursey and S. Fintan and S. Fiacre . . . and S. Brigid and S. Attracta and S. Dympna" (339), until the final cortege of this epic confluence of the totems of Catholic Ireland brings "the reverend Father O'Flynn attended by Malachi and Patrick" to bless every nook and cranny of Kiernan's pub (340).

Many aspects of the secular history of Ireland are

touched on for Joycean purposes during the events of *Ulysses*. Early in the book Mr. Deasy, whose own married life reflects the unhappy event, complains that marital infidelity led to the Anglo-Norman invasion of Ireland ("a faithless wife first brought the strangers to our shore here, Mac-Murrough's wife and her leman O'Rourke, prince of Breffni"—34–35). With a profound capacity for getting his facts wrong, Deasy has reversed the two male figures: it was MacMurrough who absconded with O'Rourke's wife (perhaps even against her will). Later that afternoon the citizen proves to be as rankled and as unforgiving about the romance of A.D. 1152, but by mentioning no names he at least avoids confusing the participants: "The adulteress and her paramour brought the Saxon robbers here" (324). Deasy's attitude, anomalous for a West Briton, is apparently the result of his own homelife, while the citizen's is intended to discomfort Bloom—who had already committed himself by a slip of the tongue regarding "the wife's admirers" (313). Bloom attempts to divert attention from the distasteful subject, but the citizen persists: "A dishonoured wife . . . that's what's the cause of all our misfortunes" (324). His dislike for Bloom is immediate (and seemingly longstanding), perhaps stemming from the canvasser's associations with the *Freeman's Journal*, the "subsidised organ" (298); the dislike takes the form of virulent xenophobia and he is adamant in questioning Bloom's national affiliations. In the newspaper office, when Professor Mac-Hugh referred to "our lovely land" (124), Bloom quite innocently asked, "Whose land?" Now the question comes back to haunt him: "What is your nation if I may ask, says the citizen" (331). "Ireland, says Bloom. I was born here. Ireland" (331).

His nation and its history are in Bloom's thoughts on occasion during the course of the day, but they are rivalled by a persistent yearning for escape to the Levant, the fertile crescent in which he senses that he has ancient roots—as he is reminded by the advertisement for a planter's company north of Jaffa. Stephen, however, feels instinctively and irrevocably trapped by his native Irish roots: as he walks along Sandymount Strand his thoughts are of Viking ships that invaded and settled Dublin, and of whales stranded ashore in 1131, and of the times the Liffey froze in winter (facts culled by Joyce from the *Dublin Annals*). He imagines his twelfth-century ancestors: "from the starving cagework city a horde of jerkined dwarfs, my people, with flayers' knives, running, scaling, hacking in green blubbery whalemeat. Famine, plague and slaughters. Their blood is in me, their lusts my waves. I moved among them on the frozen Liffey, that I, a changeling, among the spluttering resin fires. I spoke to no-one: none to me" (45). Where the citizen envisions his forebears as heroic giants, Stephen sees his as domesticated dwarfs. To Stephen, for whom history is a nightmare, there is a direct personal association between the terrifying subcurrent of centuries of Irish history and the events taking place in his own life. Mulligan's role as usurper, as the enemy, is linked with the treachery and pretense persistent in the nation's history, and as he walks along the strand the thought of Buck's primrose waistcoat and his mockery of Stephen's fear of dogs causes his mind to play ironically with history: "Pretenders: live their lives. The Bruce's brother, Thomas Fitzgerald, silken knight, Percy Warbeck, York's false scion, in breeches of silk of whiterose ivory, wonder of a day, and Lambert Simnel, with a tail of nans and sutlers, a scullion crowned. All king's sons. Paradise of pretenders then and now" (45). The history of the race repeats itself in the lives of its individuals, and Mulligan is implicated in the nefarious acts of usurpers and pretenders. In his own voice, as the trumpeter of epical catalogues in the Cyclops chapter, Joyce engages upon a list of "Irish heroes and heroines of antiquity" which begins well enough but soon lapses into delightful absurdity: "Cuchulin, Conn of hundred battles, Niall of nine hostages, Brian of Kincora, the Ardri Malachi, Art MacMurragh, Shane O'Neill, Father John Murphy, Owen Roe, Patrick Sarsfield, Red Hugh O'Donnell, Red Jim MacDermott, Soggarth Eoghan O'Growney, Michael Dwyer, Francy Higgins, Henry Joy M'Cracken, Goliath, Horace Wheatley, Thomas Conneff, Peg Woffington, the Village Blacksmith, Captain Moonlight, Captain Boycott, Dante Alighieri, Christopher Columbus" (296–97), and others. Legitimate heroes coexist here with mockfigures and failed heroes and even traitors, and the Irish vein soon runs thin.

The rebellion of silken Thomas Fitzgerald, earl of Kildare against King Henry VIII in 1534, occupies not only Stephen's momentary thought on the beach but the activities of Ned Lambert and the Reverend Hugh C. Love later in the day. They visit the remains of St. Mary's Abbey, where the young knight had assembled his Council of State to declare against the king. Reverend Love, an Anglican clergyman, is presumably writing a book about the Geraldine rebellion and is being shown the historic site by Lambert. (Love's interest in Irish history parallels Haines's fascination for Irish folklore, and Joyce gratuitously merges the two during the Black Mass celebrated in the Circe chapter into the composite figure of "the Reverend Mr

Hugh C. Haines Love M.A."—599). The Geraldines are an interesting choice for Love, since they were not Gaels but seanghalls, nobility of Anglo-Norman descent who had come as conquerors and stayed on to become more Irish than the Irish, intermarrying with Celtic nobility and developing a hatred for the English monarchy across the Irish sea. The irony doubles when it becomes obvious that the abbey described by Lambert as "the most historic spot in all Dublin" (230) is being used by the Irish as a warehouse; it triples when we next learn that the Celtophilic Anglican is a landlord who has "distrained for rent" (245) from Father Bob Cowley. The pattern that Joyce meticulously constructs involves the English landlord whose deathgrip on Irish soil had caused the Land League agitation of the nineteenth century—and even professed admirers of Ireland remain its exploiters. The final piece of irony in the pattern includes the citizen. The same patriot who fumes against foreigners "swindling the peasants . . . and the poor" (323) is revealed as an absentee landlord himself, at least according to the narrator in Kiernan's: "As much as his bloody life is worth to go down and address his tall talk to the assembled multitude in Shanagolden where he daren't show his nose with the Molly Maguires looking for him to let daylight through him for grabbing the holding of an evicted tenant" (328).

This dubious distinction notwithstanding, the citizen is a compendium of Irish lore and a voluble cataloguer of the numerous instances of British misrule in Ireland. He discourses on the "sanctimonious Cromwell and his ironsides that put the women and children of Drogheda to the sword" (334), while his fellow Dubliners contribute other reminders (John Wyse Nolan: "We fought for the royal

Stuarts that reneged us against the Williamites and they betrayed us"—330; Ned Lambert: "the poor old woman told us that the French were on the sea and landed at Killala"—330). The narrator reports that Bloom and the citizen are "having an argument about the point, the brothers Sheares and Wolfe Tone beyond on Arbour Hill and Robert Emmet and die for your country, the Tommy Moore touch about Sara Curran and she's far from the land" (305). A contrast to the citizen's viewpoint has already been introduced in the person of Garrett Deasy, the Unionist schoolmaster who attempts to lecture Stephen much as his counterpart holds forth to anyone in the pub within earshot. "You think me an old fogey and an old tory," he says to Stephen, but attempts to counter this impression with the insistent statement, "I have rebel blood in me, too" (31). But this proves to be "on the spindle side" (31), and Deasy associates women with infidelity and treachery. Actually he is most proud of the fact that he is a descendant of a supporter of the Act of Union which tightened the British control of Ireland; yet if he prides himself in this loyalty in the male branch of his family, he is again incorrect, since Sir John Blackwood voted against rather than for the Union. What Stephen thinks of Deasy is easy to estimate from a reading of his thoughts as Deasy is talking away: "Glorious, pious and immortal memory. The lodge of Diamond in Armagh the splendid behung with corpses of papishes" (31). There may be an ironic echo in Stephen's quoting the opening phrase of the Orangeman's creed (*Glorious, pious and immortal*), since earlier that morning the initials g.p.i. had been used in a different context for Stephen: "That fellow I was with in the Ship last night, said Buck Mulligan, says you have g.p.i. . . . General paralysis of the insane" (6).

Nineteenth-century Irish history, beginning with the Act of Union and the beheading of Emmet three years later, is in itself a compendium of the nation's woes, and *Ulysses* records the significant events. Deasy himself spans much of the century: "I saw three generations since O'Connell's times," he chronicles, adding the absurd statement that "the orange lodges agitated for repeal of the union twenty years before O'Connell did" (31). "I saw the famine," he also reports. To the slightly younger citizen it was not a contemporary event but one about which he is far angrier: "They were driven out of house and home in the black 47. Their mudcabins and their shielings by the roadside were laid low by the batteringram. . . . But the Sassenach tried to starve the nation at home while the land was full of crops that the British hyenas bought and sold in Rio de Janeiro" (329–30). (The keeper of the cabman's shelter, presumed to be Fitzharris the Invincible, picks up the topic many hours later, itemizing the enormous wealth of natural resources and foodstuffs that would make Ireland the richest nation in the world were it not for English thievery.) Yet it is neither O'Connell nor the Great Hunger that is the dominant aspect of the century discussed in *Ulysses,* but the person of Charles Stewart Parnell, the ghostly presence that haunted the first chapter of *A Portrait of the Artist* and "Ivy Day in the Committee Room." And it is as ghost that he reappears in *Ulysses.* "Let us go round to the chief's grave" (112) suggests the still-loyal Joe Hynes at Glasnevin, and the speculation begins again that Parnell may not actually be dead but awaiting his opportunity to return to lead the Irish once again. Jack Power's sentimental conjecture, however, is quickly deflated by the bitterly realistic Hynes, who pronounces Parnell very much dead. Two hours later Bloom sees the ghost of the chief, his lackluster brother John Howard Parnell, and recalls that when the lesser Parnell was defeated in an election by David Sheehy, "Simon Dedalus said when they put him in parliament that Parnell would come back from the grave and lead him out of the House of Commons by the arm" (165). And in the cabman's shelter the ghost looms large in the desultory conversations between Fitzharris, a jarvey, a sailor, and others (and in Bloom's thoughts thereafter). Joyce recapitulates the Parnell myth in his casual summary of the drift of the talk:

> One morning you would open the paper, the cabman affirmed, and read, *Return of Parnell.* He bet them what they liked. A Dublin fusilier was in that shelter one night and said he saw him in South Africa. Pride it was killed him. He ought to have done away with himself or lain low for a time after Committee Room No. 15 until he was his old self again with no-one to point a finger at him. Then they would all to a man have gone down on their marrowbones to him to come back when he had recovered his senses. Dead he wasn't. Simply absconded somewhere. The coffin they brought over was full of stones. He changed his name to De Wet, the Boer general. He made a mistake to fight the priests. And so forth and so on. (648–49)

Reduced to such prosaic terms and told in the weary tone of the end of a long day, the story of Parnell echoes the hopelessness of Irish political aspirations at the end of the century—and the hollow-sounding hopes of the new one.

Bloom's interest in Parnell's demise centers largely on the scandal with Kitty O'Shea which he sees as an analogue to his own marital situation. (Deasy, in his comments on the faithless Devorgilla of 1152, had added: "A woman too brought Parnell low"—35). But the incident that had previously threatened to capsize the uncrowned king, the

Phoenix Park murders, receives even greater attention from the Dubliners in *Ulysses*. It too has assumed the proportion of legend, although a contemporary event in the lives of those discussing it: "That was in eightyone, sixth of May . . . before you were born, I suppose" (136), says Myles Crawford to Stephen (he is apparently accurate about Stephen's date of birth but not about the date of the murders) and launches into an account of the journalistic feat of cabling the route taken by the murder car to a New York newspaper. The actual names of the Invincibles who committed the deed are beginning to fade, the editor listing "Tim Kelly, or Kavanagh, I mean, Joe Brady and the rest" (136). (It was Kelly not Kavanagh.) Bloom has the same difficulty in All Hallows church, where a notice of a sermon on Saint Peter Claver intrudes when he tries to remember the name of one of the assassins: "That fellow that turned queen's evidence on the invincibles he used to receive the, Carey was his name, the communion every morning. This very church. Peter Carey, No, Peter Claver I am thinking of. Denis Carey" (81). (His name was James Carey, but Peter Carey was also indicted.) Even more mysterious is the belief, voiced by O'Madden Burke in the newspaper office and assumed by Bloom in the cabman's shelter, that the shelter was run by the man who drove the getaway car for the Invincibles, Skin-the-Goat Fitzharris (his name too was James). He thus becomes a living legend, a mystery quite casually accepted by Burke, Bloom, and others; he never reveals his actual identity, but is definitely in character prophesying the return of Parnell and the imminent demise of the British Empire, insisting that he "considered no Irishman worthy of his salt that served it" (641). In his conjecture about "how much palmoil the British Government gave" (639) to engineer the wrecking of the Galway Harbour scheme, Skin-the-Goat has a strange ally in Garrett Deasy, who had averred to Stephen that morning that it was a "Liverpool ring that jockeyed the Galway harbour scheme" (33). Considering the notoriety of Fitzharris and Brady and the rest of the knife-wielding Invincibles, it is not surprising that the citizen has them already enshrined in his pantheon of martyrs for Ireland: "So of course the citizen was only waiting for the wink of a word and he starts gassing out of him about the invincibles and the old guard and the men of sixtyseven and who fears to speak of ninetyeight" (305).

More recent events for 1904 include the advocacy by the Gaelic League of the teaching of the Irish language and the new political Sinn Fein organization of Arthur Griffith. When Professor MacHugh recalls the Fitzgibbon-Taylor debate, he reminds his listeners that it took place when advocating the revival of Irish was a new issue and the movement still a weak one. To the citizen it is of paramount importance and he rails against the "shoneens that can't speak their own language" (310). But Joyce, who had begun the study of Gaelic under Patrick Pearse and given it up, was none too convinced, and in the *Evening Telegraph* for 16 June 1904 Bloom finds the delightful headline, "Lovemaking in Irish £200 damages" (647). Sinn Fein and Griffith are in the thoughts of both Bloom and Stephen during the day (and Molly at night), and of course the citizen voices his own: he is quite specific that the "Ourselves Alone" significance of Sinn Fein implies as definite exclusiveness. (*"Sinn Fein!* says the citizen. *Sinn Fein amhain!* The friends we love are by our side and the foes we hate before us"—306). He reads an anti-British spoof from Griffith's

United Irishman, and when asked if it is by Griffith he re-
plies, "No. . . . It's only initialled: P." "And a very good initial too" (334), comments Joe Hynes, to whom it signifies
Parnell. Stephen, as one might guess, is not very enthusiastic about the new movement, associating it with the type
of narrow-minded fanaticism that was responsible for the
death of Socrates: "But neither the midwife's lore nor the
caudlelectures saved him from the archons of Sinn Fein
and their noggin of hemlock" (190). Joyce, however, in
Trieste and Zurich, at times stated that Sinn Fein was indeed the only chance for Ireland.

Despite the ambivalence of his own position as a self-
exile from Ireland, Joyce was particularly mordant in his
depiction of the attitudes in his native city toward the political action necessary to implement a change. Apathy, the
handmaiden of paralysis and kin to living death, is the
prime characteristic, while vociferous talk serves as a hollow substitute for action. From his battle position on the
pub stool the citizen marshalls his armies of harangue,
denigrating the Saxon and lauding the Celt, both to absurd
degrees of exaggeration. "No music and no art and no
literature worthy of the name," he declares. "Any civilisa-
tion they have they stole from us. Tonguetied sons of bas-
tards' ghosts" (325). His excess in such instances, however,
is offset in others, when he does put his finger on an exact
symptom of the malignant situation. He excoriates the
Dublin newspapers that have sold out to the establishment,
particularly the *Irish Independent* ("founded by Parnell
to be the workingman's friend"—298). There is more humor
than he actually intends in his readings from the items of
births, marriages, and deaths, a catalogue of English names
and addresses, but the point is certainly well made—and

the humor contributes to it. In the nightmare of the Circe chapter, where Joyce concentrates his fantastic capsules of his characters, the citizen appears wearing a "huge emerald muffler" and carrying a shillalegh, and pronounces his rhymed malediction on his sworn enemies: "May the God above / Send down a [dove] / With teeth as sharp as razors / To slit the throats / Of the English dogs / That hanged our Irish leaders" (593).[3]

His patriotic bombast is no isolated example: other Dublin citizens contribute to the composite portrait of platform patriotism on display in *Ulysses*. The newspaper office, where political terrorism is discussed in the light of a journalistic coup, shows the windbag element in their glory. Professor MacHugh in particular holds forth like an only slightly better educated version of the citizen, lamenting the fact that he speaks in the language of the oppressor: "I speak the tongue of a race the acme of whose mentality is the maxim: time is money. Material domination. *Dominus!* Lord! Where is the spirituality? Lord Jesus! Lord Salisbury. A sofa in a westend club" (133). Although he scores the British for their lack of spiritual qualities, MacHugh can hardly be said to embody any of his own. Yet Joyce's caricature of the professor is not wholly lampoon, for absurd as he is MacHugh nonetheless echoes Joyce's own witticism regarding the prosaic occupations of the English: his designation of them as closetmakers and cloacamakers is Joyce's own. On numerous occasions Joyce told the anecdote about Greeks and Semites building temples, while Romans and British built waterclosets, and Frank Budgen reports that when he confronted Joyce with H. G. Wells's statement that *A Portrait* betrayed a cloacal obsession, Joyce averred that "it's Wells's countrymen who build water-closets wherever they go."[4] (The distinction should probably be made between those who are spiritual- ly obsessed with the cloacal and those who are mundanely involved with sanitation and hygiene.) Even Buck Mulli- gan makes his caustic evaluation of the British (Haines in particular): "God, these bloody English. Bursting with money and indigestion" (4). And Joyce's ultimate parody of the excess of lip service to terrorist action against the occupiers is included in the Circe chapter: when Stephen is reluctantly being pressured into defending himself against Private Carr, Old Gummy Granny steps out of the phantasmagoric void and hands him a dagger, saying: "Re- move him, acushla. At 8.35 a.m. you will be in heaven and Ireland will be free" (600). Such sentiments and such substitutes for political sophistication are the stuff of propa- gandistic drama; Stephen's compound of cowardice and resignation are closer to the reality of existence in Dublin, 1904.

Chauvinism has often been the natural concomitant of a nationalistic awakening, and has been spurred rather than discouraged by an accompanying defeatism. It is also fre- quently an outlet for frustrated aspirations. The John F. Taylor speech quoted by the failed lawyer O'Molloy likens the plight of Ireland with that of Israel in Egyptian bond- age, trumpeting the manifest destiny of a chosen Irish peo- ple, and although the rhetoric is broadcast in stentorian tones, reality intrudes when a "dumb belch of hunger cleft his speech." It is essentially a preoccupation with a glorious past (and an inflated version of that glory) that is the domi- nant motif of the patriotic rhetoric recorded in *Ulysses.* When the citizen forecasts an Irish future ("Our harbours that are empty now will be full again"—328), he relies heavily on the past ("a fleet of masts of the Galway Lynches and the Cavan O'Reillys and the O'Kennedys of Dublin when the earl of Desmond could make a treaty with the emperor Charles the Fifth himself"—328): nostalgia takes the place of precise planning when the dismal present makes the future seem rather hopeless. The empty harbors cannot be ignored, and the citizen is not always ludicrous but often pathetic in his despair. "And our eyes are on Europe," he asserts, but quickly retreats into the past again: "We had our trade with Spain and the French and with the Flemings before those mongrels were pupped" (327). The pups have become bulldogs and are now very much in command, so that when another patriotic windbag, the ablebodied seaman W. B. Murphy, indulges in the same sort of self-congratulations he betrays the inescapable facts of the present condition. "Who's the best troops in the army?" he asks rhetorically. "And the best jumpers and racers? And the best admirals and generals we've got?" His answer is obvious, but in celebrating the excellence of the "Irish Catholic peasant," Murphy reveals more than he intended by terming his champion "the backbone of our empire" (641). The empire in question is *theirs*, not *ours*.

The glorification of that archetypal peasant was a mainstay of the movement for Irish revival, and was as absurd and pathetic to Joyce as the boosting of the Russian peasant had been to Chekhov. In *Stephen Hero* Joyce revealed his mistrust of that peasant. Stephen characterized him in terms of "the calculation of coppers, the weekly debauch and the weekly piety—a life lived in cunning and fear between the shadows of the parish chapel and the asylum!"[5] and in *A Portrait* he noted in his diary: "I fear him. I fear his redrimmed horny eyes."[6] Whereas the young artist re-

cords his discomfort and antipathy, the older Joyce resorts
to burlesque, especially in the Circe chapter, where Bloom,
finding his dreams of glory beginning to pale and the popu-
lace that had exalted him now turning against him, assumes the stage-Irishman's pose ("In caubeen with clay
pipe stuck in the band, dusty brogues, an emigrant's red
handkerchief bundle in his hand, leading a black bogoak
pig by a sugaun, with a smile in his eye") and mock-Synge
diction: "Let me be going now, woman of the house, for
by all the goats in Connemara I'm after having the father
and mother of a bating" (499). (When he was running for
office he had managed to show everyone that he was wearing green socks.) Old Gummy Granny, a particularly dis-
gusting exemplar of Ireland as a poor old woman, also appears in the Circe hallucinations, and employs the cloying
language of sentimental patriotism: "Ireland's sweetheart,
the king of Spain's daughter, alanna. Strangers in my house,
bad manners to them! (*She keens with banshee woe.*)
Ochone! Ochone! Silk of the kine! (*She wails.*) You met
with poor old Ireland and how does she stand?" (595). Stephen, however, is still not prey to her lure, and pronounces
his curse as soon as he sees her, eching his aphorism from
A Portrait: "The old sow that eats her farrow" (595). Nor
is Bloom allied to her nostalgic cause. Safe at home after
the day's escapades he gloats over his retort to the citizen
and mocks the chauvinist's conception of the Irishman and
his god: "mostly they appear to imagine he came from
Carrick-on-Shannon or somewhere about in the county
Sligo" (658). To add to the deflation there is Molly Bloom's
verdict on the Irish revival movement from the female
point of view: "Kathleen Kearney and her lot of squealers
Miss This Miss That Miss Theother lot of sparrowfarts

skitting around talking about politics they know as much
as my backside anything in the world to make themselves
someway interesting Irish homemade beauties" (762).
How pitiful then is the citizen's paean to the grandeur of
the Gael and the glory of the Celt in his celebration of a
remote past that has only the remotest chance of being
revived:

Where are our missing twenty millions of Irish should be here
today instead of four, our lost tribes? And our potteries and
textiles, the finest in the whole world! And our wool that was
sold in Rome in the time of Juvenal and our flax and our damask
from the looms of Antrim and our Limerick lace, our tanneries
and our white flint glass down there by Ballybough and our
Huguenot poplin that we have since Jacquard de Lyon and our
woven silk and our Foxford tweeds and ivory raised point from
the Carmelite convent in New Ross, nothing like it in the whole
wide world! Where are the Greek merchants that came through
the pillars of Hercules, the Gibraltar now grabbed by the foe
of mankind, with gold and Tyrian purple to sell in Wexford at
the fair of Carmen? Read Tacitus and Ptolemy, even Giraldus
Cambrensis. Wine, peltries, Connemara marble, silver from
Tipperary, second to none, our far-famed horses even today,
the Irish hobbies, with king Philip of Spain offering to pay customs duties for the right to fish in our waters. What do the
yellowjohns of Anglia owe us for our ruined trade and our
ruined hearths? And the beds of the Barrow and Shannon they
won't deepen with millions of acres of marsh and bog to make
us all die of consumption. (326)

For the moment the citizen is not being the bullying bigot
that is often his primary characteristic, but an eloquent
spokesman for the pathos of the Irish condition, voicing the
legitimate complaint of the ruined Irishman, who nonetheless compounds that ruin with an attitude of self-pity and
narrow patriotism.

To compound the futility even further the Irish resorted to an internecine warfare that aided only their oppressors, a suicidal policy of dividing themselves while conquered. The religious war between Catholics and Protestants for four centuries assured the British of a successful hold on Ireland. In the Black Mass in the Circe chapter, when Carr is about to assault Stephen, "in strident discord peasants and townsmen of Orange and Green factions sing *Kick the Pope* and *Daily, daily sing to Mary*" (600). Moments before the battlelines were drawn between The Virago and The Bawd, each in turn shouting her Irish slogan: "Green above the red, says he. Wolfe Tone"; "The red's as good as the green, and better. Up the soldiers! Up King Edward!" (593). Such factionalism existed as a historic condition, one which has been a plague to Ireland always. The inability of the Irish to unite in common cause gives rise to another Joycean catalogue, in this case of the historic antagonists in the nation's internal struggle. Joyce's technique is a familiar one by now: the list begins with actual figures from history but dissolves into comic absurdity in a development from the factual to the ridiculous: "Armed heroes spring up from furrows. They exchange in amity the pass of knights of the red cross and fight duels with cavalry sabres: Wolfe Tone against Henry Grattan, Smith O'Brien against Daniel O'Connell, Michael Davitt against Isaac Butt, Justin M'Carthy against Parnell, Arthur Griffith against John Redmond, John O'Leary against Lear O'-Johnny, Lord Edward Fitzgerald against Lord Gerald Fitzedward, The O'Donoghue of the Glens against The Glens of the O'Donoghue" (598–99). Worse still than this self-destructive fratricide is the long history of treachery that accompanied the struggles, the endless dynasty of traitors and informers and police spies. In Oxen of the Sun Joyce employs the style of Edmund Burke to indict the typical opportunist: "During the recent war whenever the enemy had a temporary advantage with his granados did this traitor to his kind not seize the moment to discharge his piece against the empire of which he is a tenant at will while he trembled for the security of his four per cents?" (409). The condition of a divided nation was a fixed one long before the political partition of 1922. The citizens of Dublin in 1904 went about their daily business in a city of invisible walls, some owing their allegiance to an empire which designated Dublin as its second city, while others saw it as the seventh city of Christendom destined to take its place as the capital of a reborn nation. Some of Joyce's people skirt the boundaries of the two countries or live ambiguously in both. When the totem of British Ireland, the lord lieutenant and governor-general, William Humble, earl of Dudley, wends his way in the leading carriage of the viceregal cortege across the face of the city, he is respectfully greeted by Tom Kernan, Simon Dedalus, Reverend Love, Tom Rochford, Denis Breen, the Trinity College porter, and the son of Paddy Dignam. Dudley's opposite number is the citizen, that self-appointed guardian of the national spirit, who holds his court later that afternoon in Barney Kiernan's, where he accepts tribute in the form of pints of stout from his loyal subjects. But neither Stephen Dedalus nor Leopold Bloom bends the knee to either pretender, although each finds himself governed by ambiguous and conflicting motives in their reluctance to serve.

In *A Portrait of the Artist as a Young Man* Stephen had already declared himself against those voices that made demands upon him: "when the movement towards national revival had begun to be felt in the college yet another voice had bidden him be true to his country and help to raise up her language and tradition."[7] In a conversation with Haines he again asserts his independence from all claims being made upon him, and he reacts against the pressures that he feels as an Irishman under English domination. "I am the servant of two masters" (20), he notes; "an English and an Italian." Haines has no difficulty understanding the first allusion, but not being an Irish Catholic he is nonplussed by the second. Not waiting for him to comprehend, Stephen adds: "And a third . . . there is who wants me for odd jobs" (20). Stephen goes on to explicate the first two, but the concept that a resurgent Hibernia is calling upon him to serve is never explained to the dense Englishman. True to his position as a conscripted servant of English lords Stephen remains uncommonly civil in his conversation with Haines (his attitude toward Mulligan is decidedly more sullen). Haines, after all, has money, and Stephen somehow hopes to barter the product of his wit. Haines's weak apology for British treatment of subject Ireland ("It seems history is to blame"—20) goes unchallenged, and it is only after his departure from Haines, when the Englishman had smiled at him, that Stephen silently declares his mistrust: "Horn of a bull, hoof of a horse, smile of a Saxon" (23).

The drunken Dedalus in nighttown finds himself in open confrontation with the muscle of British authority, having inadvertently infuriated a drunken soldier. In affixing to the Tommy the name of his Zurich *bête noire* (Henry Carr of the British consular service), Joyce identifies himself strongly with Stephen against the English tormentor. A self-professed coward, Stephen hopes to extricate himself without having to fight, but he cannot bring himself to be

sufficiently obsequious. His comments might pass as innocent enough under ordinary circumstances, but they are
hardly the sort to assuage Private Carr. "I understand your
point of view" (591), Stephen says, "though I have no king
myself for the moment." This denial of loyalty to the British monarch becomes an obsession to Carr, despite the otherwise conciliatory tone of Stephen's subsequent remarks.
But in a moment of exasperation he "*throws up his hands*"
in resignation, "O, this is too monstrous! Nothing. He wants
my money and my life, though want must be his master,
for some brutish empire of his" (594). The trivial incident,
in itself only a personal and accidental clash between a
drunken Dubliner and a drunken Tommy, takes on this
universalized context as Stephen declares the enemy to be
not the individual bully but the "brutish empire" making
unreasonable demands upon him. Stephen has resigned
himself to being knocked down by Carr, a token act of
harassment symbolic of his subject position as an Irishman.

Lord Dudley, Haines, and Privates Carr and Compton
are the only significant Englishmen present in *Ulysses*;
Carr's sergeant-major, the Portobello bruiser Percy Bennett, is mentioned often. Several weeks earlier he had been
defeated in a boxing match with "Dublin's pet lamb"
(250), Myler Keogh, an odd instance of an Irish victory
over the English, offsetting the numerous occasions in
in which the English or their surrogates reasserted their
superior positions. In *Dubliners* orange-cravated Gallaher
returns from London to lord it over little Chandler; a Bel-
fast man buys up the lot on which Eveline had played
happily as a child; Jimmy Doyle loses disastrously at cards,
the heavy winner being Routh the Englishman; Mr. Alleyne from the north of Ireland is intent on hounding Far-

rington out of his job, while the Englishman Weathers bests him in a trial of strength. Little Keogh's defeat of Sergeant-Major Bennett has a David-Goliath significance, although Private Harry Carr reestablishes dominance by knocking down the pacifistic Stephen.

Stephen is conscious throughout of the unequal battle between his native land and the wardens of the empire: in his thoughts he designates conqueror England as "the seas' ruler." An echo of Shakespeare's John of Gaunt might underlie an important motif here, Gaunt's panegyric for blessed England, "This precious stone set in the silver sea,"[8] is reflected in Haines's cigarette case ("a smooth silver case in which twinkled a green stone"—19–20). Stephen had just dubbed him "the seas' ruler" as Haines "gazed southward over the bay, empty save for the smokeplume of the mailboat vague on the bright skyline, and a sail tacking by the Muglins" (18). He offers Stephen a cigarette from his case, which Stephen accepts. In colloquy with pro-British Deasy, Stephen is asked what the Englishman is most proud of; immediately his mind reverts back to Haines: "The seas' ruler. His seacold eyes looked on the empty bay: history is to blame: on me and my words, unhating" (30). In the National Library that afternoon Stephen learns that Haines has gone off to buy a copy of Douglas Hyde's *Lovesongs of Connacht* and will therefore not be present to hear him hold forth on *Hamlet.* "Penitent thief," he muses; "Gone. I smoked his baccy. Green twinkling stone. An emerald set in the ring of the sea" (186). The silver case has become Gaunt's silver sea and the precious stone a green emerald. Shakespeare's designation for his native England was in itself an usurpation, since an Irishman would insist that it is Ireland that is the Emerald Isle, and during the patriotic blather in the newspaper office the Joycean subheading reads: "ERIN, GREEN GEM OF THE SILVER SEA" (123). It is left to the chauvinistic citizen to dethrone England's eminence as the seas' ruler: "That's the glorious British navy, says the citizen, that bosses the earth. The fellows that never will be slaves. . . . That's the great empire they boast about of drudges and whipped slaves" (329). To the zealous citizen the ruler of the seas, having to command allegiance from conscript sailors by corporal punishment, is weakening; Stephen during the first hour of 17 June nonetheless feels the full impact of Private Carr's punch.

The resentment at having to serve his brutish master is complicated by Stephen's refusal to align himself with the citizen's faction. The boy who sought to ignore all voices and the youth who hoped to fly by all nets is now a young man declaring his *non-serviam* to his native land. His father hypocritically acknowledges all masters who claim his allegiance, without bothering himself much about any of the claims: he willingly doffed his hat to King Edward's viceroy (as had Kernan) and sauntered on into the Ormond bar for a musical interlude. When Kernan requests that Ben Dollard sing *The Croppy Boy*—"Our native Doric" (282)—Dedalus concurs, "Ay do, Ben. . . . Good men and true" (282). In the cabman's shelter Murphy mentions Simon Dedalus to Stephen (or a mysterious namesake of his) and credits him with being a paragon of his race: "He's Irish, the seaman boldly affirmed. . . . All Irish" (623). Stephen is quick to comment, "All too Irish" (623), a rejoinder that needs no amplification, although it is reinforced by Joyce's remark in a 1904 letter to Nora about J. F. Byrne: "He was Irish, that is to say, he was false to me."[9] Bloom is rather mystified by much of Stephen's cryptic commentary in the shelter, having incorrectly assumed certain orthodox attitudes on the part of the young intellectual. He is completely perplexed, therefore, when Stephen makes his highly individualistic declaration about his relationship to his country: "You suspect . . . that I may be important because I belong to the *faubourg Saint Patrice* called Ireland for short. . . . But I suspect . . . that Ireland must be important because it belongs to me" (645). This assertive credo stands as Stephen Dedalus's conclusive statement on the subject, despite Bloom's plea for an explication. All that the youthful solipsist adds is a termination to the topic: "We can't change the country. Let us change the subject" (645).

Leopold Bloom's attitudes on the subject are neither as clearcut nor as conscious; nor have they remained as fixed as Stephen's. His status in the Dublin community is of course a dubious one: he has kept his innermost thoughts to himself and become a subject of wild speculation among those who know him. Few have taken the trouble to get to know him well, and he has therefore become almost a mythic figure. It is not surprising in a city of blarney and Irish bull to hear a citizen like John Wyse Nolan, in an attempt to refute the xenophobic citizen's sneers, insist that "it was Bloom gave the idea for Sinn Fein to Griffith to put in his paper all kinds of jerrymandering, packed juries and swindling taxes off of the Government and appointing consuls all over the world to walk about selling Irish industries" (335–36). Martin Cunningham, already seen as protective of maligned Bloom, arrives in time to act as corroborator: "it was he drew up all the plans according to the Hungarian system. We know that in the castle" (337).

If Cunningham is really convinced that Bloom is highly positioned in Sinn Fein circles, he is unfazed in associating with a potential subversive, considering his situation as a castle employee, and goes off with Bloom to the Dignam house to take care of the insurance problem. Bloom's respect for Griffith seems real enough. Nonpolitical Molly indicates that Bloom pointed him out in the street and asserted that Griffith is "very intelligent the coming man" (748) and "so capable and sincerely Irish" (772). In fact Molly assumes that her husband has been "going about with some of them Sinner Fein lately or whatever they call themselves talking his usual trash and nonsense" (748), but of course she has difficulty being accurate about technicalities, at one instance confusing "those Sinners Fein or the Freemasons" (772). What delights Bloom the most about Griffith is one of his witticisms: "What Arthur Griffith said about the headpiece over the *Freeman* leader: a homerule sun rising up in the northwest from the laneway behind the bank of Ireland. He prolonged his pleased smile. Ikey touch that: homerule sun rising up in the northwest" (57). (Bloom's use of the epithet "Ikey" will have an ironic echo later when Buck Mulligan looks at Bloom's calling card and asks, "What's his name? Ikey Moses? Bloom" [201]. Did Leopold Bloom know that Griffith was as antisemitic as the citizen?)

Bloom's morning musing over Griffith is recapitulated in the early afternoon, and although a "Home Rule sun rising up in the northwest" (164) is still good for a smile, his thoughts are now somewhat more extensively political. It is apparent that he has not allied himself with Sinn Fein to any committed extent and is in fact leery of that sort of commitment: "Sinn Fein. Back out you get the knife. Hidden

hand. Stay in, the firing squad" (163). Bloom is thinking about the nineteenth-century Fenians, but he immediately focuses on Griffith and concludes that he "is a square-
headed fellow but he has no go in him for the mob. Want
to gas about our lovely land" (164). Bloom's square-
headed Griffith is somewhat removed from Molly's neckless
Griffith, as is the actuality of Bloom's carefully uncom-
mitted politics from the speculations of either the Nolan-
Cunningham faction or Mrs. Bloom herself.

Tracing Bloom's political vacillations produces a pattern
and a patterned inconsistency. In his dialogue with Stephen he thinks back to when he was Stephen's age and remembers the extent of his radical views at the time of the
campaign for the rights of evicted tenants. His attitudes
then were not only "in sympathy with peasant possession"
(657), but went even "a step further than Michael Davitt
in the striking views he at one time inculcated as a backto-
thelander" (657). He does not date the retreat from this
extreme position but does indicate that this was "a partial-
ity, however, which, realising his mistake, he was subse-
quently partially cured of" (657). The movement away
from youthful enthusiasms toward caution is already noted
here by the 38-year-old Bloom, who admits that "in 1885
he had publicly expressed his adherence to the collective
and national economic programme advocated by James
Fintan Lalor, John Fisher Murray, John Mitchel, J. F. X.
O'Brien and others, the agrarian policy of Michael Davitt,
the constitutional agitation of Charles Stewart Parnell
(M. P. for Cork City), the programme of peace retrench-
ment and reform of William Ewart Gladstone" (716). His
position as a political pundit at the time still remains a mystery, for although he has kept the sealed envelope contain-

ing his predictions "written by Leopold Bloom in 1886 concerning the consequences of the passing into law of William Ewart Gladstone's Home Rule bill of 1886" (721), he never reveals its contents to the reader—nor was the bill ever passed. Molly again has the last word on the political stance of the young Leopold as she recollects the days of their courtship: "wasnt I the born fool to believe all his blather about home rule and the land league" (771).

Bloom's career as a Parnellite can be discerned from his thoughts in the cabman's shelter. It is a personal recollection rather than an objectively political one: Parnell's hat had been knocked off in a fracas and Bloom returned it to him. Parnell's simple "Thank you" is accepted by Bloom as dignified and gracious, "excited as he undoubtedly was under his frigid expression notwithstanding the little misadventure mentioned between the cup and the lip—what's bred in the bone" (650). (John Henry Menton's "Thank you" that morning under similar circumstances, however, is regarded by Bloom as pompous hauteur—"How grand we are this morning"—115). The mature Bloom is not uncritical of Parnell, conceding that he "used men as pawns" (165), but also convinced that he had a "certain fascination" (163) that made him a leader of men—a quality that Bloom denies to Griffith. Thirteen years after the death of Parnell, he is still aware of the man's qualities in contrast to those who betrayed him and those who succeeded him. "It was in fact a stoning to death on the part of seventytwo out of eighty constituencies that ratted at the time of the split" (660–61), he recalls. Those who replaced the fallen chief are "Messrs So-and-So who, though they weren't even a patch on the former man, ruled the roost after their redeeming features were very few and far between" (649).

He acknowledges that Parnell's death was a disappointing anticlimax for so tempestuous a career, that speculation regarding the coffin filled with stones stems from that disappointment, but he allows himself the luxury of a chance that Parnell is alive and planning a comeback. Yet he is astute enough to add: "Still, as regards return, you were a lucky dog if they didn't set the terrier at you directly you got back. Then a lot of shillyshally usually followed. Tom for and Dick and Harry against" (649).

By 1892, a year after Parnell's death and two years after his disgrace, Bloom was already having second thoughts about nationalism. An avid contemplator of a literary vocation he was tempted to enter a competition to write a skit for the Gaiety Theatre on *"If Brian Boru could but come back and see old Dublin now"* (678), but rationalizes his literary inactivity by acknowledging "apprehension of opposition from extreme circles on the questions of the respective visits of Their Royal Highnesses, the duke and duchess of York (real), and of His Majesty King Brian Boru (imaginary)" (679). By the time of the Boer War this ambivalence was thoroughly rooted in Bloom, who was then in his early thirties. He had found himself swept along by the crowd during a demonstration against Prime Minister Joseph Chamberlain and was nearly "souped" by a mounted policeman. He records his disdain for the demonstrators, the "Trinity jibs in their mortarboards. Looking for trouble" and the "silly billies: mob of young cubs yelling their guts out" (163). There is Joycean irony in his prediction about the durability of their protest ("Few years' time half of them magistrates and civil servants. War comes on: into the army helterskelter: same fellows used to whether on the scaffold high"—163), since he himself had made a similar transition in just a few years' time from his position left of Davitt. Commiserating that a policeman's lot is not a happy one, especially the horse policeman who cracked his head in his fall when attempting to "soup" the fleeing Bloom, he nonetheless maintains "that a lot of those policemen, whom he cordially disliked, were admittedly unscrupulous in the service of the crown and . . . prepared to swear a hole through a ten gallon pot" (615). Yet in his hallucinatory self-defense in nighttown he feels it necessary to claim world-famed greatness for the Royal Dublin Fusiliers, and a local version of the same for the Dublin Metropolitan Police, "guardians of our homes, the pluckiest lads and the finest body of men, as physique, in the service of our sovereign" (457). (Later he muses resignedly that Irish soldiers have seen more action fighting for the empire than have ever taken up arms against it.) It is one matter that when backed into a corner by the watch during a hallucination for Bloom to insist, "I'm as staunch a Britisher as you are, sir" (457), but it is another for him in the privacy of his thoughts to contemplate a list of serious criminal offenses and include "intelligence with the king's enemies" (733), and to keep a furled Union Jack in the parlor of 7 Eccles Street.

Much of Joyce's own ambivalence is invested not only in Stephen Dedalus but in Leopold Bloom as well. The quarrel with Consulate flunkey Carr and Consul General Bennett in Zurich, in the midst of his work on *Ulysses*, may have crystallized for Joyce an attitude toward the British hegemony, but his concern with the incipient Irish nation remained clouded—so much so that Stephen's fixed position, the position of the *young* artist, was not sufficient to contain the whirlpool of Joyce's intellectual involvement and the many-headed monster of his emotional ties. In one breath he can tell Frank Budgen that "Ireland is what she is . . . and therefore I am what I am because of the relations that have existed between England and Ireland. Tell me why you think I ought to wish to change the conditions that gave Ireland and me a shape and a destiny," and in the next breath he can concede that *Ulysses* "is the work of a sceptic, but I don't want it to appear the work of a cynic. I don't want to hurt or offend those of my countrymen who are devoting their lives to a cause they feel to be necessary and just."[10] Budgen is concise in his differentiation between the political stances of the younger and older protagonists of Joyce's novel: "Bloom hoists a flag of his own, whereas Stephen refuses to serve or govern under any flag. Bloom does not deny his responsibility for the just government of the city. He is political and belongs to a party, but there is only one in it—himself. He throws the whole weight of his party into the scale on the side of reason and justice, but it weighs only eleven stone four. Stephen is anarchist, Bloom is Utopian. Utopia and Anarchy are old neighbors and near of kin, but they have never got on well together."[11] Yet the duality of Joyce's attempted view does not allow for the extremes of chauvinism and exclusiveness, nor has Joyce much patience with the sentimentality of patriotism. Even Emmet's sacrosanct words to the court are suspect as inflated pomposity as Bloom conjures them up in his mind—without comment—while trying to relieve himself of a bothersome flatulence, so that both wind and quotation break simultaneously with a final "*Done*" (291).

NOTES

1. All parenthetical references are to the Random House edition of *Ulysses* published in 1961.

2.   Frank Budgen, *James Joyce and the Making of "Ulysses"* (Bloomington: Indiana University Press, 1960), pp. 67–68.

3.   An important correction of the text, from *cove* to *dove*, has been made, in compliance with the suggestion of Norman Silverstein, "Toward a Corrected Text of *Ulysses*," *James Joyce Quarterly* 6 (Summer 1969): 355.

4.   Budgen, *James Joyce and the Making of "Ulysses,"* p. 106.

5.   *Stephen Hero* (New York: New Directions, 1963), pp. 54–55.

6.   *A Portrait of the Artist as a Young Man* (New York: Compass Books, 1964), p. 252.

7.   Ibid., pp. 83–84.

8.   *Richard II*, II, i, 46.

9.   *Letters of James Joyce*, vol. 2, ed. Richard Ellmann (New York: Viking Press, 1966), p. 50.

10.   Budgen, *James Joyce and the Making of "Ulysses,"* p. 152.

11.   Ibid., p. 150.

The Allusive Method
in *Ulysses*

WELDON THORNTON

I

ONE OF THE MOST STRIKING FEATURES of the development of
James Joyce's work from *Dubliners* through *Finnegans
Wake* is his increasing use of allusion. Each successive work
shows a more and more pervasive use of the technique: the
several dozen allusions in *Dubliners* become several score
in *A Portrait*, several hundred in *Ulysses*, several thousand
in *Finnegans Wake*. But in addition to an increase in number, there is also a change in how the technique of allusion
functions, from the more or less traditional disposal of it
in the early works to an innovative, almost revolutionary,
use of it in *Ulysses* and *Finnegans Wake*. In the earlier
works—*Dubliners* and *A Portrait*—allusion is used skillfully
but traditionally; it remains a device, subservient to and
separable from the core of the work. *Ulysses* is Joyce's first
work involving a significantly innovative use of the technique. Here the novel's themes and structures are embodied by allusion and dependent upon it, and the allusions
are an integral and organic part of the novel. But *Ulysses* is

still a novel, not an encyclopedic montage: there are observable events, the characters are persons, and some thematic and structural elements are not totally dependent on allusion. When we move to *Finnegans Wake*, however, we see for better or worse the end point of this revolutionary use of allusion. In *Finnegans Wake* allusion has become the substance of the work, and we cannot separate the characters, themes, and structures from the allusions that form them. Ordinary plot elements or events are almost impossible to discover, and Shem and Shaun, among the most distinguishable "characters" in the book, are not so much persons as archetypal conglomerates made up of all the historical and literary personages they coalesce.

Since *Ulysses* does blend traditional and innovative uses of the device, it offers an ample field for the exploration of almost any facet of allusion. We might if we wished consider some ways that allusion serves rather traditionally to reveal character. We might, for example, compare the percentage of popular song allusions in the minds of Molly and Stephen, or scrutinize the errors and imprecisions in Bloom's allusions, or we might study the several instances when a character fails to complete, or distorts, an allusion because of its unpleasant associations.[1] But interesting and necessary as these specific, piecemeal considerations are, they run the risk of losing the forest in the trees. There is as much challenge, and perhaps more profit, in the larger questions of why Joyce came to rely on allusion so heavily and use it so distinctively, and what effects he hoped to achieve by it. Certainly this increasing, developing use of the technique is not an accidental or trivial part of Joyce's growth. It is, rather, an important part of his answer to the problem of creating art in the modern age.

II

In the twentieth century, several writers—Joyce, Yeats, and Eliot among them—have taken a new attitude toward allusion. They have seen capacities in allusion which earlier writers were unaware of or unresponsive to—perhaps because earlier times did not require it—and they have relied on allusion in ways that would puzzle their predecessors. We can understand these modern writers' interest in allusion better if we examine the trope closely. Allusion—the casual reference to some prior figure or event in history or art—is an old, respected literary technique that has had several traditionally recognized functions. In some instances allusion has been used primarily to show the writer's erudition or to signal to his audience that he and they are members of some elite. Skillful writers always chose allusions that augmented rather than diminished their themes, but allusion was generally an ornament or flourish rather than an integral part of the work. There was little inclination to take the technique very seriously or to make it more than it obviously was—a means of embellishing the more basic literary dimensions of character, theme, and structure.

But two particular capacities of allusion have attracted modern writers and caused them to take it more seriously. First, an allusion involves an element of comparison and contrast, of analogy, so that it can be made to invite a comparison and contrast of its present context (for example, *Ulysses*) with its previous context (for example, *Hamlet*). It asks the reader to consider how the present context and the earlier one are comparable, to think through the implied analogy and test its validity. In this respect the analogy that allusion implies differs from that of metaphor by evoking an almost inexhaustible number of points of comparison and contrast. No matter how skillfully an author uses an ordinary metaphor, such as a rose, there are only a limited number of comparisons that offer themselves for development—color, beauty, length of life, etc. But an allusion to Hamlet or Icarus or Christ brings with it a large array of relationships among characters, qualities of personality, themes, structural patterns, all of which may be put to use if the author has the desire and the genius to do so. When Stephen, in *Ulysses*, alludes to Icarus' cry to his father, for example, we may think first of the analogy between Icarus' flight from Crete and Stephen's from Ireland, and then of their similarities of character; but we have not fully explored the allusion until we have compared their respective fathers, asked why Stephen identifies with Icarus rather than Daedalus, and so on.[2]

But there is a second, more important, basis for the appeal of allusion to modern writers. Again in contrast to ordinary metaphor, an allusion comes to us trailing clouds of glory from some prior existence in art or history. For this reason it is not merely a more complex metaphor; it contains a potential link between the past and the present, between an earlier culture and our own, between tradition and the modern world. This prospect of some kind of cultural continuity, of a link with tradition, has a special appeal to many modern writers. It has fulfilled a need that could not otherwise be fulfilled. It has provided the main impetus behind their innovative use of an old device, and their elevation of a relatively minor technique to major importance.

III

The reasons behind Joyce's fascination with allusion and his responsiveness to it seem to lie both within his own personality and within the modern situation. By nature, and perhaps by training, Joyce was inclined to be comprehensive; he wished to incorporate as much of life and reality into his works as possible. For this reason *Ulysses* has many archetypal aspects and it includes the most basic events and patterns of human experience—birth and burial, day and night, ingestion and defecation, the search for a father and the search for a son. But Joyce felt that to be truly comprehensive his "chaffering allincluding most farraginous chronicle" (423)[3] must do more than this. It must also incorporate the earlier works of Western art and literature by which man has defined these events and patterns. And so, in order to make *Ulysses* the most comprehensive Word ever uttered in our culture, Joyce used allusion to incorporate into his own work of art the patterns and essences of many earlier ones, especially those classic definitions of Western man such as the *Odyssey*, the life and passion of Christ, and *Hamlet*.[4]

Joyce's own personal, and perhaps jesuitical, need for comprehensiveness was complemented and enforced by his view of the modern world and his wish to be the complete twentieth-century artist. To Joyce as to many of his contemporaries, the modern age seemed characterized by cultural dissolution and schizophrenia. The modern world was in need of some synthesizing, unifying force, some cultural stay against chaos, and since the traditional institutions of state and church seemed incapable of the synthesis, it fell to the artist to provide it.

More specifically, the artist as sensitive modern man found himself torn between the demands of the inner, "subjective" world of value and quality, and the outer, "objective" world of fact and quantity. He needed some valid foundation for his art that would do justice to each without neglecting the other. Nor could Joyce be satisfied with the answers offered by the two major camps of nineteenth-century literature, symbolism and naturalism, for these were merely manifestations and aggravations of the schizophrenia. Naturalism, bowing to the dictates of prestigious scientific empiricism, attempted to make literature as quantitative as physiology, and consequently neglected or denigrated the distinctive qualities of the inner, value-oriented world. Symbolism, appalled by the implications of science for man's life, retreated into the inner world of the mind and emotions and avoided the intractable world of fact outside.

How then to achieve the satisfactory synthesis of fact and value, naturalism and symbolism? This was the task Joyce himself faced, and it is the major dilemma he depicts Stephen Dedalus as facing. And though Stephen does not solve the problem, he does, in *Ulysses*, come to understand it, and he shows a strong inclination to fight the battle through to a positive conclusion. In *A Portrait*, Stephen comes to see that his destiny is to be an artist, but he never fully understands what this involves. This is largely because he remains too inner-oriented, too *symboliste*, and has no adequate awareness of the intractable reality of the physical world. In *Ulysses* we find him almost at the other extreme, so buffeted by the material world—his mother's agonizing death and Mulligan's cynicism—that he barely maintains his faith in the inner realities which he so facilely espoused in *A Portrait*. His effete symbolist villanelle is now replaced by his naturalistic vignette of Dublin's ancient virgins, and he seems in danger of succumbing to a materialistic world view. But Stephen's strength, and the basis for our hope in him, is that though he has taken the Icarean plunge into the material world, he has not accepted Mulligan's verdict that the mother is merely "beastly dead." Death and material reality are powerful forces, more so than he realized in his youthful exuberance, but they are not the only realities. Hopefully Stephen will find a way to reconcile the demands of inner and outer reality without sacrificing one to the other.

An important part of Joyce's own solution to this dilemma, this burgeoning schizophrenia in our culture, lay in his realization of the capacities of allusion. He saw in it one means to span the chasm between naturalism and symbolism, between the present and the past, between the individual and the typical or archetypal, and he put this new understanding into practice in *Ulysses*. Interestingly enough, Joyce's effort, his response to the modern challenge, was understood and articulately described by one of his fellow artists. T. S. Eliot was in an especially good position to appreciate Joyce's method since he saw the modern dilemma similarly and found similar answers in his own poetry. In a perceptive review of *Ulysses* which appeared in *The Dial* in November 1923, Eliot emphasized and praised the radically new methods of the novel. In the opening paragraph of his review, Eliot says forthrightly "I hold this book to be the most important expression which the present age has found; it is a book to which we are all indebted, and from which none of us can escape." He then calls attention to what interests him most in the novel:

"Amongst all the criticisms I have seen of the book, I have seen nothing . . . which seemed to me to appreciate the significance of the method employed—the parallel to the *Odyssey*, and the use of appropriate styles and symbols to each division." Later in the review, Eliot deals more specifically with this aspect of the novel. I quote the pertinent sentences from the last three paragraphs of the review:

The question, then, about Mr Joyce, is: how much living material does he deal with, and how does he deal with it: deal with, not as legislator or exhorter, but as an artist?

It is here that Mr Joyce's parallel use of the Odyssey has a great importance. It has the importance of a scientific discovery. No one else has built a novel upon such a foundation before: it has never before been necessary. . . .

In using the myth, in manipulating a continuous parallel between contemporaneity and antiquity, Mr Joyce is pursuing a method which others must pursue after him. . . . It is simply a way of controlling, of ordering, of giving a shape and a significance to the immense panorama of futility and anarchy which is contemporary history. It is a method already adumbrated by Mr Yeats, and of the need for which I believe Mr Yeats to have been the first contemporary to be conscious. It is a method for which the horoscope is auspicious. Psychology (such as it is, and whether our reaction to it be comic or serious) ethnology, and *The Golden Bough* have concurred to make possible what was impossible even a few years ago. Instead of narrative method, we may now use the mythical method. It is, I seriously believe, a step toward making the modern world possible for art.[5]

Eliot's comment is a perceptive response to the implications of Joyce's method and accomplishment. And for our purposes the assumptions of this response may be as important as its conclusions. These assumptions are that modern experience is not culture in any organic sense, but an "immense panorama of futility and anarchy"; that the modern world is not, without some adjustment, "possible for art"; and that only now for the first time has something like the "mythical method" become necessary.

Eliot's comment about the mythical method in *Ulysses* focuses upon the *Odyssey* parallels, but it does not apply solely to the *Odyssey*. The key to the mythical method is not in the use of something mythological, but in "manipulating a continuous parallel between contemporaneity and antiquity," and we could with justification and accuracy rechristen it the "allusive method." For while the *Odyssey* parallel is one of the most pervasive in the novel, its function is not essentially different from that of many others, including *Hamlet*, the Daedalus myth, Shakespeare's biography, Christ's life and passion, Mozart's *Don Giovanni*, or Goethe's "Walpurgisnacht." In evoking an earlier context for comparison and contrast, this method imports some of that earlier milieu, some of its values and norms, into the present work. It gives us a means of rising above the exigencies of our present, particular situation by suggesting what it shares with the past. This is especially true of those allusions which occur repeatedly in *Ulysses*, so that we sense a pattern of history or art being continually held up against the present.

Only in the context of Eliot's assumptions can the importance of this new method be appreciated. By clarifying its milieu he clarifies its distinctiveness and its necessity. Earlier writers may on occasion have used allusion similarly, but few ever used it so systematically and pervasively, and none ever used it with this need and purpose. The central theme of *Ulysses* is the need for an adequate synthesis of all the dichotomies of modern experience—the split between inner and outer, fact and value, present and past, individual experience and larger human experience, anarchy and culture, naturalism and symbolism. Through the allusive method Joyce embodies the needed synthesis in many of the structures, themes, and characters in the novel. Without the allusive parallel to the *Odyssey*, for example, the structure of *Ulysses* would be severely changed and depleted. The most important remaining structural elements would be the city of Dublin, the carefully controlled chronology of the novel, and the counterpointing of the main characters—the standard equipment of the realistic or naturalistic novel. Gone would be that sense of implicit pattern constantly on the verge of manifesting itself in these events. Absent would be the continual question of how the life of an ordinary modern man has anything in common with that of an ancient hero, and of whether, though we may have lost sight of it, the lives of modern men, frenetically separate and individual as they are, gain value from their participation in some larger human experience. In such a case the novel might be built upon the foiling of Stephen and Bloom and be called *Blephen Stoom*, but it could not be called *Ulysses*.

But even this counterpointing of the characters blends into structure and theme, and all are intimately dependent on allusion. The foiling of Stephen and Bloom would have little force or meaning if the allusive contexts of Ulysses-Telemachus, God-Christ, Shakespeare-Hamnet, Hamlet *père*-Hamlet *fils* were absent. We could of course still see Stephen and Bloom as young man and old man and perhaps as paired opposites in personality, but our sense of their mutual need and their complementary quest would be severely damaged. So much of their character is tied up

with the theme of fatherhood and sonship that without it
their natures would be essentially altered. And this theme
is present in the novel primarily through the allusive contexts that embody and validate it. Without those contexts,
the mutual quest of Stephen and Bloom would be, not a
theme, but an idiosyncrasy of personality, another instance
of the isolation and solipsism of the modern individual.

IV

What effect are these allusive parallels intended to have
on our attitude toward the characters and events of the
novel? Most discussions of this question have assumed that
the allusive correspondences either elevate or denigrate
the characters and events of the novel or have offered some
variation of this view. But this approach usually involves
an oversimplification into an inadequate either-or choice,
and it distorts Joyce's emphasis. Joyce is not primarily concerned with either elevating or denigrating his characters.
The most relevant point to be made about the parallels the
allusions incorporate is that they are *there*, deeply implicit
in human nature and experience and fairly explicit in literature. Our individual lives do reenact patterns enacted a
thousand times before, however aware or unaware of this
we may be. Not of course that the mere repetition of a pattern endows it with value; a meaningless act is still meaningless even if it is repeated thousands of times. But the
ultimate question of whether life is meaningful in itself is
not really Joyce's concern in *Ulysses*. He assumes it is and
addresses himself to why modern man is so out of rapport
with the meaning that is potentially there. He does not ask
whether it is worthwhile to heal man's schizophrenia; he

presumes that it is and faces the problem of how it is to be done.

This leads to a second point about the effect of the allusive parallels. We have said that Joyce's aim in using the allusive method was to heal the splits in the modern psyche, to restore some measure of unity and fullness to human experience. This is a positive aim and it suggests that some degree of hope and optimism lies behind the novel. But this does not manifest itself in any elevation of the characters so much as in a concern for them. The second relevant point about these parallels is that neither Stephen nor Bloom draws upon them, derives substance from them, as fully as he should. Though their acts reiterate the acts of earlier men, neither of them seems adequately aware that his individual, seemingly separate existence is given potential form, depth, and meaning by his participation in the perennial, archetypal patterns of man's experience. But *aware* is of course the wrong word here, for it implies a high degree of consciousness, and Joyce does not intend that his characters or his readers will begin thinking "Ah! How like Hamlet was that last gesture of mine!" Too keen a consciousness parodies and destroys the needed rapport. What Joyce does wish is that modern man were not so isolated—that he had, if not an *awareness*, at least a *sense* that his particular experience is deeply rooted in general, traditional human experience and that this root taps sources of meaning.

But before we become too enamoured of blending our selfhood into that of past ages, we need to redress the balance by making a distinction. For Joyce's point is certainly not that we should disparage our present situation in favor of some generalized human experience or of the life of some prior age. Life has never been more available, more actual, than it is in Dublin in 1904 or in our own city in our own time. The point is not that we should sacrifice the present to eternity or to the past, but that we should put the past to its proper use as basis and enhancer of the present; not disparage our present life but get the fullest possible value from it. Joyce was certainly wily enough to know that if we disdain this present life we disdain our share in existence. And if Dublin in 1904 seemed to Stephen the most ordinary, even unreal, of places, no doubt Telemachus found Ithaca fretfully restraining and frequently pined to be somewhere where life was being lived more fully.

V

In *Ulysses* Joyce set out to create the culmination of the realistic-naturalistic movement, and he succeeded. He also set out to create the culmination of the symbolic movement, and here again he succeeded. He produced the most fully documented account of one day in one city the world has ever seen. And he entitled it *Ulysses*. The major device by which the blend of naturalism and symbolism, of surface and symbol, is achieved, is the mythical, allusive method. By supplementing and qualifying the naturalistic dimension of the novel with the symbolic, Joyce performs within the work of art the model of the synthesis our culture needs.

But if the proximate purpose of the allusive method in *Ulysses* is "to make the modern world possible for art," the further purpose is to show us, the readers, something about the quality of modern life—not to disparage it, but to show us its solipsism and depletion, and to suggest a remedy for these qualities. If the characters of the novel remain oblivious to the reverberations of their actions within the chambers of human experience, if they are deceived and depleted by the dichotomies and misemphases of modern life, that is no reason we, the discerning readers, should remain victims. As a matter of fact, it is all the more reason we should not. Our role in the novel is to complete the synthesis which Joyce has provided the basis for: to see and join the incompleteness of Stephen and Telemachus, Bloom and Ulysses, and Molly and Penelope into a more satisfactory whole, to reconcile present with past, Dublin with Ithaca, our individuality with our humanity.

NOTES

1. Errors by Bloom have been noted by several commentators. For examples, see entries 113.18, 280.23, 179.35, 387.26, and 661.14 in my *Allusions in "Ulysses": An Annotated List* (Chapel Hill: University of North Carolina Press, 1968). For examples of suppressed or distorted allusions, see entries 26.33 and 45.31 (entry numbers refer to page and line in the 1961 Random House edition of *Ulysses*).

2. William York Tindall also sees this allusion as suggesting Jesus, another forsaken son calling to his father in extremity, which opens up another array of analogies (*A Reader's Guide to James Joyce* [New York: Farrar, Strauss and Giroux, 1959], p. 179).

3. Numbers in parentheses refer to the Random House edition of *Ulysses* published in 1961.

4. The idea of *Ulysses* as a complex mode of the Word deserves fuller presentation than space permits. I explore the idea more fully in a recently completed essay entitled "James Joyce and the Power of the Word."

5. *The Dial* 75 (November 1923): 482–83.

FRITZ SENN

10

THE PROCESS OF TRANSLATION involves an approach—every translator of *Ulysses* approaches the novel in his own unique way. The results, the individual translations, are approximations, not, in themselves, approaches. Readers can of course use them in their struggle with the original text, as many do whose native language is not English. At some time bilingual editions of *Ulysses* (as of many other classics) will no doubt be published abroad.

Translations can, however, also be turned into an approach—if we compare them with the original and among themselves. This is a somewhat academic exercise and really a misuse of the translations, whose purpose is not mutual comparison and which, at any rate, are not written for the study or the classroom. But it can be a rewarding exercise. It will tell us something about the nature of translation and about its limitations; on the other hand it will oblige us to take a close look at the original, from perhaps a few different angles. When we speak of "translating *Ulysses*" we pretend that we know what either *translating* or *Ulysses* means when in fact the novel means something different to every one of us and we may not have a very clear conception of what the translation of a complex work of literature amounts to or should amount to. If we had such a conception and could agree on it we would be prepared to answer the ultimate question of whether *Ulysses* can be translated at all. Joyce himself said that only the original was authentic,[1] but then he also helped and encouraged translations.

The following remarks are based on passages selected from a handful of translations of *Ulysses* into what is really an extremely narrow range of languages.[2] They ought to be supplemented by a summary of the problems and perspectives of translators working in languages that are fundamentally different from the Indo-European ones. The aim is not to establish principles of translation, or to evaluate the existing translations, but to analyze what has actually been done by the translators and to find out, if possible, what their intentions were. Apart from each translator's skill and sensibility, the translations reflect their cultural background, the potentialities and confines of the language the translations are written in. They also represent diverse points of view, reflections in mirrors throwing back light on the original. Every translation will highlight some characteristics, either where it succeeds in re-creating a particular effect or where, sometimes by a painstaking effort, a purpose becomes manifest. Even where it fails, the comparison, by contrast, will throw some feature of the original into distinct relief. Passages that appear typically Joycean and by their complexity compel the translator to make decisions naturally deserve the greatest attention.

By necessity a comparison of this kind is concerned with

details, and the details have to be separated from much of their larger context. The translations as a whole, their intrinsic artistic merit, will not be considered. Such decisive, but elusive concepts as the tone, the feel, the total impact of a translation have to be neglected as well as the question of whether a translation catches the spirit of the original, whatever that means. These aspects are essentially matters for the critic within his own language. The comparison of isolated passages, even words, with the vision sharpened, I hope, by the juxtaposition, often boils down to just a close reading which always comes dangerously close to an over-reading since it cannot help being a verbalization of what are ultimately subjective impressions. Nevertheless, no valid approach can be made without, in the last resort, taking account of what is actually on the page. The translator is a close reader too, perhaps the closest there is. He is almost the only one who is professionally obliged to examine every single word. We do not grant him the selectivity of the critic; he is not allowed the luxury of omission.

Since translations are, at least quantitatively, a complete running commentary of the original, we may call them in as witnesses to help determine some puzzling questions in Joyce's text. There is particular temptation to make such use of the two translations that came into being under Joyce's supervision. In 1927 the German translation was published and announced as "vom Verfasser geprüfte Ausgabe von Georg Goyert."[3] In spite of this claim, it had to be revised at Joyce's insistence, and the second edition of 1930 bears an even prouder imprint: "vom Verfasser geprüfte definitive deutsche Ausgabe."[4] In the meantime, in 1929, the renowned French translation had come out,

Ulysse, "traduit de l'anglais par M. Auguste Morel, assisté par M. Stuart Gilbert. Traduction entièrement revue par M. Valery Larbaud avec la collaboration de l'auteur."[5] These formulae seem to imply something beyond a merely legal placet, and we may fancy ourselves in the fortunate position of having two authorized commentaries, all the more so since one of the co-translators and advisors, Stuart Gilbert, became the first extensive commentator of *Ulysses*. There is, however, no evidence that Joyce's supervision entailed a careful examination of every word. In the late twenties Joyce, preoccupied with *Work in Progress*, with Lucia's illness, and troubled by failing eyesight, even if he had had the inclination, could hardly have found the time and the energy that the task evidently required. We know that he relegated some of the responsibilities of the German translation to friends.[6] There are instances of the two authorized translations clearly contradicting each other. In fact the German and the French translation are the least accurate of all, which is understandable enough in view of their early origin, but clearly precludes too hasty a notion—suggested strongly in *geprüfte, definitive*, and *entièrement revue*—of Joyce providing a reliable commentary himself.[7] It is safe to say that neither the celebrated French translation nor the German one (which has come in for severe criticism) can be adduced to settle controversial points even if, in exceptional cases, they might corroborate conclusions for which there is other evidence as well.

Translation comes into the novel as a rather minor theme. A few sparse attempts made at translating a few phrases, while not very serious, are either faulty or incomplete. Bloom comes to grief over two lines from *Don Giovanni*, for the most elementary of reasons, insufficient knowledge of the language: "What does that *teco* mean. Tonight perhaps" (180). Bloom's subjective reading "doesn't go properly." Translation often doesn't. Stephen's two renderings of a Latin misquotation, *"Descende, calve, ut ne nimium decalveris,"* are primarily facetious: "Get down, bald poll!" (40);[8] "Down, baldynoddle, or we'll wool your wool" (243). Both versions are defective or paraphrastic and partly subjective again. Protean metamorphosis too can come near to translation: "She trudges, schlepps, trains, drags, trascines her load" (47), just as translation often results in a metamorphosis. The near-synonyms which Stephen culls from four languages and which he mentally tries for effect have similar meanings but different suggestiveness.

An intentionally literal, word-for-word translation of a common French phrase ("Mais c'est bien triste, ça, ma foi, oui") is, and, according to Joyce's stated view, must be, quite unconvincing: "But it is well sad, that, my faith, yes" (427).[9] The pedantic accuracy and hopeless inadequacy of this version as well as the imaginative woolliness of Stephen's earlier mock translations are extremes not unknown to most practitioners of the art.

The rapid transformations of style which go to make up the Oxen of the Sun chapter could also be taken to be a series of translations, not horizontally from one language into another, but vertically through progressive stages of the literary language, and of course into the idiom of highly individualistic writers. This is one of the reasons why translators find the Oxen of the Sun chapter particularly frustrating.

It may be significant that in the library chapter, whose

art is literature, Stephen makes a point of reading the
"gorbellied works" of Saint Thomas "in the original" (205),
implying perhaps that even in philosophical discourse,
which, on the whole, tends to be lucid and unambiguous,
there is a difference between a translation and the original.
Joyce himself studied Norwegian and German in order to
read two favorite authors.

In general we rarely trouble to distinguish between
reading the original and reading a translation. For obvious
reasons we could only sample a small fraction of the world's
literature if we had no translations to fall back on. We often
have no means of knowing what translations, necessarily
substitutes, cut us off from, and we may forget that they do.
Courses in comparative literature, for example, usually
have to be conducted in only one language, on the tacit
assumption that literary works can be discussed and compared in translation. Thousands of readers who do not
know English have "read" *Ulysses* when in point of fact
they have not been exposed to a single word as Joyce wrote
it. It is worth pausing a moment to realize that a translation
changes the whole of a literary work, with the exception
of, usually, the names. What is the relation between a new,
entirely changed surface and the original one? And how
much of the "meaning" is thus affected? Translation pre-
supposes that the content can be dissociated from its
linguistic form. Whatever the epistemological position to
be taken, we know that the presupposition can be acted
on—up to a point. Communication would be difficult to
attain unless in large areas of human speech expression
could be changed within the same or into another language
without seriously altering the meaning. On the other hand,
language does not consist of simple labels for clearly defined

things, actions, and relations that could be replaced and interchanged. In the highly subtle and sophisticated use of language that is called literature all the resources of language are drawn upon, including its formal qualities, and the more ambitious a writer is the more he will also integrate all those secondary functions that escape categorization and go beyond mere designation. We have come to accept as a truism that with Joyce form and content become one. If they really and completely did, translation, by its drastic change of form, would indeed be impossible. The more language approximates the condition expressed in Samuel Beckett's view of Joyce's later prose ("His writing is not *about* something; *it is that something itself*"),[10] the more it is put out of the translator's reach.

Fortunately (for the translator) this complete identification remains an ideal rather than an achievement, but even so, and even in *Ulysses*, Joyce approximates it often enough, in what has been called "expressive form," to make *Ulysses* a borderline case and to push *Finnegans Wake* out of the translator's province. The problems and difficulties encountered in *Ulysses* are not even new ones, but most of the problems assume a greater importance. Hardly anything can be discounted as inessential. There seems to be always more at stake.

From the early beginnings Joyce's protagonists are portrayed as unusually conscious of the value of words, and they devote much of their attention to language itself. *Ulysses* is very much concerned with language; it is even largely *about* language. Many of the book's characters join in the game. When Bloom meditates "There is a word throstle that expressed that" (93), this observation about a word cannot just be taken over into any other language.

Mere probability goes against the semantic equivalent of another language expressing the same thing that Bloom has in mind. The Spanish translation, for example, cannot continue with its word for *throstle* (*zorzal*), but has to remain vague: "Hay una palabra que lo expresaba" (SP 127). Similarly, Molly's comment on the name of a congenial author: "Paul de Kock's. Nice name he has" (64), is too firmly grounded in the English language to enable reproduction. The chances are, again, that the nicety of the name—assuming for the moment that the name of an actual author must remain as it is in translation —may disappear or change its character in, say, German, Czech, or Japanese. If the translation still claims that the name is nice the reader may be led to suppose that Molly refers to its sound.

The spotlight may be turned on language in a less explicit manner: "Do ptake some ptarmigan" (175) appears among other evocations of banquet scenes in Bloom's imagination. By the mere addition of a superfluous letter the sentence has become a playful comment on an oddity of English spelling. "Nehmen Sie doch etwas Schneehuhn" (G 199– 200) remains on the level of table talk and leaves what may be the more important part of Bloom's idea out of consideration. If a spelling peculiarity is simply imitated, as in "Ptrendete un ptò di ptarmigan" (I 238), a comment on language is included, but there is little point to it in its non-English context. The word *ptarmigan* has not really been translated, but transplanted without its lexical background, and without it *ptake* is not really ptranslatable.

Ever so often, the translator has to be content with an accurate rendering of the surface. Even this he can only do if he knows what the basic meaning is, and he will often guess wrongly. The search for errors in translations, though deeply gratifying to our malevolence and a gleeful pastime of fellow translators, is perhaps the least profitable pursuit. There must be many mistakes in all translations of a book so challenging and, partly, still obscure as *Ulysses*. Small wonder that "Dunlop, Judge" (185) appears as "Dunlop, Juge" (F 182), "Dunlop, juez" (SP 221), "Dunlop, Richter" (G 211), or "Dunlop, domaren" (SW 194)—it may take extensive research to establish if *Judge* is the profession of Dunlop or a proper name, which more recent commentators have told us that it is. That Joyce did not, apparently, notice, or point out, the misreading in either the French or the German translation would indicate that his supervision was more superficial or intermittent than it might have been. Nor did Joyce, if he really looked closely at these passages, communicate his superior knowledge to the translators when he allowed them to render "lousy Lucy" in Stephen's thoughts (215) by "die lausige Lucy" (G 245) and "L'ignoble Lucie la pouilleuse" (F 211). The translators, not being Shakespearean scholars, turned lousy Lucy, whom they could not expect to be Sir Thomas Lucy, reasonably enough, into a girl. Errors of this kind will decrease in number as the bulk of scholarship grows, but the exposure of ignorance remains one of the translator's professional risks.

Apart from errors of fact or glaring linguistic howlers (the German version "des dunklen Arbeitszimmers" for "in a brown study"—354—was still chuckled over long after it had been corrected in the second edition[11]), however numerous, the concept of "correctness" does not apply too well to *Ulysses*. Sometimes a rather narrow view has to be taken to label a rendering "wrong." A few years ago, in a harsh attack on the German translation, the use of *bogenförmig* was objected to: "Bending archly she reckoned fat pears" (228), which reads: "Sie beugte sich bogenförmig" (G 237).[12] As any dictionary can tell, and as the French and the Danish translations bear out (*coquette*— F 222, *kokett*–D 237), *archly* does not mean *like an arch*. The wrong translation nevertheless catches some undercurrent. Architectural expansion in space is one of the features of the Wandering Rocks chapter, which already contains "Merchant's Arch" and various other arches. *Bogenförmig* may be a wrong turn, in a chapter which is intentionally full of wrong turnings, but it archly refers to at least a remote possibility that Joyce may have had in mind. The Spanish and the Portuguese translations, incidentally, also settle for an architectural reading: *arqueadamente* (SP 264), *em arco* (P 259). This may be a case of over-interpretation at the cost of a more important basic meaning. If we call it an error, translators' errors too may serve as useful portals of discovery.[13]

The choice of a word is often not a matter of correctness but of a careful balance of various effects. To illustrate in concrete terms some of the questions involved, a word shall be presented that does not complicate the issue by too many semantic problems, that is free of ambiguities and not affected by auctorial convergences (as in the cluster made up of "Throwaway," "a throwaway" and "I was just going to throw it away") or interfered with by homonymy (such as "arch," "grave," "race," "massproduct," etc.). The word has some definite and important functions within the novel; it is moreover the "organ" assigned to a whole chapter: "Womb." Anyone undertaking a study of, say, Stephen's preoccupations, his psychology (and, for that matter, perhaps Joyce's too), his esthetics, or some theological interpretation could hardly afford to bypass the motif *womb* in *Ulysses.*

For the translator this motif is a word. It occurs some twenty times in the novel. One of the dilemmas is whether, for the sake of unity, the translator ought to stick by a given choice or whether the optimal effect of each passage is to be preferred. It is easy to state dogmatically and naively that a word like *womb* must be translated consistently by the same word wherever it occurs. So it should, but in practice this is not feasible. The French translation, for example, usually gets by with *ventre,* but has to deviate to *matrice, les limbes,* and an occasional paraphrase. In Italian the convenient word *grembo* ensures some continuity, but *ventre* as well as *utero* are substituted at times. Every vocabulary imposes its own restrictions. They seem to be particularly baffling in German.

In the Proteus chapter Stephen's speculations range from midwives via navelcords to Eve, to "belly without blemish" and on to "womb of sin" (38). In German this latter becomes "Leib der Sünde" (G 46). Now *Leib* is not a felicitous choice; it is ambiguous and the meaning most likely to be understood here is the rather general one of *body.* The sinfulness of the flesh will be suggested to the reader rather than original sin. The misconception might have been evaded by the more unequivocal *Mutterleib,* but this pedantic composite would have been clumsily out of place. Another possibility is *Bauch;* it corresponds to *belly* and has already been used for "belly without blemish" and would be confusing. Finally there is *Schoss,* which would fit the context, even if it is predominantly figurative. It is the word that was used by the same translator to do duty for "the virgin womb of the imagination" in *A Portrait*: "im jungfräulichen Schosse der Imagination."[14] But it lacks the presence of a body. So the German vocabulary —a very rich one, on the whole—does not contain a suitable word. It might be argued that there is not really any choice, that, in keeping with the biblical tone of the passage, the Old Testament word must be taken over, which happens to be *Leib*. It also fits the relevant phrasing in the account of the Annunciation (Luke 1:44).

But *Leib* does not at all lend itself to the Protean change immediately following: "Wombed in sin darkness," where the word is made verb. *Leib* does not permit this change, nor, for that matter, would *Bauch*, *Mutterleib*, or *Schoss*. The womb, then, is simply refined out of existence: "In sündiger Dunkelheit." A translation that does follow the original rather closely here is the Portuguese one: "Matriz do pecado. Matrizado em pecadora escuridade" (P 43); *matriz* is not, however, the prevalent word for *womb* in *Ulisses*.

Neither *Leib* nor *matriz* are continued into the next ventral reference in Proteus: "mouth to her womb" (48). The German translator chose *Bauch*: "Mund auf ihren Bauch" (G 58). There is some justification for this; *Leib* would have been far too general and would only have been understood to mean *body*; of the other possible words, only *Bauch* offers the necessary physical surface for a mouth. But there is no echo of "womb of sin." Nor does "Mund auf ihren Bauch" serve as a basis for the rhyming experiment to which Stephen subjects *womb*: "Oomb, allwombing tomb." The translator does not aim higher than at mere repetition, and a flat paraphrase of *allwombing*: "Bauch, allumschliessendes Grab." There is neither rhyme nor too much reason, but it is, as always, easier to disapprove than to suggest a satisfactory solution. The French translation uses an ingenious detour: "ventre. Antre, tombe où tout entre" (50). Some device is obviously called for, such as "suo grembo. Onbo, tomba omnigrembo" (I 70). "Antre: ventre" as well as "tomba: grembo" can be taken up later, in the Aeolus chapter, when Stephen recalls the rhyme: "mouth south: tomb womb" (138). The German translator has no rhyme to fall back on, but aware that Stephen here is clearly pondering on the rationale of rhymes, introduces a parallel structure: "Mund Hund: Erdmutter Gebärmutter" (G 158), which is entirely without precedent, containing two words the reader never met before in the book, therefore not possibly a recall of an earlier thought. The physiological term *Gebärmutter* (*uterus*) is an odd choice in the context of the rather traditional sort of poetry that Stephen is imitating. The word is much more appropriate later on, in a Bloom passage, "in blutroten Gebärmüttern" (G 266), relating to an illustration of Aristotle's *Master-piece*: "infants cuddled in a ball in bloodred wombs" (235). Most of the other translations also become more anatomical here, using *matrices* (F 230), *uteri* (I 318), and so on.

The word *womb* has also a career in Bloom's thoughts, starting with a maternal "womb of warmth" in the Lotus Eaters chapter (86). In German it is "im warmen Leib der Wanne" (G 100), while it is psychologically glossed over in French: "dans une chaleur d'eaux maternelles" (F 85). Bloom returns to it in the Sirens chapter: "Because their wombs. / A liquid womb of woman eyeball" (286). The German translation decides for the more clinical term (as does the French one, *matrice*): "Weil ihre Gebärmütter. /

Ein feuchter gebärmütterlicher Augapfel" (G 321). These words do not charm the ear, but in spite of their clumsiness, as associations to birth and Mrs. Purefoy, they are not quite out of tone. The dark-vowelled monosyllable *womb* allows Joyce more auditory scope than the translators have with equivalents like *matrice*, *Leib* or *Gebärmutter*. If they take care of the sense, the sounds will not always take care of themselves. A translator might, for example, consider using *Bauch* instead of *Gebärmutter* in the above sentence, and, for the sake of the experiment, we might balance the resonant gains against the semantic losses in an otherwise unchanged rendering: "Weil ihre B*äu*che. Ein f*eu*chter geb*auch*ter *Au*gapfel."

The hospital scene, Oxen of the Sun, above all, is dominated by the organ womb. The German translation continues with *Leib* as far as possible. "Leibesfrucht" (G 432) is the inevitable and suitable word for *wombfruit* in the invocation (383). "Im Leibe des Weibes" (G 441) translates "In woman's womb" (391), where *Leib* will hardly be misunderstood though it may be distracting that *Leib* has already had to serve for the liturgical and eucharistic *my body* in the same paragraph. "Im Leibe schon wurde es geliebt" (G 432) is a pale imitation of the heavy cadences of "Within womb won he worship" (384), in marked contrast to a strongly alliterative sequence in Portuguese: "Verso ventre vencia veneração" (P 436). Sometimes *Bauch* is preferred to *Leib*, and *Gebärmutter*, which is of course thematically appropriate, recurs twice.

The resources of the German language then proved insufficient to provide a word to cover all the uses of *womb*, and few of the words selected for each occasion fit their immediate context too well. In none of the translations examined here was it possible to preserve the thematic unity, which is so much a matter of course in the original, by one and the same word (the German and the French translators did not, of course, have a word index to trace any given motif through the entire novel). Even if some improvements look possible, the semantic distribution alone prevents the delineation of a motif which takes such a simple form in English (there are some further twists like the Shakespearean "uneared wombs"—202—which pose yet another problem). In every language at least three different nouns had to be called in; distinctions like the one between *womb* and *belly* cannot be upheld; some of the music has been silenced and odd side-effects creep in. Neither *Leib, Bauch, Gebärmütter,* nor *Schoss* (in *A Portrait*) can become as fertile a source of conception, whether literary or embryonic, as *womb.*

Fortunately, not all the words of *Ulysses* are saddled with such heavy thematic burdens. Or are they? No one would insist, ordinarily, on the exact translation of a particular word within an idiomatic phrase like "But Dignam's put the boots on it" (380). There is nothing wrong, except, perhaps, a certain flatness, with "la visite chez Dignam m'a achevé" (F 374), "Ma la visita a Dignam è stata l'ultima goccia" (I 514), or "Aber Dignam das war zuviel" (G 429). It would be idle to complain about the absence of (merely metaphorical) boots. But, out of a wide array of idiomatic possibilities, Joyce selected boots, and this at least allows the reader to recall that the late Patrick Dignam, as his son remembers, in his last mundane appearance was "bawling for his boots" (251). And it seems to be the selfsame pair of boots that Dignam's ghost singles out for particular attention in the séance parody on page 302.

These potential memories and overtones give the sentence a different ring, a slightly humorous touch, and at least a suspicion that there is, as usual, more to it. And they help to tighten the closed world of *Ulysses* just a little bit more. It may not amount to much, but the little flutter in the reader's response was probably Joyce's aim.

A figure of speech, if taken literally, sometimes serves an ironic turn. Bloom's advice to Stephen is couched in the choicest inappropriate terms: "I wouldn't personally repose much trust in that boon companion of yours . . . , Dr Mulligan, as a guide, philosopher, and friend, if I were in your shoes" (620). The translations, "si j'étais de vous" (F 545) and "ich an Ihrer Stelle" (G 621), being entirely neutral, fail to drive home just how much Bloom is out of touch with the reality he tries to influence: Stephen happens to be wearing, as the reader will remember, but as the reader of the translations has no cause to remember, the shoes of the very person that he is being warned against. The Italian translation, a late one, did not miss the pointed reference: "se fossi nelle sue scarpe" (I 800).

The correct, literal translation can falsify a meaning. A telling example can be taken from a passage made up of the simplest of words, in Molly's monologue. A woman who has poisoned her husband occupies Molly's thoughts:

take that Mrs Maybrick that poisoned her husband for what I wonder . . . white Arsenic she put in his tea off flypaper wasnt it I wonder why they call it that if I asked him hed say its from the Greek leave us as wise as we were before. (744)

Not a word here that mightn't be translated without much effort. In fact a translator would have very little choice— there is certainly no choice whatever for the word that arouses Molly's curiosity *as a word* for the moment, the name of the poison, which has its given form in all European languages: *Arsenik, arsenico,* and so forth. But in none of these languages (with the exception of the Scandinavian ones) does the inevitable word permit the same association. And without this association Molly's interest must appear more purely philological. Molly is never, as far as we know her, curious about etymologies—though, oddly enough, the etymology of *arsenic* is revealing too: the word was assimilated to a Greek one, *arseneikon,* literally meaning *male* (due to its potency as a poison), and so also something worthy of Molly's attention, though she wouldn't know (this remote etymological benefit is theoretically contained in the translations). But to turn Molly momentarily into a linguist makes her a different human being. The "correct" translation results in a distortion of character. To put it differently: if Molly were thinking in a language other than English, she would never bother about a word like *arsenic*; it might not even occur to her in the first place. Only in the original, not in the translations, does a word, once more, become flesh through Molly, almost literally so. The identical word in translation becomes a sterile one. Joyce's humor could hardly be called "cerebral" here; it is rather down to earth, characteristic of both Molly Bloom and the whole Penelope chapter—it goes to the bottom of things. The point that is lost in the other languages happens to be a cardinal one in the structure of the chapter. We have Joyce's word for it that its "four cardinal points are the female breasts, arse, womb and sex."[15]

The reader of the translation is indeed as wise as he was before; he will not be induced to stop and wonder "why they call it that." The translation does not condition him to look for implications and correspondences, and if he does look for them, he may be led astray. This amounts to a change in the reading process. The detail does not stimulate the reader to respond, and his concentration will be turned more to action and plot, things relatively unaffected by translation. *Ulysses* becomes thereby a more ordinary, more traditional novel.

The loss of overtones and ambiguities in translation is normally taken for granted, but the stripping of a phrase to its bare semantic bones may occasionally render it incongruous in its own context even as a piece of realism. Buck Mulligan's smooth quip "Monsieur Moore . . . , lecturer on French letters to the youth of Ireland" (214) is one that some translators can only simplify: "conférencier ès lettres françaises" (F 210), "Lektor der französischen Literatur" (G 244), "uppfostrare i fransk litteraturen" (SW 223). This is a different characterization of George Moore. But the chief drawback of the straightforward translation is that it misrepresents the speaker too who would probably never wish to be caught uttering as innocuous a statement as that, and one as devoid of informative content for the erudite audience that he is addressing (the French translation, by referring somewhat equivocally to Moore as a *conférencier*, at least hints at some malice). For the contraceptive undercurrent is the point of Mulligan's remark. If there were no point to it, he would keep silent. But this alternative—silence—is one that the translator is forbidden to use, and of course omission would mutilate the text even more.

When Mulligan's saying is taken up by Stephen in the hospital scene, "regius professor of French letters" (393), some translators inconsistently, but with good reason, go out of their way to reinsert the missing component: "königlicher Professor für französische Kondoms" (G 443), "professor i preservativologi" (SW 399). There is thematic justification for limiting the meaning to literature in the library episode and for pushing it toward contraception in the Oxen of the Sun chapter, but the correspondence between the two passages may be lost sight of (it certainly is in the Swedish translation). The link (between literature and fertility/sterility) has been severed.

The rather narrow focus employed here, which tends to reduce the whole novel to a web of small, interconnected verbal units—and fails to see the novel as a whole—largely coincides with the translator's own. Whatever his theories or ambitions, in the actual workshop the problems manifest themselves often as nothing more exalted than a choice among available words and forms. Technically, a giveaway like Bloom's tripping up over "the wife's admirers" for "the wife's advisers" (313) depends on the similarity of two words. If *admirers* and *advisers* are faithfully rendered into other languages, the resulting pairs evince a varying degree of similarity, due on the whole to common prefixes, suffixes, and endings: *admiradores/consejeros* (SP 352), *admiradores/consultores* (P 356), *beundrere/behjaelpelige* (D 320), *pretendenti/consulenti* (I 422), *beundrare/rådgivare* (SW 319), *Bewunderer/Berater* (G 351), *courtiseurs/conseilleurs* (F 306–07). The opportunity for a slip of the tongue diminishes with the loss of phonetic proximity. The Italian and the French translators took some pains to achieve closer resemblance than would have resulted from a literal rendering; they prefer *pretendenti* and *courtiseurs* to *ammiratori* or *admirateurs* (by which *admirers* is translated in a previous occurrence, page 309).

Both *pretendenti* and *courtiseurs* are closer to the meaning *suitors*. Thus the translators, when endeavouring to provide more linguistic basis for a psychological slip, were able to push the text nearer to a Homeric analogy, Penelope's suitors, than the original—no doubt a legitimate device.

An instructive alternative solution was adopted by the Dutch translator. In an interview, he insisted on the relevance of the Freudian slip, to which the dictionary renderings, *bewonderars* and *raadgevers*, would fail to do justice —the sort of pair that would find its place in the list quoted above. In Dutch then Bloom says *zaadgevers* instead of *raadgevers*.[16] This certainly comes as close as the language will allow and is technically much more pertinent than all the other translations. But, as the translator himself pointed out, *zaadgevers* (literally *seed-givers*) bluntly overstates the sexual component and even adds another dimension. The word is, moreover, not common in Dutch, not one that would easily slip out in conversation, and for this reason as well as for its grossness it sounds odd on the lips of prudent Leopold Bloom (outside, maybe, an episode like the Circe chapter). If Bloom did use the word it might well startle the regulars of Barney Kiernan's pub a great deal.

Here, then, is a common dilemma. A straightforward, correct translation often deprives a passage of an essential function. If an artifice is resorted to, some requirements may be fulfilled, but the emphasis may shift; the passage may be distorted in other respects. In order to save the plausibility of a slip of the tongue, an unusual and strong word, *zaadgevers*, has to be put into Bloom's mouth. The insertion of *seed* also enlarges the spectrum of associations in the perceptive reader (if the reader is not perceptive a great many of the translator's efforts are wasted anyway and not even worth discussing): he might well imagine some significance where none is warranted. It has to be remembered, however, that the translation that does *not* try to re-create some particular effects can also distort the context—by default.

The increasing volume of studies of *Ulysses* will ensure that a present-day translator is very alert. Where earlier translators had to grope their way courageously in partial darkness through what they often took to be chaos, their successors, with an abundance of illumination at their disposal, can afford to choose consciously, to weigh the various advantages and sacrifices of every solution on the various levels they think relevant. Perhaps all that can be required is that the translator choose in lucid awareness of what is at stake. On the other hand some naive insouciance, or an intuitive grasp, might prepare the translator better to square the Joycean excentric circles than the necessarily fearful tread of the systematic scholar. A conscious choice was plainly involved in the version *zaadgevers*: the attendant misconceptions must have appeared less weighty in the balance than the alternative sacrifices. This is a question of interpretation.

Interpretation and the translator's own views come into play whenever there is a parting of the ways, irrespective of whether the verbal complications are profound or superficially shallow. The predilection for words and language in all its coincidences, which Joyce's characters share with their author, accounts for the high percentage of riddles, double entendres, puzzles, spelling bees, and other verbal fireworks that crop up in their conversations. These outward and visible signs of the spell, the mysteriousness but also the deceptiveness of language, are a formidable challenge if they are witty; but even if they are not they oblige the translator to make decisions. Prominent among the facile punsters is Lenehan with his repertoire; and the Aeolus chapter, with its variations of rhetorical noises, is a suitable playground. A few lines sung, and quoted, from Balfe's *The Rose of Castille* (130) prompt him to force a riddle upon a rather reluctant audience:

What opera is like a railway line? . . . *The Rose of Castille.* See the wheeze? Rows of cast steel. Gee! (132, 134)

Lenehan's wheezy joke, for which Stuart Gilbert has supplied the technical term, *paronomasia*,[17] is not an example of supreme wit and might deserve offhand treatment in translation if Joyce did not integrate it into the texture of the novel. The opera is a recurrent motif in the Sirens chapter, where its title is mentioned six times. The riddle is repeated in the chaotic verbiage that closes the Oxen of the Sun chapter: "With a railway bloke . . . Opera he'd like? Rose of Castille. Rows of cast" (426). In the Circe chapter it recurs twice, first intimately connected with *flower* and Bloom: "This is the flower in question. . . . You know that old joke, rose of Castille. Bloom" (455). Then it is linked to Gibraltar: "What railway opera is like a tramline in Gibraltar? The Rows of Casteele" (491).

For the translator the task can be described very simply: he should include Balfe's opera, which was popular in Ireland in the second half of last century. If its title is not susceptible of riddling transformation, the name of another opera, preferably Irish (or known to the Dubliners of 1904) is to be substituted. It should be Spanish in content and title. And be associated with a railway line, or something equivalent. What is the equivalent of a railway line for a translator? Do we actually need an opera? Isn't it perhaps enough to have some sort of verbal resemblance? The translators give various answers.

The Danish, Swedish, and German translations take the easy way out: they retain the name of the opera, untranslated, and also the paronomastic version in italicized English: "*rows of cast steel.*" This leaves the entire motif and its full significance (whatever it may be) intact, but it also puts them out of the readers' grasp. In the non-English context, Lenehan's contribution to the general amusement takes on a different color; he is credited with linguistic knowledge extending to double entendres in a foreign tongue. On the surface of it, there is the odd and somewhat anticlimactic effect of a character mustering an untypical amount of sophistication to give voice to a witticism lacking almost all sophistication.

But even the wholesale retention of its English guise cannot safeguard all the potential correspondences in the motif's further exfoliations. The Castilian rose cannot be blended with a homonymous "rose" in the Sirens chapter, nor is it possible for the equivalent of *steelyringing* to induce the name of the opera, via the rows of cast steel, in the overture of the Sirens chapter (256). In all three translations, the name of the opera *is* translated in this chapter, so that "*The Rose of Castille*" occurs alongside of "Kastiliens ros" (SW 264), and so on.

The fact that some translators took over the whole riddle in its original form, in spite of some marring effects, testifies to the importance they attributed to it, as well as to their admission of its untranslatability. They also took for granted a certain willingness of their readers to accept foreign words and phrases. This is less true within the Romance languages. There the obstacle has to be overcome by some means, and the translators' inventiveness produces interesting results.

In Italian it was possible to retain the title of the opera and to give it an entirely native reading:

Quale opera assomiglia a una donna frigida? . . . *La Rosa di Castiglia.* . . . La Rosa casti li ha. (185)

The riddle, however, is different, it refers to a woman, not a railway line. The correspondence of the *Rose of Castille*, Irish opera in a Spanish setting, with Molly Bloom, Irish singer of Spanish origin, is stressed more than in Joyce's wording. But this emphasis also alerts us that the ingredients of the new riddle, frigidity and chastity, have changed both the temperature and the temperament. If we are to think of Molly as a Castilian rose—which the personified version rather invites us to do—*frigida* and *casti* are hardly *mots justes*.

In the French translation the opera is replaced:

Quel est l'opéra qui ressemble à une filature? . . . *L'Etoile du Nord.* . . . Les Toiles du Nord. (132)

This preserves Lenehan's *kind* of wit, but little else. With a different opera, there is no possible connection with the snatches from Balfe's aria that went before, and we may wonder what put the thought of that particular riddle into Lenehan's mind at this instant. This, it is true, may also happen to the reader of the original who is unlikely to recognize and place " 'Twas rank and fame" (130) and to connect it with Lenehan's flash of inspiration. But the reader of the French translation does not even have the *possibility* of detecting this detail of Joycean motivation. The railway line too has disappeared, and there is no longer a rose. The

missing rose causes some difficulty in the Circe chapter
where the transition from a flower to the riddle looks arbitrary: "Voici la fleur en question. . . . Vous connaissez bien
cette vieille plaisanterie, les Toiles du Nord. Bloom" (F
440). And later on, still in Circe, it is difficult to infer why
the riddle should recur to Bloom in connection with trams
and Gibraltar:

Quel opéra tramatique ressemble à une filature de Gibraltar?
Les Toiles du Nord. (F 464)

Since there never was a railway line associated to the riddle, the otherwise clever *opéra tramatique* is unmotivated
--the reader in translation will not expect much motivation
in Circe, and the chapter will appear more fitful to him
than in fact it might be. On the other hand, both *filature*
and *toiles* in the French translation could take the alert
reader, by devious paths, to Penelope's web and thus on to
Molly Bloom, née Tweedy. But a reader who regards these
words as valid clues and starting points for interpretative
flights would be rather nonplussed if he wanted, consistently, to apply the same method to *étoile* and tie this
bright particular star to other Ulyssean constellations. And,
still acting on the same principle, what is he to make of the
North? Wouldn't there be temptation to dig for hidden
depths when Bloom and Stephen pass the North Star Hotel
(613) on their way to the cabmen's shelter? If *filature* and
toile could theoretically—be trusted (all the more so since
they imply a web, a texture, interrelatedness), *Nord* probably could not, and the reader has no guiding principle to
tell him which words do deserve the interpreter's zeal.

The Spanish translation removes the riddle yet farther
from the original combination. There is no longer an opera:

Cuál es el país que tiene más hoteles? . . . Suiza. . . . La patria de Guillermo-hotel. (SP 169)

Guillermo Tell might, but hardly does, include Rossini's opera; the reference is primarily to the Swiss legendary hero (who puts in a transitory appearance among the Irish and Hibernicized heroes in one of the Cyclopean catalogues, p. 297). But William Tell doesn't fit into any contexts. Switzerland is, as far as *Ulysses* is concerned, a dead end. The riddle in Spanish is attuned to Lenehan's mental capacity but remains otherwise almost completely unintegrated.

Though the opera is changed in French, and in Portuguese ("Que opera é vegetal e mineral? . . . *Palhaço*. . . . Palha e aço," P 152) and dispensed with altogether in Spanish, all three translations allude to the title of the original *Rose of Castille* throughout the Sirens episode, and not to *Etoile du Nord*, *Palhaço* or Swiss hotels. The motif has been split up into two unrelated parts. One consequence is again that no explanation is provided why Lenehan should introduce the opera during his vain overtures to the barmaid (264).

All the different solutions, while circumscribed by the linguistic potential, also reflect different emphases. Some translators were more intent upon a network of associations than others. The Spanish translator set store by the immediate effect alone; in the Germanic languages the motif seemed so important as to justify its total but unassimilated inclusion. This principle, carried to its logical extreme, would bring us back to the original (the reader, instead of struggling with mutilated, distorted translations, could be advised to learn the language of the original). The opposite extreme is radical change. It would be interesting to speculate upon the outcome of such a translation experiment that would rigorously apply the principle of change. *The Rose of Castille* might be replaced by *L'Etoile du Nord*, or by Switzerland and William Tell, and railway lines and cast steel by *filatures* and *toiles*, and these substitutes could be consistently adhered to so that ultimately an entirely different texture would emerge. Translation might, after all, be understood to mean more than just an exchange of words—a transference of names, places, allusions, of the whole cultural background. In some such sense *Ulysses* is such a radical translation of the *Odyssey*, from ancient Greek into modern Irish.

The pedantic insistence on the necessary distortions of every translation raises the question of their relevance. The losses may be negligible. The Dutch translator, who also settled for a different opera ("*Herodias*: hierodiejas"),[18] indicated that there are, after all, other ways to refer to Molly. So perhaps we need neither railway lines, nor Spanish operas, nor music, but just some sort of facile pun. Since values are involved, no objective answer can be given; and the proof of the translation is in the reading. There is no doubt that the implications of the motifs that were either dropped or newly introduced by the various translations have been overrated. In all probability we are not meant to take every word as a sign to be interpreted, connected with every other part of the translation. Which is, of course, exactly the point. Joyce always seems to imply, to suggest, to provide clues that we *can* take up (which is no blanket justification for every conceivable fanciful interpretation). In translation it is not possible to play the same game. The reader has fewer opportunities to read with the sort of creative cooperation that seems to be a characteristic Joycean activity.

Considered as a quotation, "*The Rose of Castille*" is not

much of a problem. In the translations an opera is clearly referred to, and its title is quoted. But quotations are often much longer, and not clearly marked, shading off into the numerous allusions whose functions are dealt with in another essay of this volume. The translator is at a loss as soon as the same preformed verbal matter which we call a quotation or, if it is more indirect, an allusion, is not available in his own language and literature. And of course it usually is not. Even where a quotation is available, the form it takes may prevent its incorporation into the translated context. For a familiar Shakespearean tag like the one contained in "But how to get there was the rub" (613), there *is* a rendering in German, but it has never become familiar at all, and its form (the standard translation of *Hamlet* turns it into a flat and unspecific "Ja, da liegt's") makes it entirely unsuitable for a passage in the Eumaeus chapter. So there is no inkling of *Hamlet* or poetry in "Aber der Haken war nun, wie sie dahin komen sollten" (G 615) and consequently no feeling of the distance between the literary tradition and the marketplace. And yet, the translator no doubt recognized the allusion.

The recognition of familiar elements in new surroundings is a pleasure the reader of the translation often has to forego. When Joe Hynes, in the Cyclops chapter, being informed with the rest of the company that the victims of hanging die with an erection, comes out with a slick comment: "Ruling passion strong in death" (304), the reader is likely to be startled and amused. Whether he knows the line or simply feels it as being part of a heritage of poetic wisdom, or whether he considers *ruling passion* no more than a cliché, its sudden new application puts the barroom scene in a different light and Pope's verse[19] in turn acquires a new meaning and will never be the same again. No corresponding relationship will be set up in the translations that, with no possibility of referring to the literary tradition, content themselves with a faithful rendering of the sense. Versions like "La passion maîtresse forte encore dans la mort" (F 298) or "Lidenskab i doden" (D 311), though they might have a poetic ring, must appear more like simple elaborations of the preceding topic than as a sudden oblique sidelight, and they hardly electrify the text.

Beyond the loss of resonance, an untranslated allusion or quotation may become unintelligible or downright misleading. Imagine a reader coming upon the following sentence (Bloom has just left the Burton restaurant in disgust and thinks, with vivid illustrations, of a communal kitchen for all Dublin):

Le Père O'Flynn leur donnerait des ailes. (F 167)

Padre O'Flynn li farebbe correre tutti. (I 231)

El padre O'Flynn haría liebres de todos ellos." (SP 205)

O padre O'Flynn diria cobras e lagartos dêles. (P 193)

Pater O'Flynn würde sie alle auf den Schwung bringen. (G 194)

Fader O'Flynn skulla skrämma dem alla. (SW 178)

A clerical person, not met with before, is thought capable of doing something (and not, it seems, the same thing) to an unspecified group of people. The readers of the above translations will be hard put to find out who *they* (*leur, li, sie, dem*) are; there is no trace of *them* in the sentences immediately preceding. Not all translations succeed too well in catching the meaning of Joyce's sentence: "Father O'Flynn would make hares of them all" (170). It would take an unusually intuitive reader to relate Father O'Flynn back to the phrases with which the translators come to terms with "don't talk of your provosts and provost of Trinity":

sans parler des professeurs et Principal de Trinity. (F 167)

non parliamo di provosti e di quello di Trinity. (I 231)

fragt kein Mensch danach, ob einer Probst oder Direktor des Trinity. (G 194)

The German version, without any plural, does not even have an antecedent for *sie alle*. Now the English-speaking reader, too, may not know the song which links the idea of such potential communicants of the common feast as the Provost of Trinity (whose house Bloom has just passed a few minutes ago) to Father O'Flynn:

> Talk of your Provost and Fellows of Trinity
> Far renowned for Greek and Latinity
> Gad and the divils and all at Divinity,
>   Father O'Flynn would make hares of them all.[20]

But he will at least suspect the presence of something more than plain prose, and it is fairly obvious that Father O'Flynn is not just one of Bloom's acquaintances. If the reader is inquisitive enough he may find the relevant song. The most inquisitive spirit would do the reader of the translations little good. Father O'Flynn, a strange and unaccountable character, remains unintegrated, and so are the lines that translate the song fragments (but not *as* song fragments). The German version *fragt kein Mensch danach* . . . is on a completely wrong track, hinting at some philosophical bent in Bloom's thought. In some translations *would make hares of them all* is interpreted to mean *would put them to fright*. The Spanish translation, remaining literal, works in some possible cannibalistic overtones (this

is the Lestrygonians chapter), but *haria liebres* may be
something quite different from *make hares*. There is no
tension between the original meaning of the song (which
could not possibly be evoked in any translation) and the
new deflected one that Bloom gives the lines.

Most of the translators obviously did not know the song
about Father O'Flynn. But even if they did, could they
somehow indicate that Bloom remembers a song, perhaps
by formal devices like italics, quotation marks, or even a
footnote? All of these outward marks go against the very
grain of *Ulysses*. Some translators have found the separate
publication of a companion volume with annotation the
best solution.[21]

Since "Father O'Flynn would make hares of them all"
cannot be adequately translated as a recognizable line from
a particular song, with all its implications, a translator
might be grateful to be told, by the critics, what then are
the most important functions of the sentence that ought to
be preserved. Not, probably, the literal meaning of the potential metamorphosis of a group of people into hares?
Rather the fancy that Father O'Flynn is superior to some
learned people at some sort of activity? Is the connection
with the previous fragment to be made obvious, even if
the reader can have no idea what the relation is? Is the
main function of the sentence that it is a memory of a different sort from the surrounding ones, not from Bloom's
everyday experience, but from the realm of imagination,
of poetry? Should a distinctive rhythm or jingle characterize the sentence as non-prosy, the content as fictional? Or
is, perhaps, the melody that may accompany the words in
Bloom's mind more important than any sense? Should
some sort of musical notation be provided? Or should the

translator aim chiefly at the tone—one of genial and facetious admiration (if that's what it is)? Or again, do we
need a reference to something edible to account for this
particular association within its context? Questions of this
sort may help to assess priorities in translation, but an
analysis of the component functions would also contribute
to our understanding of *Ulysses.*

Theoretically an entirely different background could be
substituted, some allusion that would evoke associations
with which Danish or French readers could replace Father
O'Flynn. A transplantation of this sort would not be easy
to perform, especially if the connection with Trinity College, part of Bloom's immediate experience, is to be upheld.
Father O'Flynn, moreover, reappears in the Circe chapter.
So none of the translators have replaced him, even if his
public appearance is utterly cryptic. A legendary figure is
occasionally replaced by an indigenous one, especially in
the French translation, by far the freest of them all. "Sir
Lout's toys" (44) became "les joujoux du Grand Pitaud"
(F 47). The French translators were not too timid to bring
"Ham and his descendants mustered and bred there"
(171), without regard to Old Testament references, much
closer to the French cuisine: "Toute la famille Cochon
emmourtadée chez Madame Tartine" (F 168). Joyce may
well have encouraged this procedure himself. In his own
playful translation of a little poem by James Stephens into
five languages, he freely introduced Boreas, Fra Vento,
Ragnarok, and a German proverb as well as some puns of
his own.[22] Joyce who, for all we know, would have made
hares of them (the translators) all, did not, however, give
us his views about changing specific allusions in *Ulysses*
that are tightly interlaced with the whole surrounding
texture.

The translations could be examined, furthermore, with regard to sound, rhythm, alliteration, onomatopoetic effect, musical qualities of the prose, and especially to matters of style. There are, for example, no real and adequate equivalents to the literary styles whose progression makes up the Oxen of the Sun chapter. And still less can the styles of individual and highly characteristic writers be parodied. The results of further comparison would bear out what we knew all along, that a translation becomes inevitably flatter, that every one of its particles is less capable of an epiphany than those of the original, that motifs and overtones have been lost in transit. But perhaps the premises themselves ought to be questioned: in the perspective adopted here the ideal translation has been assumed to be the one that could be subjected to the same sort of scrutiny that Joyce scholars devote to *Ulysses* and that it would yield the same results. These demands are utopian. Translations are not undertaken for scholars—even if scholars are no more, ultimately, than ordinary readers with better training, slightly better equipment and more time at their disposal.

But once we acknowledge that a translation cannot, in the nature of language, be all things to all readers (as *Ulysses* seems to be), we may come to realize that we do not know what can reasonably be expected of a translation. What are its prime requirements? If principles like correctness, accuracy, internal consistency, preservation of motifs, correspondences, overtones, symbolic superstructures, tone, music, and many others are at variance, as they undoubtedly are, what are the preferences? The translator is really left to fend for himself as best he can; it is only afterwards, when we see the results, that we come and say, "Now *this* won't do." The theory and the principles of translation will probably get more scholarly attention than they have received so far, and some guiding lines that are more than the vaguest of general rules will emerge in the course of research that is being conducted now at several universities. One of the more practical problems is to make the complete resources of every language more readily available than they are now, when every translator is still dependent on his own memory and a shelf of reference books that he will find inadequate for his purposes.

Translation, too, is the art of the possible, and the perpetual squint at the original cannot do justice to its full achievement. The only facts it brings out are the deficiencies. Even a theoretically perfect imitation, rendering faithfully each shade of meaning and re-assembling all the constituent parts of the original in the other language, if it were possible, might, for all we know, fall completely flat and lack all life. For all its numerous inaccuracies, the French *Ulysse* is generally considered a work of literature almost in its own right. It also contains some splendid details, like an ingenious "Yeux pochés à la blême" (F 161) for Bloom's "Poached eyes on ghost" (165), which skillfully combines *yeux* and *œufs* in its sound, alludes to the paleness of a ghost (*blême*) and is yet pertinently culinary, by suggesting *à la crême*. This is brilliant and delightful even if it still falls short of Joyce's ingenuity (which could be demonstrated). The German translation, which generally fares worst in any comparative study, at any rate received Joyce's approval as well as his praise. He is reported to have said that he preferred some of its passages to the original.[23] Both the French and the German translations have had a lasting influence on contemporary writers.

Joyce's *Ulysses* has not yet yielded up all its secrets, and most of its readers concede that it may have more surprises in store for them. Critics of the translations are far less ready to grant, with equal humility, that they may not have exhausted at a first reading all the meanings that the translators put in. Not all the subtleties of a translation are obvious at once, and our minds, quick to notice errors, may fail to perceive hidden allusions and touches that would, if we but knew, enrich their context. The translator does not normally authorize a commentator to point out *his* intentions and *his* finesses to the uninitiated. So some of his best achievement may well pass unacknowledged. Every translator will moreover arrive at a point where he realizes, with resignation, that any further exertion of time, research, and ingenuity would be a waste for all practical purposes since no reader would be patient or sensitive enough to appreciate the result. And then, of course, hardly a translator is given seven years to devote to his work and few publishers encourage extensive revision and rewriting at the galley and page proof stage.

Ulysses has been translated more than a dozen times already, and more attempts will be made.[24] As a bibliographical fact, *Ulysses* is translatable, but a more differentiated answer is needed if the possibility is called into question. The enthusiasm with which translations of *Ulysses* have been received (even where they have been gravely criticized) is proof that the book has a great deal to offer in the refraction of a different and perhaps unsuitable language as well. At the same time there is ample documentation for the view that not all the qualities of *Ulysses* can be recreated in translation. That the task is not worth doing is usually said by those privileged to have access to the original anyway. For the alternative to reading *Ulysses* in translation is not, in practice, to turn to the undiminished splendor of the original, but not to read *Ulysses* at all. Even a pale reflection of the real thing is better than nothing, and certainly better than being fed with the half-truths and clichés *about* the book.

The student of *Ulysses* can learn from the translator, who is a neglected expert, often a modest one, more concerned about getting on with the job at hand than talking about it and not inclined to make a display of his insights and discoveries. He is also a creator, remaining within or behind or beyond or above his handiwork. He gives us a commentary, not an authorized one, but a complete one, even if every individual gloss is incomplete (and some are wrong). We can benefit from his predicament and learn from his frustrations—because it is in ascertaining the limitations of the translator's art that we learn just what makes *Ulysses* tick.

NOTES

1. Jan Parandowski, "Begegnung mit Joyce," *Die Weltwoche* (Zurich), 11 February 1949.

2. The translations used and referred to by abbreviations and page numbers are:

D   Danish   *Ulysses*, paa dansk ved Mogens Boisen (Copenhagen: Martins Forlag, 1964), 5th ed. First published in 1949. See note 24.

F   French   *Ulysse*, traduction intégrale par Auguste Morel, assisté de Stuart Gilbert, entièrement revue par Valery Larbaud et l'auteur (Paris: Gallimard, 1948). First published in 1929 by La Maison des Amis des Livres, Paris.

G   German   *Ulysses*, vom Verfasser autorisierte Übersetzung von

Georg Goyert (Zurich: Rhein Verlag, 1956). First published privately in Basel, 1927, in three volumes, but substantially revised in 1930.

I   Italian   *Ulisse*, unica traduzione integrale autorizzata di Giulio de Angelis, consulenti: Glauco Cambon, Carlo Izzo, Giorgio Melchiori (Milan: Arnoldo Mondadori Editore, 1961), 4th ed. First published in 1960.

P   Portuguese   *Ulisses*, tradução Antônio Houaiss (Rio de Janeiro: Editôra Civilização Brasileira, 1966).

SP   Spanish   *Ulises*, traducción por J. Salas Subirat (Buenos Aires: Santiago Rueda, Editor, 1959), 3rd ed. First published in 1945.

SW   Swedish   *Odysseus*, oversattning av Th. Warburton (Stockholm: Albert Bonniers Förlag, 1964). First published in 1946.

3.   Privatdruck (Basel: Rhein Verlag, 1927).

4.   (Zurich: Rhein Verlag, 1930). In subsequent editions the only claim made was "von Verfasser autorisierte Übersetzung."

5.   (Paris: La Maison des Amis des Livres, 1929). Later editions simplify the imprint: "traduction intégrale par Auguste Morel, assisté de Stuart Gilbert, entièrement revue par Valery Larbaud et l'auteur."

6.   Letter to Claud W. Sykes, 10 February 1927, *Letters of James Joyce*, vol. 3, ed. Richard Ellmann (New York: Viking Press, 1966), pp. 153–54. Madame Maria Jolas has informed me that Joyce also asked her husband, Eugene Jolas, to help check the translation but that he did not have the time necessary for it.

7.   See Breon Mitchell, "A Note on the Status of the Authorized Translation," *James Joyce Quarterly* 4 (Spring 1967): 202–05; and Jack P. Dalton, " 'Stately, plump Buck Mulligan' in Djoytsch," *James Joyce Quarterly* 4 (Spring 1967): 206–08.

8.   Numbers in parentheses refer to the Random House edition of *Ulysses* published in 1961.

9.   Alan M. Cohn, ed., "Joyce's Notes on the End of 'Oxen of the Sun'," *James Joyce Quarterly* 4 (Spring 1967): 198–99.

10.   Samuel Beckett, "Dante . . . Bruno. Vico . . . Joyce," in *Our Examination Round His Factification For Incamination of Work in Progress* (London: Faber and Faber, 1936), p. 14.

11.   *Ulysses*, vol. 2 (Basel: Rhein Verlag, 1927), p. 293. The phrase was changed to "wenn sie *dumpf* grübelte" (G 208).

12.   Arno Schmidt, "*Ulysses* in Deutschland, kritische Anmerkung zu

einer James-Joyce-Übersetzung," *Frankfurter Allgemeine Zeitung*, 26 October 1957, no. 249.

13.   See the discussion of "built of breeze" (164) in the translation issue of *James Joyce Quarterly* 4 (Spring 1967); 176–77.

14.   *A Portrait of the Artist as a Young Man* (New York: Viking Press, 1966), p. 217; *Jugendbildnis* (Zurich: Rhein Verlag, n.d.), p. 321.

15.   Frank Budgen, *James Joyce and the Making of "Ulysses"* (Bloomington: Indiana University Press, 1960), p. 263.

16.   "De Vertaling van *Ulysses*: Interview met J. Vandenbergh," *Utopia* (Eindhoven), 6 June 1969 (James Joyce issue), p. 11.

17.   Stuart Gilbert, *James Joyce's "Ulysses,"* (London: Faber and Faber, 1952), p. 193.

18.   "De Vertaling van *Ulysses*." p. 11.

19.   *Moral Essays*, Epistle I.

20.   Alfred Percival Graves, "Father O'Flynn," *Irish Minstrelsy*, ed. H. Halliday Sparling (London: Walter Scott Ltd., n.d.), p. 330.

21.   Giulio de Angelis, *Guida alla lettura dell'Ulisse di J. Joyce* (Milan: Lerici Editori, 1961); John Vandenbergh, *Aantekeningen bij James Joyce's Ulysses* (Amsterdam: Uitgeverij De Bezige Bij, 1969).

22.   See Richard Ellmann, *James Joyce* (New York: Oxford University Press, 1959), pp. 668–69; and *Letters of James Joyce*, vol. 1, ed. Stuart Gilbert (New York: Viking Press, 1957), pp. 317–19; as well as my article, "Seven Against *Ulysses*," *James Joyce Quarterly* 4 (Spring 1967): 189.

23.   Daniel Brody reported that Joyce "erklärte mir persönlich, dass er die deutsche Übersetzung für die beste halte, sie sogar an manchen Stellen seinem Original vorziehe." Quoted from *Frankfurter Allgemeine*, 5 November 1957, in *James Joyce Quarterly* 4 (Spring 1967): 205.

24.   Since the completion of this essay two more European translations have come out: *Ulysses*, translated into Dutch by John Vandenbergh (Amsterdam: Uitgeverij de Bezige Bij, 1969) (see notes 16 and 18); *Ulisses*, translated into Polish by Maciej Słomczyński (Warsaw: Państwowy Instytut Wydawniczy, 1969). The Danish translation by Mogens Boisen was heavily revised and republished in 1970: *Ulysses* (Martins Forlag, Copenhagen). These translations were widely reviewed and helped to reawaken interest in the various problems involved.

Biographical Notes

BERNARD BENSTOCK is professor of English and chairman of graduate studies at Kent State University. He is the author of *Joyce-again's Wake: An Analysis of Finnegans Wake* and of the forthcoming *Sean O'Casey*. His articles on Joyce have appeared in *PMLA, Modern Fiction Studies,* the *James Joyce Quarterly,* and other journals.

ROBERT BOYLE, S.J., is professor of English at Marquette University. He has contributed articles to the *James Joyce Quarterly, Victorian Poetry, America,* and other journals, and is the author of *Metaphor in Hopkins.*

DAVID HAYMAN is professor of English and comparative literature at the University of Iowa. His books on Joyce include *Joyce et Mallarmé, A First-Draft Version of Finnegans Wake,* and *Ulysses: The Mechanics of Meaning.* He has published many articles on Joyce and is currently editing a volume of essays devoted to the individual chapters of *Ulysses* (with Clive Hart).

RICHARD M. KAIN is professor of English at the University of Louisville. His books include *Fabulous Voyager,* an early study of *Ulysses,* and *Dublin in the Age of W. B. Yeats and James Joyce.* He is co-author with Marvin Magalaner of *Joyce: the Man, the Work, the Reputation,* and co-editor with Robert Scholes of *The Workshop of Daedalus.* He has contributed critical articles, reviews, and notes to numerous books and periodicals.

DARCY O'BRIEN is associate professor of English at Pomona College. He is the author of *The Conscience of James Joyce*, and *W. R. Rodgers*. His articles on Joyce and other Irish writers have been published in several periodicals and he is a contributor to the *Irish Times* (Dublin).

WILLIAM M. SCHUTTE, Lucia R. Briggs Professor of English at Lawrence University, is currently senior faculty fellow in literature with the Newberry Library Seminar in the Humanities of the Associated Colleges of the Midwest. He has also served as consultant in communication for industrial corporations. Among his books are *Joyce and Shakespeare: A Study in the Meaning of "Ulysses," Communication in Business and Industry* (with Erwin R. Steinberg), and *Twentieth Century Interpretations of "A Portrait of the Artist as a Young Man."* He has published on Joyce, on Shakespeare, and on communication problems.

FRITZ SENN is lecturer at the University of Zurich and a fellow of the School of Letters, Indiana University. With Clive Hart he is the co-founder and co-editor of *A Wake Newslitter*. He has written over fifty articles and notes on James Joyce. He co-edits and supervises the new German translation of Joyce's works now in progress.

THOMAS F. STALEY is professor of English and dean of the graduate school at the University of Tulsa. He is editor of the *James Joyce Quarterly* and on the editorial board of *Twentieth Century Literature*. He has published *James Joyce Today* and *Essays on Italo Svevo*, and co-edited (with Harry Mooney, Jr.) *The Shapeless God: Essays on Modern Fiction*. He has contributed to numerous periodicals both in the United States and Europe.

ERWIN R. STEINBERG is professor of English and dean of the College of Humanities and Social Sciences at Carnegie-Mellon

University. He is editor of *The Rule of Force* and of the Noble and Noble *Insight* series, author of *Needed Research in the Teaching of English.* With William M. Schutte he is co-author of *Communication in Business and Industry* and co-editor of *Personal Integrity* and *Communication Problems From Business and Industry.* He has published numerous articles, monographs, and chapters in communications and literature.

WELDON THORNTON is currently associate professor of English at the University of North Carolina. He is the author of *Allusions in "Ulysses": An Annotated List* and of articles on various modern writers, including Joyce, Faulkner, and Frost.

H. FREW WAIDNER, III, teaches the English and Continental novel at the University of Tulsa, where he is assistant professor. He has been associate editor of the *James Joyce Quarterly* since its inception. He is currently writing articles on Svevo and Gide, and editing a comparative study of Joyce and Thomas Mann.